"This excellent book shows in a hi[gh] neuro-scientism trades upon a not[ion] in order to deny the very ground c[...] making capacity of spiritual creat[ion] God. No previous book has so su[...] trades on the incoherence of legal positivis[m ...] way round. It seriously illuminates the vicious biopolitics of ou[r ...] [a]nd indicates the way beyond."

—JOHN MILBANK, author of Theology and Social Theory

"Opderbeck's is an argument of great originality and profundity. Modern attempts to reduce the human capacity for law and lawfulness—our capacity, that is, for transcending mere material necessity and evolutionary imperatives, as well as for failing before a standard at once within and beyond our nature—are ultimately as contradictory as all other forms of dogmatic naturalism. Opderbeck bracingly contends that this curious condition instead testifies to our relationship with and participation in a God of boundless love, and that its true and 'natural' explanation is found in Christology."

—DAVID BENTLEY HART, author of The Experience of God:
Being, Consciousness, Bliss

"If human moral agency is an illusion, perhaps law is merely a tool for the manipulation of human behavior. This is the perspective defended by reductionistic 'neurolaw,' drawing on recent developments in neuroscience. In this extraordinarily wide-ranging and vigorously argued book, legal theorist and theologian David Opderbeck shows how reductive neurolaw is self-defeating and how the emergentism and non-reductive physicalism embraced by many contemporary theologians continue to employ a problematically physicalist notion of causality. Building instead on the new Aristotelianism in the philosophy of science, with its non-reductive understanding of the relationship between brain states and human decisions, Opderbeck defends an approach that recovers formal and final causes, pointing unapologetically to love as the reason and end of creation, and to the law of love as a constituent element of human nature. Only if the order of creation flows from the order of love that is the law of God's own being, he contends, is it possible to recover an adequately non-reductive account of how accountable human persons exist within the context of physical laws of nature. A vital contribution to an important cluster of debates."

—JENNIFER A. HERDT, Yale Divinity School

"One of the major concerns raised by recent neurolaw has to do with the legal consequences of skepticism about human agency raised by the neurosciences. This has important legal, philosophical, and theological implications. David Opderbeck is well placed to tackle these issues as both a lawyer and theologian. He has written an accessible and erudite study that tackles the historical dimension to the current debate as well as providing incisive criticism and a constructive theological response. This is an important interdisciplinary contribution to a pressing contemporary discussion with which lawyers, philosophers, and theologians working in this area will have to engage."

—Oliver D. Crisp, University of St Andrews

"This is an erudite, closely reasoned, well-written, and wide-ranging study of the real and imagined problems for traditional Christian thought raised by the development of materialistic, biological, and now neurological theories about human nature and the possibility of an objective law to be discerned and obeyed by rational intelligences. Professor Opderbeck shows how a simply neurological account of our thoughts, motives and actions does more than contradict the Christian story: it is at odds with our ordinary self-understanding, with the possibility of a humane civil order, and with the scientific and scholarly enterprise itself: if all that we think, desire, and do is merely the effect of material events determined by the behavior of physical particles and the long effects of natural selection, there is no sense in supposing that we are capable of learning any objective truth, or amending our thoughts and actions in the light of an objective moral law. Only if we can in some way come to transcend our own physical nature can we hope even to learn what that nature is, and the Christian story at least offers a rational account of how that might occur. Scientists and theologians alike have a lot to learn from Professor Opderbeck."

—Stephen R. L. Clark, University of Liverpool

"'Follow the science' is the saving message of pandemic times. And for good reason. But how do we follow the science while keeping our souls intact? Better yet, how do we follow science into goodness, truth, and beauty? Legal theorist and theologian David Opderbeck offers a way. Refusing the reductionist terms on offer, he presses toward a wonderfully bodied account of how our moral habits of speech, rather than flattening out as so much epiphenomenal noise, tell us about the sorts of creatures we are and the kind of world we live in. Especially useful is his Thomistic revision of neo-Aristotelian powers and properties to frame what evolutionary theory comes to regarding our most cherished commitments. Learned, sharp, disciplined, and absolutely needed."

—JONATHAN TRAN, Baylor University

The End of the Law?

VERITAS
Series Introduction

"... the truth will set you free" (John 8:32)

In much contemporary discourse, Pilate's question has been taken to mark the absolute boundary of human thought. Beyond this boundary, it is often suggested, is an intellectual hinterland into which we must not venture. This terrain is an agnosticism of thought: because truth cannot be possessed, it must not be spoken. Thus, it is argued that the defenders of "truth" in our day are often traffickers in ideology, merchants of counterfeits, or anti-liberal. They are, because it is somewhat taken for granted that Nietzsche's word is final: truth is the domain of tyranny.

Is this indeed the case, or might another vision of truth offer itself? The ancient Greeks named the love of wisdom as *philia*, or friendship. The one who would become wise, they argued, would be a "friend of truth." For both philosophy and theology might be conceived as schools in the friendship of truth, as a kind of relation. For like friendship, truth is as much discovered as it is made. If truth is then so elusive, if its domain is *terra incognita*, perhaps this is because it arrives to us—unannounced—as gift, as a person, and not some thing.

The aim of the Veritas book series is to publish incisive and original current scholarly work that inhabits "the between" and "the beyond" of theology and philosophy. These volumes will all share a common aspiration to transcend the institutional divorce in which these two disciplines often find themselves, and to engage questions of pressing concern to both philosophers and theologians in such a way as to reinvigorate both disciplines with a kind of interdisciplinary desire, often so absent in contemporary academe. In a word, these volumes represent collective efforts in the befriending of truth, doing so beyond the simulacra of pretend tolerance, the violent, yet insipid reasoning of liberalism that asks with Pilate, "What is truth?"—expecting a consensus of non-commitment; one that encourages the commodification of the mind, now sedated by the civil service of career, ministered by the frightened patrons of position.

The series will therefore consist of two "wings": (1) original monographs; and (2) essay collections on a range of topics in theology and philosophy. The latter will principally be the products of the annual conferences of the Centre of Theology and Philosophy (www.theologyphilosophycentre .co.uk).

Conor Cunningham and Eric Austin Lee, *Series editors*

The End of the Law?

Law, Theology, and Neuroscience

DAVID W. OPDERBECK

CASCADE *Books* · Eugene, Oregon

THE END OF THE LAW?
Law, Theology, and Neuroscience

Veritas Series

Cascade Books
An Imprint of Wipf and Stock Publishers
199 W. 8th Ave., Suite 3
Eugene, OR 97401

www.wipfandstock.com

PAPERBACK ISBN: 978-1-4982-2389-8
HARDCOVER ISBN: 978-1-4982-2391-1
EBOOK ISBN: 978-1-4982-2390-4

Cataloguing-in-Publication data:

Names: Opderbeck, David W.

Title: The end of the law : law, theology, and neuroscience / David W. Opderbeck.

Description: Eugene, OR: Cascade Books, 2021 | Series: Veritas | Includes bibliographical references and index.

Identifiers: ISBN 978-1-4982-2389-8 (paperback) | ISBN 978-1-4982-2391-1 (hardcover) | ISBN 978-1-4982-2390-4 (ebook)

Subjects: LCSH: Christianity and law | Law (Theology) | Neurosciences—ethics | Neurology—ethics | Cognitive neuroscience—Moral and ethical aspects | Evolution (Biology)—Philosophy | Christian ethics

Classification: BJ1311 O63 2021 (print) | BJ1311 (ebook)

Table of Contents

Acknowledgements xi

Introduction 1

Chapter 1. The Origins of Western Law 9

Chapter 2. Progress and/or Decline? 20

Chapter 3. The Path of Reductive Neurolaw 40

Chapter 4. Method in Theology and Science 52

Chapter 5. Paleo-Law: Have We Always Been Human? 106

Chapter 6. Towards a Philosophical Critique of Neurolaw 130

Chapter 7. Mind, Law, Theology 157

Chapter 8. The Soul of the Law

Chapter 9. Law, Violence, and Original Sin 203

Conclusion 221

Bibliography 225

Index 239

Acknowledgements

THIS BOOK BEGAN ITS life as a doctoral thesis at the University of Nottingham. I am grateful to my doctoral advisor, Conor Cunningham, without whom I never could have completed the Ph.D. or this book. John Milbank and Robert Song examined my thesis and provided helpful criticisms. Steven Horst read a version of the manuscript and provided invaluable comments. I also wish to thank Bem and Julio Culiat, who helped support the early phases of my research. Finally, I am grateful to my wife Susan and my children for allowing me the time and freedom to pursue this project. Any errors or omissions, of course, are only my own.

Introduction

POPULAR SCIENCE WRITERS AND scholars alike often suggest that the "mind" is the last unopened black box in the universe.[1] Modern neuroscience promises to crack open this box by unlocking and demystifying human consciousness, conscience, and will. It seems that each day reveals a new discovery, from the identification of brain regions associated with specific emotions, perceptions, and memories to the translation of human visual impulses onto computer screens.[2] Such research offers the hope of new treatments for debilitating neurological diseases such as epilepsy and Parkinson's, better therapies for depression, anxiety, sleep disorders, and other maladies, more effective reconstructive techniques and prosthetic devices for disabilities caused by stroke, brain damage and other traumatic injuries, and deeper insights into cognition, mental performance, and learning, among other benefits. The rapid progress of brain and neuroscientific research therefore is rightly a cause for celebration.

There are, however, dangers lurking within this framework of progress. Modern neuroscience operates under a presumption of scientific naturalism. In part, this reflects the methodological presupposition of all modern natural science: a "scientific" explanation is one that refers

1. See, e.g., Güzeldere, "Introduction: The Many Faces of Consciousness" (stating "[t]here is perhaps no other phenomenon besides consciousness that is so familiar to each of us and yet has been so elusive to any systematic study, philosophical or scientific . . . are we facing a phenomenon the understanding of which lies forever beyond our intellectual capacities?"); Big Think, "The Ghost in the Machine: Unraveling the Mystery of Consciousness," (asking, "[i]f physicists can find the 'God particle' with a Hadron collider, then why, given their sophisticated tools, have neuroscientists failed to unlock the black box of consciousness?").

2. See Nishimoto, "Reconstructing Visual Experiences from Brain Activity Evoked by Natural Movies."

only to "natural" phenomena.[3] In significant part, it is also a metaphysical assumption about what is real, or at least what is possible. The "mind" or "will," many neuroscientists argue, is simply an epiphenomenal product of lower level processes that are hidden from what we (mistakenly) call "consciousness." Human beings do not have any real "freedom." We are entirely creatures of "law"—the laws of nature.[4]

This connection between neuroscience and the laws of nature has informed the emerging discourse in "neurolaw."[5] In the relevant literature, "neurolaw" encompasses a wide variety of research programs and perspectives. Many neurolaw scholars are exploring how the new insights drawn from brain scans and other neuroscientific findings might be used as evidence in a courtroom.[6] These generally are salutary efforts consistent with traditional scholarship and practice on the use of scientific evidence in the courtroom. Neurolaw scholars are seeking to better understand, for example, how diagnostic tools such as functional magnetic resonance imaging (fMRI) might or might not be useful as evidence in the courtroom.[7] Such evidence might help determine the presence of brain injury in a negligence case, assess mental capacity in a competency hearing, or define "brain death" for purposes of interpreting a medical advance directive.[8] More controversially, fMRI evidence could bear on the *mens rea* requirement in criminal law when the defendant suffers from some mental defect, or on whether a witness is telling the truth.[9] Such use of the best available empirical science to help clarify the application of legal rules represents the way in which the law's general principles become instantiated in particular situated contexts.

But "neurolaw" also refers to efforts to explain and reform the legal system from the ground up based on neuroscience. If the human "mind"

---

3. See, e.g., *Merriam-Webster Dictionary*, "Science" (defining "science" as "knowledge about or study of the natural world based on facts learned through experiments and observation").

4. See chapter 3.5.

5. See chapter 3. The term "neurolaw" was coined by attorney Sherrod Taylor, whose work focused mostly on the use of neuropsychological evidence in personal injury cases. See Shen, "The Overlooked History of Neurolaw."

6. See Jones et al., *Law and Neuroscience*; MacArthur Foundation Research Network on Law and Neuroscience Website.

7. See, e.g., Feigenson, "Brain Imaging and Courtroom Evidence."

8. Feigenson, "Brain Imaging and Courtroom Evidence," 25.

9. Feigenson, "Brain Imaging and Courtroom Evidence," 25.

or "will" is reducible to the laws of nature, then the cultural artifacts of the human mind that relate to reason and the will—in particular, positive law—likewise are reducible to the laws of nature. If positive law is reducible to the laws of nature, then Ockham's Razor suggests that the unnecessary term should be elided and we should acknowledge that jurisprudence is really only the study of human behavior from the bottom up. "Jurisprudence" is actually just "sociology," or more accurately, "jurisprudence" is actually just "sociobiology."

Some of the more candid neurolaw scholars acknowledge and celebrate this reductionistic program. Neurolaw, for them, represents an opportunity to erase the final traces of jurisprudential moralism that seem irrepressible in commonsense "folk" conceptions of positive law. Mainstream modern academic legal scholarship has long been suspicious of connections between "law" and "morality." Since the nineteenth century, American legal scholarship has been deeply influenced by "legal realism" (not to be confused with metaphysical realism), which holds that positive law is produced "from below," in the concrete realms of sociology, economics, and evolutionary psychology, and not "from above," in the ethereal realm of transcendent ethics. Neurolaw presents an opportunity to fill this gap empirically with the hard data of brain scans.

This reductionistic version of neurolaw conflicts with classical Christian accounts of law. The great thinkers about law in the Christian tradition broadly agree that positive law is a function of human reason and that positive law to some degree connects present human persons and societies with God's transcendent purposes for creation. There are disagreements in the tradition, of course, about many important issues— for example, is there a natural law that can be ascertained by any person, apart from revelation, or does positive law in any way contribute to the sanctification and salvation of believers, or should "law" be set in opposition to "grace?" From the patristic era through the Reformation, however, the best Christian minds claimed that positive law points beyond itself to its source of truth and justice in God.

The conflict between neurolaw and classical Christian accounts of positive law seems to invoke the warfare thesis between theology and science. Serious scholars of theology and science have long argued, persuasively, that the warfare thesis is misplaced. Although pre-modern Christian thinkers knew nothing of modern evolutionary biology, most of them were not biblical literalists about the mechanisms of creation. Within their own frames of reference, they incorporated the proto-scientific knowledge of their times into their biblical interpretations and theological arguments.

The fathers and doctors of the church did, however, emphasize that the aspects of human nature they attributed to the "soul"—reason, will, and purpose—transcended the physical. They believed human beings possess a capacity to grasp transcendent truths through reason, and that this capacity informs our ability, among other things, to formulate positive law. In articulating this belief, they drew on the Hebrew scriptures as well as on Platonist and Aristotelian concepts. If the neurolawyers are right, however, what we think of as "mind" or "reason" boils down to biology after all, and "law" is just a term applied to the complex working out of brain states among one group of primates. The warfare between theology and science would appear alive and well.

The neurolawyers are wrong. One reason it is obvious they are wrong is the argument we can have about whether they are "right" or "wrong." If the neurolawyers were "right," the concept of "right" would be meaningless. The argument would not be about who is "right" or "wrong," but would only represent an epiphenomenal illusion produced by brain chemistry bound by impersonal physical laws. But the neurolawyers are wrong in even more profound ways. Their story not only fails to account for positive law—it fails to consider what may comprise the "laws of nature" that supposedly govern brain chemistry, if there are even any such "laws."

Many theology and science scholars, along with thinkers who want to account for human reason and freedom apart from theology, appeal to nonreductive physicalism to address the obviously self-defeating arguments of deterministic neurobiology. I will argue that nonreductive physicalism is inadequate on philosophical and theological grounds. Nonreductive physicalism accepts a physicalist account of causality and the laws of nature that is problematic on many levels. From a Christian theological perspective, nonreductive physicalism seems to create insuperable theological problems for Christology. On a physicalist account—even a nonreductive one—it is hard to see how Christ is savingly related to "humanity" because the universal category "humanity" would have no ontological status.

The question whether there are "laws of nature," and if so how such "laws" could be identified, is subject to intense debate in the philosophy of science. One important stream of that literature embraces a "new Aristotelianism," which focuses on the causal powers and capacities of things rather than on law statements derived through modal reasoning or some other means. This approach opens up the possibility of a nonreductive understanding of causality, including concerning the relationship between brain states and human decisions. But the new Aristotelianism concerning laws of nature tries to avoid important questions addressed by the *old* Aristotelianism, not least as taken up in the Christian tradition by Thomas Aquinas—that is, the questions of primary and final causes famously picked up in Aquinas' "five ways."

Once freed from the strictures of physicalist metaphysics, the observation that "law" occupies the liminal space between science and metaphysics opens some new and fruitful avenues for the conversation between science, philosophy, and theology. Theology here can suggest that Aquinas, as well as earlier Christian thought in dialogue with Plato, offers an even more robustly nonreductive understanding of how thinking, acting, accountable human *persons* exist within the field of "natural laws" without reduction to mere law or dissolution into mere matter. In turn, law's place as a mediating structure between physics and metaphysics can help Christian theology account for humanity—for "Adam and Eve"—in our post-Darwinian age.

Among the creatures of the earth, only human beings formulate positive law. Humans alone create specified contingent rules that refer to transcendent norms and are promulgated by duly recognized authorities. Other creatures exhibit social norms, in some cases elaborately so, but none of these capacities approach the human power to formulate positive law. I will argue, *this power to formulate positive law helps makes us human*, at least in some significant part. Moreover, the power to formulate positive law was acquired only recently in the history of our evolutionary development. While we cannot identify a "historical Adam and Eve" in any literalistic or concordist sense, we can meaningfully speak of an advent of humanity standing "before the law," in a first encounter with God, when God first made himself know to humanity through the mediating structure of law. And while we cannot identify "Eden" as a literal geographic location, we can also meaningfully speak of an initial state of harmony with God and his law and a subsequent fall away from that harmonious state. Finally, we can trace this theme through the biblical witness to observe how Christ, the true Adam, fulfilled the law of love and thereby restores humanity's capacity to live as authentically human, free from the law of sin and death.

There is, of course, no way to "prove" that this theological account is true over against the neurolawyers, if "proof" is restricted to certain kinds of empirical evidences or logical propositions. But thinking about the human capacity to formulate positive law uncovers facets of the premodern tradition concerning human beings and our relationship to each other and to God that have been obscured by the dust of modernity. When uncovered, they shine welcome light into many corners of our understanding of theology, science, and human nature.

Chapter 1 provides a brief survey of Western thought about the sources of law. Greek, Roman, Jewish, and Christian sources offered rich accounts of a transcendent source of ethical norms that informed how positive law should be shaped. The sources, of course, often assumed hierarchies—for example, between men and women, or between free persons and slaves—that we would reject today. But the principle that the positive law relates to a higher natural law fostered reflection on enduring purposes and values connected to human flourishing.

Chapter 2 describes how this sense of transcendence began to break down with the rise of nominalism and voluntarism in the late Middle Ages. This, of course, is a familiar and contested decline narrative. This chapter attempts to read the leading villains in this decline narrative— John Duns Scotus and William of Ockham—charitably, but critically. They and their counterparts on the theology faculty at the University of Paris sought to preserve divine freedom against an increasingly encrusted Aristotelian system that also was being challenged in the arts and sciences faculty on the eve of the Renaissance. But, this chapter argues, some of their ideas did filter through the matrix of history to help make possible the proto-legal positivism of sixteenth- and seventeenth-century thinkers such as Hugo Grotius and Thomas Hobbes.

Chapter 3 describes reductive neurolaw and places it within a broader context of the modern rejection of natural law. Reductive neurolaw argues that our "folk" conceptions of law based on intentionality, responsibility, and justice are merely epiphenomena of biology. This sociobiological concept of law connects reductive neurolaw with the legal realist program begun in the nineteenth century, following on the heels of thinkers such as Grotius and Hobbes. Although that program sought to rationalize law through sociology and economics, today behavioral law and economics is demonstrating that actual human behavior often confounds the expectations of rational-choice theorists.

Chapter 4 begins a transition from a historical account to a constructive effort to address neurolaw philosophically and theologically. This chapter provides an extended discussion of method in theology and science. Reductive neurolaw is an effort to make law scientific rather than humanistic, so it is important to outline a methodological framework for how theology and philosophy relate to the natural sciences. I explore the well-known parameters of that conversation and also try to reflect on seldom-referenced resources from strands of modern theology, including radical orthodoxy and postliberalism.

Chapter 5 begins to apply the constructive theological method discussed in chapter 4 to the central question of how positive law relates to human uniqueness in light of human evolution. Neurolaw is an application of evolutionary psychology and sociobiology to the positive law. The paleoanthropological record shows that our genetic ancestors were remarkable creatures but that they did not possess the capacity to formulate positive law. Positive law seems to have developed well after the "cultural explosion" along with the development of writing and cities. It seems that positive law is a cultural product unique to modern humans.

Chapter 6 continues the discussion begun in chapter 5 with a philosophical critique of neurolaw. Reductive neurolaw is one expression of reductionism in the philosophy of mind, which in turn is an expression of evolutionary psychology and sociobiology. Neuroscientists often assume reductionism in the philosophy of mind is the only defensible, mainstream view within analytic philosophy, but that assumption is false. This chapter explores some other mainstream theories in analytic philosophy, but suggests that they, too, conclude with a kind of pragmatism that is insufficient to support a concept of the rule of law.

Chapter 7 relates the philosophical debate to theology—recognizing, consistent with the methodology developed in chapter 4, that philosophy is always theological. This chapter critiques the nonreductive physicalism that seems to have become the favored view among modern theologians addressing the problem of the mind and soul. I argue in this chapter that the "new Aristotelianism" in the analytic philosophy of science coheres well with classical Christian metaphysics. Returning to the roots of classical Christian metaphysics provides us with fresh resources for addressing the claims of reductive neurolaw and for revitalizing the philosophy of science.

Chapter 8 extends the theological discussion to link a concept of law with Christian theological anthropology and ontolog·
neurolaw, like all regimes founded only on materialism, ulti·
us with nothing but violence. Christian theological antl
contrast, offers a view of law not as a violent imposition b
of love. Although this does not offer some kind of supp·

non-traditioned proof of a Christian account of law over neurolaw, it presents a narrative that is more consistent with the phenomena of human nature and the goal of human flourishing, and therefore much closer to the truth.

Chapter 9 addresses a core problem for this Christian ontology in relation to law: law seems inherently violent. In figures such as Jacques Derrida, Blaise Pascal, and Giorgio Agamben, however, we can see hints that the violence of the law is, in fact, the *absence* or *suspension* of the law. This absence or suspension connects our theory of law with the Christian doctrine of "original" sin. We examine this doctrine through the great patristic thinker Athanasius to conclude that the original law was and remains the law of love, flowing from the life of the Trinity and donated to the being of creation. The law of love finds its fulfillment in the true Adam, Christ, who returns creation to its proper nature. The proper purpose of the law, including human positive law, is to nudge us closer to the law of love.

1

The Origins of Western Law

THE NATURE OF LAW—ITS purposes, authority, and legitimacy—is an enduring question in human civilization. Law relates to political and religious authority. It claims that some people or entities—including, in religious cultures, God or the gods—possess the competence to identify and define principles and rules that compel or restrict the members of a human society. A philosophy of law therefore invokes a philosophy of society, that is, a political philosophy.

In Western civilization, prior to modernity, the philosophy of law drew deeply from three streams: Greek/Roman, Hebrew, and Christian.[1] The Christian stream, which was the dominant one in Western legal thought from the beginnings of medieval Europe through the Enlightenment, borrowed from and incorporated elements of the Greek/Roman and Hebrew streams. Each of these streams was rich, diverse, and internally contested, and their legacy and interpretation remain contested today. This section offers a very brief sketch of their salient features for purposes of contrasting theories of law after modernity.

1. This is not to suggest Western legal theory is the only legal theory that matters. The focus of this book is Western legal theory because that is the locus of the author's work and expertise. It also is not to suggest that these three influences were the only influences on Western legal thought. They were, however, the main streams from which Western legal thought developed.

1. Greek

As Shirley Letwin has noted, "[t]he idea of law has been at the heart of Western civilization since its beginnings in ancient Greece."[2] The most significant elements of the Greek stream of legal thought for our purposes are Socrates' legal naturalism, Plato's idealistic concept of just government, Aristotle's ethics based in his notions of causation and virtue, the Stoic's deterministic views leading to a deontological concept of duty, and the refinement of Stoic thought by Roman jurisprudes.

Socrates' ideas are mediated to us through dialogues presented by Plato. In those dialogues, Socrates develops a rationalistic account of knowledge and virtue that leads to a kind of natural law theory: that there are principles of reason that are true for everyone, including in the area of morality.[3] One of these principles of reason is that citizens are obligated to obey the laws promulgated by the state. The laws of the state are not always consistent with the laws of reason, so the laws of reason can be employed to argue for changes in the laws of the state. However, a citizen does not have a right to disobey a law he believes unjust, because the citizen is obligated to the city for his existence—a position that led Socrates to accept his death sentence for allegedly corrupting the youth of Athens.[4]

Socrates' student Plato considered the realm of ideas to be more real than the material world. The governance of a city, like anything else, could be compared to the ideal form of a city through the exercise of reason. But not just anyone can exercise right reason. The capacity to reason, for Plato, related to the quality of a person's soul. For Plato, the soul participated in the world of forms and descended into bodies in cycles of birth and rebirth. A properly disciplined person remembers what his soul has learned and thereby has a greater capacity for reason. Plato considered philosophers to possess this sort of discipline and therefore suggested that the ideal city would be ruled by a philosopher-king who can create good laws.[5]

As Shirley Letwin notes, this does not mean Plato's view of the source and nature of law was always consistent. At times, Plato spoke

---

2. Letwin, *On the History of the Idea of Law*, 1.

3. Dore, *The Epistemological Foundations of Law*, 268–69.

4. Dore, *The Epistemological Foundations of Law*, 263–69; Reynolds, *On the History of the Idea of Law*, 10–15.

5. Dore, *The Epistemological Foundations of Law*, 270.

of positive law as a particular set of rules designed to maintain the *polis* by mediating conflict, without necessarily eliminating all difference and conflict. At other times, Plato spoke of positive law as a set of principles closely connected with universal ideals, with the goal of reducing difference and moving the community as a whole closer to the ideal. In either case, however, Plato understood positive law to be a product of reason, which referred beyond the law's immediate circumstances to a higher reality.[6]

While Plato's philosophy wrestled with the relationship between the particular and the universal, Aristotle's metaphysics and ethics emphasized teleology. At the same time, "Aristotle, like Plato, understood the character of law by analogy with a conception of the universe as a cosmos in which the elements of disorder are reduced to unity by reason."[7] The purpose of the *polis*, for Aristotle, was the "good life." The law imposes a "system of order" that teaches members of the *polis* a way of life by helping them form good habits—a help backed by coercion.[8] Aristotle agreed with Plato that the good lawmaker must understand the eternal, transcendent truths the underlie the concept of the good life in order to form good laws. However, Aristotle recognized that an actual society will not fully reach the ideal and that a good lawmaker also must possess the practical reason required to know which laws will work and which will not at any point in a society's development.[9]

Aristotle's ideas about law and practical reason were tied to his concept of causality. For Aristotle, the entire universe, and each thing in it, including human beings, can be explained by its four "causes": the material, formal, efficient, and final causes. The material cause is the matter of which a thing is composed, such as the marble of a statute. The formal cause is the arrangement, appearance, or form of a thing, such as the shape of the goddess into which the marble block is formed. The efficient cause is the action that causes a change in a thing, such as the sculptor's hand shaping the marble block into the form of a goddess. The final cause is the end or purpose of a thing, such as the invocation of the goddess' presence by the statue.

6. Letwin, *On the History of the Idea of Law*, 17–20.

7. Letwin, *On the History of the Idea of Law*, 21.

8. Letwin, *On the History of the Idea of Law*, 24.

9. Letwin, *On the History of the Idea of Law*, 25–27.

The relative excellence of anything can be discerned by considering whether and to what extent it reflects its formal cause and is moving towards its final cause.[10] The purpose of the state, Aristotle said, is justice: "In all sciences and arts the end is a good, and the greatest good and in the highest degree a good in the most authoritative of all—this is the political science of which the good is justice."[11] For Aristotle, human flourishing, and more broadly the harmony of the universe, was comprised by extremes of excess and deficiency. Virtue, then, usually was a "golden mean," a choice between extremes, although some actions, like murder, were inherently bad and could never reflect a mean between extremes.[12] A good state produces just laws based on a constitution that orders the state towards basic ends that lead to human flourishing. A good constitution and laws, reflecting the principle of the golden mean, avoids extremes—for example, the extremes of either indulging the population with food without work vs. starvation. In Aristotle, then, there are always "closely knit connections between the constitution, happiness, virtue, reason, and law."[13]

Aristotle recognized a distinction between natural law and positive law. Natural law involves basic, universal principles. Positive law is the particular law of a state, which reasonably might vary from place to place.[14] According to Aristotle, "[o]f political justice part is natural, part legal—natural, that which everywhere has the same force and does not exist by people's thinking this or that; legal, that which is originally indifferent, but when it has been laid down is not indifferent, e.g. that a prisoner's ransom shall be a mina, or that a goat and not two sheep shall be sacrificed . . . "[15]

2. Roman

Law was foundational to the Roman Republic. Even in the Imperial period, Roman political theory retained the fiction that a legal instrument, the *lex regia*, provided the citizenry's necessary consent for the Emperor's

---

10. See Dore, *The Epistemological Foundations of Law*, 270–71.

11. Aristotle, *Politics*, 1252a–1252a5.

12. Dore, *The Epistemological Foundations of Law*, 216–17.

13. Dore, *The Epistemological Foundations of Law*, 228.

14. Dore, *The Epistemological Foundations of Law*, 230.

15. Aristotle, *Nicomachean Ethics*, 1334b-18–1135a4.

authority. According to the third-century Roman jurist Ulpian, "a decision given by the emperor has the force of a statute . . . because the populace commits to him and into him its own entire authority and power, doing this by the *lex regia* which is passed anent [concerning] his authority."[16] Although the *lex regia* was a fiction, it demonstrates the importance of at least a concept of the rule of law in Roman society.[17]

Roman jurisprudes, drawing on Plato and the Stoic school, developed a strong version of natural law theory. This is evident in the work of one of the greatest Roman lawyer-politicians of the late Republican period, Cicero. Cicero's *Treatise on the Laws*, presented in the form of a Socratic dialogue, was written in 51 BCE to accompany the dialogue on *The Republic* written in 54 BCE. This combination of *The Republic* and *The Laws* intentionally mirrors Plato's works by the same name.

Cicero said a republic was "the property of the public" (*res publica res publici*) and defined a true republic as "a numerous gathering brought together by legal consent and community of interest."[18] In *The Republic*, Cicero argued that the best form of government is based in a mixed constitution balancing elements of aristocracy, monarchy, and democracy.[19] The legal consent that binds together the elements of a true republic requires the right kind of law.

In his *Treatise on Law*, Cicero said that the word "law"—in Latin *lex*—means "selection or discrimination" and implies "an equitable discrimination between good and evil."[20] This means law is connected to justice, and for Cicero, "the origin of justice is to be sought in the divine law of eternal and immutable morality."[21] This "eternal and immutable morality" is a principle of reason that connects humans to God. Cicero described the "human animal" as "prescient, sagacious, complex, acute, full of memory, reason and counsel."[22] Among the animals, only humans are endowed with "superior reason and thought," which is "the common

---

16. *The Digest of Justinian*, 1.4.1.

17. See Lee, *Popular Sovereignty in Early Modern Constitutional Thought*, 27–28.

18. Cicero, *The Republic*, 39–42.

19. Cicero, *The Republic*, 69.

20. Cicero, *Treatise on Law*, 37.

21. Cicero, *Treatise on Law*, 37.

22. Cicero, *Treatise on Law*, 40.

property of God and man."[23] Reason forms mortals and gods into "one immeasurable commonwealth and city" governed by "universal law."[24]

Cicero's interlocutor in the dialogue, Atticus, echoes what many modern readers might think about this: "Good heavens, my Cicero! From what a tremendous distance are you deducing the principles of justice!"[25] Cicero, however, insists that these metaphysical foundations are necessary to show "that man is born for justice, and that law and equity are not a mere establishment of opinion, but an institution of nature."[26] Nature, Cicero argued, "made us just that we might participate our goods with each other, and supply each others' wants."[27] But "[i]f nature does not ratify law," Cicero says,

> all the virtues lose their sway. What becomes of generosity, patriotism, or friendship? Where should we find the desire of benefitting our neighbors, or the gratitude that acknowledges kindness? For all these virtues proceed from our natural inclination to love and cherish our associates. This is the true basis of justice . . . .[28]

These brief summaries illustrate that Plato, Aristotle, and Cicero "all understood the universe as a cosmos, that is to say, as a unity governed by a single pattern or principle."[29] The temporal order of human society on earth connected with this bigger cosmic order, which supplied a metaphysical basis for the relationship between law, morality, and justice. Human beings participated in the ideal (Plato), were drawn to the perfection of the divine as a final cause (Aristotle), or were citizens with the gods in a cosmic commonwealth governed by reason (Cicero). A good human society was ordered by law that reflected these transcendent truths.

3. Hebrew

In his otherwise excellent text *The Epistemological Foundations of Law*, Isaak Dore states that "[b]efore the arrival of the Greek rationalist era,

23. Cicero, *Treatise on Law*, 40.

24. Cicero, *Treatise on Law*, 41.

25. Cicero, *Treatise on Law*, 44.

26. Cicero, *Treatise on Law*, 45.

27. Cicero, *Treatise on Law*, 48.

28. Cicero, *Treatise on Law*, 56.

29. Reynolds, *On the History of the Idea of Law*, 55.

the natural and moral dimensions of the world were understood in the haphazard passions and beliefs of the moment, without the benefit of a unifying theory."[30] Dore suggests that "[t]hese beliefs were based on a combination of myth, superstition, religion, and intuition."[31] These unfortunate statements dismiss the entire Hebrew tradition of *Torah*, Wisdom, and Prophets, which itself has roots in older ancient Near Eastern traditions.

The Hebrew tradition reflected in the Bible pictures one God who created and ordered the universe, with humanity as the high point of his creation.[32] Humanity, however, quickly becomes rebellious and violent. The first humans, Adam and Eve, are expelled from Eden, followed quickly by the first murder by their son Cain against his brother Abel. Violence increases until God destroys the world with a flood, sparing only the righteous Noah and his family. After the flood, humanity continues its rebellious ways, and at the Tower of Babel God scatters the nations. But God does not give up on humanity, and soon promises to build a nation that will redeem the world through one seemingly randomly chosen person, Abraham. The people God begin through Abraham and end up enslaved by the Egyptians, but God miraculously delivers them through Moses. After the exodus from Egypt, God gives Moses the *Torah*, beginning with the Ten Commandments. The *Torah* includes extensive law codes, often related to law codes in surrounding Assyria, Babylon, and Egypt.

Although many aspects of these law codes are harsh to modern ears, and the cultures from which they arose were far from open or egalitarian, the codes embed principles of equity, justice, and concern for the poor and oppressed. The Hebrew words *tsedeq* ("justice" or "righteousness"), *mishpat* ("judgment"), *shalom* ("peace"), and *hesed* ("lovingkindness") appear frequently in the Hebrew scriptures and offer a political theology in which God establishes a peaceable and just rule in which each person is appropriately cared for.[33]

---

30. Dore, *The Epistemological Foundations of Law*, 253.

31. Dore, *The Epistemological Foundations of Law*, 253.

32. For a fuller discussion, see Opderbeck, *Law and Theology*, chapter 1.

33. The word "appropriately" here is loaded, from our contemporary perspective. The *Torah* allowed for slavery, women did not have anything like equal rights, total holy war was permitted and even commanded, sexual roles and identities were rigidly enforced, and so-on—at least it seems so without delving into the more casuistic gloss of Rabbinic commentary in the *Mishnah*. These were features of ancient Near Eastern

The nation and its leaders rarely keep *Torah*, however, and after a long and tumultuous history, as an act of judgment, God allows the nation to be divided and then overrun by Assyria and Babylon. The root causes of this judgment include mistreatment of the poor, oppression of the common people by its rulers, and worship of foreign gods. The Bible's prophetic literature reflects on this disaster and offers glimpses of hope that the nation will again return to the principles of the *Torah* and be restored under God's reign.

It is crucial to recognize that God's judgment of Israel for failing to keep *Torah* is not pictured in the Hebrew scriptures, or in later Rabbinic literature, as merely an act of divine pique or willfulness. Rather, the *Torah* was the principle of creation, the order of the goodness of God's free gift of life given to the world and to human beings. Failure to keep *Torah* was an act of de-creation, which destroyed the goodness of the world and of the human life within it. Although the Hebrew scriptures do not contain a theory of natural law based in a rationalistic Greek concept of reason, they relate the order of creation to the divine *wisdom* (*hokmah*). This is summed up eloquently in Proverbs 8:22-31:

> The LORD created me at the beginning of his work,
>   the first of his acts of old.
> Ages ago I was set up,
>   at the first, before the beginning of the earth.
> When there were no depths I was brought forth,
>   when there were no springs abounding with water.
> Before the mountains had been shaped,
>   before the hills, I was brought forth;
> before he had made the earth with its fields,
>   or the first of the dust of the world.
> When he established the heavens, I was there,
>   when he drew a circle on the face of the deep,
> when he made firm the skies above,
>   when he established the fountains of the deep,
> when he assigned to the sea its limit,
>   so that the waters might not transgress his command,
> when he marked out the foundations of the earth,
>   then I was beside him, like a master workman;
> and I was daily his delight,
>   rejoicing before him always,

culture that the *Torah* did not eliminate. However, from the Hebrew scriptures' internal perspective, the focus is on how the *Torah* mitigates the harshest aspects of life for vulnerable members of society.

> rejoicing in his inhabited world
> and delighting in the sons of men.

Tsedeq, mishpat, hesed, and *shalom* were found in the *Torah* that was part of the *hokmah* of creation.

4. Christian

These Hebrew themes are taken up and modified in diverse ways in the New Testament.[34] The Synoptic Gospels present Jesus as a Jewish prophet recalling the community to a *Torah* of the heart, with a new twist of non-violent resistance. The Gospel of John seems to echo some Platonic/Hellenistic themes, with its famous opening line of "In the beginning was the Word (*Logos*), and the Word was with God, and the Word was God." The book of Acts depicts an early Christian community centered in Jerusalem and spreading into the civilized world, navigating tensions between its Jewish heritage and the new mores of gentile followers of Jesus. Paul's epistles wrestle with how the *Torah* relates to the new Christian community, picturing the *Torah* as a teacher that prepared the way for a deeper participation in the divine life through Jesus.

There is an eschatological cast to all the New Testament literature, not least in the Apocalypse of John, with many of the texts seeming to anticipate an imminent return of the risen Christ to establish his final kingdom. The New Testament's attitude towards temporal authorities therefore is ambiguous at best, often depicting the Roman state as demonic, but also urging the Christian community not to seek trouble and to respect legal authority.

As decades and centuries went by and Christ did not return, Christian thinkers began to interact deeply with the Hellenistic culture and philosophy of Roman antiquity.[35] Clement of Alexandria, Origen, Tertullian, and others in the centuries before Constantine offered various arguments rooted in classical natural law concepts in defense of Christians against charges that Christian impiety towards the ancient gods was corrupting the Empire. In the fourth century, Lactantius, the "Christian Cicero," served as a kind of transitional figure for Christian thought about law and justice prior to Constantine and as a figure in Constantine's court. Lactantius reframed the Republican golden-age mythology

---

34. For a fuller discussion, see Opderbeck, *Law and Theology,* chapter 1.
35. For a fuller discussion, see Opderbeck, *Law and Theology,* chapter 2.

found in Roman jurisprudence and argued that Christians, connected to the true God through Christ, could fulfill the requirements of the natural law for a just society in a way earlier Romans could not. Although these thinkers all drew on Platonic and Roman thought about law and justice, they also were deeply immersed in the Hebrew scriptures and the New Testament, and sought to demonstrate how these sources perfected or (particularly in the case of Tertullian) refuted pagan thought by emphasizing the central themes of wisdom, peace, and love.

In the declining stage of the Roman Empire in late antiquity, St. Augustine further developed this interplay of Platonic, Roman, and Hebrew-Christian thought about law and society. In his *City of God*, Augustine modified Cicero's definition of a commonwealth, suggesting that a commonwealth is "a gathered multitude of rational beings united by agreeing to share the things they love."[36] A human commonwealth could love good things or bad things. Augustine agreed with the pagan sources that human law should be connected to natural law with a source in God, but his particularly strong Christian concepts of sin and grace led him to conclude that no human society could ever achieve the fullness of justice prior to the eschaton. He therefore connected human positive law not only to natural law but also to the reality of sin. Human law could only ever be incomplete, provisional, and indeed pragmatic, because no human society on this side of the eschaton would ever be perfect. Augustine thereby tied his thinking about law and politics into a broader theology of history.[37]

Augustine's political theology was deeply influenced by later Platonic and Roman/Stoic sources available in Latin. The Aristotelian stream of Greek thought was not as influential because Aristotle's works were not accessible to scholars who worked in Latin and did not know Greek. As the Roman Empire collapsed and antiquity gave way to the medieval period, Augustine's thought continued to pervade the Christian West. In the twelfth and thirteenth centuries, however, many of Aristotle's works were "rediscovered" by Latin theologians who found the texts in Arabic through Islamic scholars. The rediscovery of Aristotle deeply influenced the great medieval theologian Thomas Aquinas.

In his *Summa Theologica*, Aquinas included an entire "Treatise on Law." Aquinas suggested a stronger link between law and reason than

36. Augustine, *City of God*, 19.21–24.
37. Opderbeck, *Law and Theology*.

Augustine, although Aquinas agreed with Augustine's pragmatic approach to the limits of positive law short of the eschaton. Like Cicero, Aquinas thought "the whole community of the universe" is governed by God and participates to some degree in the eternal law.[38] Aquinas' pragmatism, though, also reflected his Aristotelian sense of causality, in that he believed human society, most directly through the church, was drawn to its final cause, which was the beatific vision of God. This meant that humans could progress, by grace, in virtue, and that the positive law had a role to play: "the purpose of human law," he said, "is to lead men to virtue, not suddenly, but gradually."[39]

Figures such as Lactantius, Augustine, and Aquinas, of course, were not the only Christian thinkers before modernity to develop a theology of law in conversation with biblical and classical notions of natural law. It is fair to say that reflection on the nature and purposes of law was one of the primary contributions of Christianity to Western civilization.[40] From ancient Greece, to the Roman Republic, to the Hebrew scriptures and the New Testament, through Christian antiquity and the Middle Ages, Western legal thought centered on the notion that human beings, through the capacity for reason, occupied a unique place in a cosmos suffused with divinity and laden with purpose. This is not to suggest, of course, that law on the ground always operated according to such lofty concepts, or that opportunistic rulers never deployed these notions for their own gain. It also is not to suggest that these ancient and medieval societies would satisfy contemporary ideas about gender equality, the cruelty of torture and capital punishment, protection of sexual minorities, freedoms of speech, religion, and association, and other important developments in Western law. But at least, in its best ideals, Western legal thought from antiquity through the early Middle Ages was richly humanistic—a humanism supported by philosophical and religious concepts of human nature.

38. *ST* I-II, 91, art. 1.

39. *ST* I-II, 96.

40. See, e.g., Berman, *Law and Revolution; Law and Revolution II*; McConnell et al., *Christian Perspectives on Legal Thought*; Witte Jr., *God's Joust, God's Justice; The Reformation of Rights*; O'Donovan and Lockwood O'Donovan, *From Irenaeus to Grotius*; Witte and Alexander, *The Teachings of Modern Christianity on Law, Politics and Human Nature; The Teachings of Modern Roman Catholicism on Law, Politics, and Human Nature; The Teachings of Modern Orthodox Christianity on Law, Politics and Human Nature; Christianity and Law: An Introduction*.

2

Progress and/or Decline?

1. Contending with Greek Metaphysics

A s THE INTRODUCTION TO this book suggests, reductive neurolaw is
the apotheosis of a "scientific" view of law that elides the notions
of natural law, metaphysics, and human uniqueness evident in the
strands of legal thought profiled in chapter 1. Reductive neurolaw is one
manifestation of a contemporary "metaphysical naturalism" that seeks
to bring all questions of ethics, religion, and morals within the domain
of the natural sciences.[1] It is part of a broader rejection of any notion of
transcendence, including in particular notions of transcendence informed
by religious traditions, which might relate to universal ethical principles
for social ordering, whether through social norms or through positive law.

From the perspective of many contemporary thinkers, this move
away from metaphysics is a sanguine development. As historian of science Peter Harrison suggests, a "particular version of the history of
science" is supposed to support the contemporary commitment to
both methodological and metaphysical naturalism.[2] As Harrison notes,
"[m]ost often this is a narrative that sees naturalism beginning with the
ancient Greeks, going into decline in the Middle Ages, and being restored

1. Hunter and Nedelisky, *Science and the Good*; Harrison and Roberts, *Science without God?*.

2. Harrison, *Science without God?* 6.

20

in the 'scientific revolution' of the seventeenth century."[3] As Harrison suggests, "[e]ssentially, this is a story about the connection between naturalism and human progress—one that not only attributes the success of the sciences to their naturalistic assumptions, but which also regards commitment to the supernatural as inimical to scientific progress."[4]

But, as the essays in Harrison's book demonstrate, and as the narrative in section 1.3 above suggests, ancient Greek thought certainly was not naturalistic in the modern sense. Both Plato's and Aristotle's metaphysics obviously were committed to the reality of non-material entities, including the soul. The Christian thought of late Roman antiquity developed in deep dialogue with Platonism, moving the ideal realm of Plato's forms into ideas in the mind of God, and the "rediscovery" of Aristotle in medieval scholastic Christian thought via Islamic sources gave rise to a new synthesis of Christian and Greek concepts.

A related narrative to that suggested by Harrison is that the medieval synthesis held back scientific progress because the Aristotelian view of the cosmos became part of religious orthodoxy. Aristotle's cosmology placed the earth at the center of the universe and, the narrative goes, eschewed careful empirical investigation in favor of abstract speculation along with incorrect ideas about the fixity of species and the hierarchy of being. When Galileo challenged the Aristotelian view of the cosmos, he was punished by the church, but ultimately outdated Aristotelian ideas wedded to religious dogma could not stop the progress of empirical science.

It is true that the natural sciences needed to break free from some of the details of the medieval synthesis to advance, and that related changes were required to move beyond the statically hierarchical medieval view of society. But a move away from Aristotle's (supposedly) static cosmology did not require the wholesale rejection of Platonic ideas about universals, Aristotle's concepts of formal and primary causes, or related Christian metaphysical ideas about *esse* and essence or act and potency. Indeed, both during the Renaissance and after, there were neo-Platonist and other idealist movements, which eventually informed German idealism's reaction against Kant. Different kinds of idealism remain important today, and in the modern philosophy of science, an important neo-Aristotelian school of thought about "laws of nature" could help inform a view that escapes today's dogma of metaphysical naturalism—a dogma

3. Harrison, *Science without God?* 6.

4. Harrison, *Science without God?* 6.

that pulverizes the possibility of human freedom along with the legal institutions and frameworks that foster human freedom in society. Yet idealism and neo-Aristotelian perspectives on the philosophy of science remain far less influential today than reductive scientism. So why *did* the intellectual center from the Renaissance through modernity elide all causes and entities outside the material, instead of taking a more fulsome path forward?

There were many powerful currents at work. Plague, famine, and war rent the social and economic fabric, and neither the existing ecclesial or political orders were equipped to lead productive change. The Protestant Reformation, the printing press, and political and religious writing in vernacular languages fractured the religious elites' hegemony over information. The discovery of the New World and, despite the church's condemnation, Galileo's proof of the Copernican cosmology disoriented the orderly medieval universe.[5] The rediscovery of ancient texts and new humanistic learning questioned how canonical writings were interpreted and the authority accorded to them. The Wars of Religion—motived by intra-Christian differences, but also by long-simmering political and economic rivalries—devastated Europe.

2. Nominalism, Voluntarism, and the Decline of Universals: Scotus and Ockham

Such epochal changes were far larger than any change in intellectual fashion. But these epochal changes were augured and accompanied by a shift in the medieval synthesis away from the thick metaphysics of Aquinas and Augustine and towards nominalism and voluntarism. Duns Scotus provided a key impetus for this shift through his arguments for the univocity of being. William of Ockham kicked the shift into overdrive through his much more explicit nominalism and voluntarism. It is unfair to place the "blame" for modernity's deficiencies at the feet of Scotus and Ockham, much less to trace a clear, straight line between them and something like reductionism in contemporary neuroscience. Yet if we want to offer a theological appraisal of how we got where we are, and to suggest some ways forward, we need to attend to the nominalism and voluntarism expressed by Scotus, Ockham, and their later followers.

---

5. See Lohr, "The Medieval Interpretation of Aristotle," 91–98.

Christian theology (along with Jewish and Islamic theology) must contend with a set of related problems concerning God and creation. God alone is God. Creation is not God; God is not creation. God is absolute, undetermined, and free, without any contingency. Creation is finite and contingent. Creation depends utterly upon God for its existence. God simply exists and depends upon nothing. God is perfect and his perfections reflect no division in God—God's goodness, love, justice, power, glory are interchangeable and one.

These sets of beliefs raise the question how human beings, who are created, can have meaningful knowledge of God. How can finite humans know anything about the infinite God? They also raise the questions about God's freedom in creating and in the history of creation. How can God's decision to create be utterly free and undetermined if God only acts according to his perfections? How can God freely relate to creation if, within creation, including among human creatures, there is any freedom? Does God's free action lead to determinism in creation? Alternatively, does even contingent freedom in creation limit God's freedom? These questions obviously are not unique to Christian theology—they are among the oldest and deepest philosophical questions about the finite and the infinite, freedom and determinism. But the doctrines of God and creation require Christian theology to seek ways through the questions.

On the question of knowledge, a strand of Christian thought influenced by Platonism emphasized God's inherent unknowability, while accounting for the innate sense that God exists and for the biblical language that describes him. Gregory of Nyssa, for example, said that

> All the words found in holy scripture to indicate God's glory describe some feature of God, each providing its particular emphasis, whereby we learn that he is powerful, or not susceptible to evil, that he is without cause, or comes to no finite end, that he has control of the universe, or anything else about him. His being itself, however, scripture leaves uninvestigated, as beyond the reach of mind and inexpressible in word, decreeing that it should be honoured in silence by prohibiting enquiry into the deepest things and by saying that one ought not to "utter a word in the presence of God."[6]

Likewise, Gregory of Nazianzus said, "No one has yet discovered or ever shall discover what God is in his essence."[7]

---

6. Gregory of Nyssa, *Contra Eunomium II*, ¶ 105.

7. Gregory of Nazianzus, *Oration* 28.17 (tr. Wickham).

Augustine emphasized our innate knowledge of God through our sense of longing for something we cannot grasp: "you have made us for yourself, and our hearts are restless until they find their rest in you."[8] Because of sin, we now often experience this intuitive knowledge as a sense of lack. God was present with us in the Garden, but the immediate sense of God's presence has been lost to us. That sense is now more like a dim memory, something we know should be there but feels absent. This Augustinian strand re-emphasized the earlier Greek church fathers, who stressed negative theology—that we cannot make affirmative statements about what God *is* like but that we can make negative statements about what God is *not* like.[9]

The rediscovery of Aristotle led to the development of an Aristotelian-Thomistic response to the problem of knowledge, which emphasized the human intellect's capacity to observe meaning and purpose in the universe that points to a source of the universe's beginning and a cause towards which it moves.[10] The Aristotelian-Thomistic response suggested the possibility of some natural knowledge of God without special divine illumination. However, the concepts human beings can form about God are inadequate because of God's absolute difference from creation. Our understanding of God and language about God therefore is equivocal. A human term such as "good" or "wise" can mean various things, while God, in his own essence, simply *is* "good" and "wise." As the word "is" here suggests, the problem for Aquinas was how to speak of "being" in human terms. Aquinas employed the Aristotelian concept of analogy to provide the means for humans to reason about God.

For Aquinas, an analogical term is something that is said of two things in a prior and posterior sense connected by an attribution or relationship.[11] For example, "food" is "healthy" when it is used to cause health in the animal that consumes it. We cannot know God's essence because of God's absolute difference from us, but we can know of God's goodness, wisdom, and the like because of the causal relation between God and the creature. A creature possesses goodness, wisdom, and the like insofar as it participates in God's essential goodness, wisdom, and the like.[12] The words we use about God, such as goodness and wisdom,

8. Augustine, *Confessions*, 1.1.1.

9. Mahoney, "Sense, Intellect, and Imagination," 605–11.

10. Dod, "Aristoteles Latinus."

11. Ashworth, "Medieval Theories of Analogy."

12. Ashworth, "Medieval Theories of Analogy."

cannot be purely equivocal, or else we could known *nothing* of God, but they also cannot be purely univocal, because God infinitely exceeds creation. These words, therefore, are analogical.[13]

Although, for Aquinas, our understanding of God is only analogical, he obviously believed God really existed apart from human concepts, and he further believed in the reality of creation external to human sensation. The human imagination, located in the brain, Aquinas thought, serves as a storehouse of forms or "phantasms" of sensible things when those things are not present to the external senses.[14] The potential intellect is the capacity to know an individual sensed thing through reflection on a phantasm by the active intellect.[15] This means humans can know immaterial things only through comparison to phantasms of material things—the mental process of analogy.[16] But through this process humans can receive certain knowledge of God without divine illumination.[17]

As this very brief discussion of Augustine and Aquinas suggests, knowledge of God through either illumination or analogy requires the related concept of "participation"—a concept that, in turn, relates to the question of universals. Plato and Aristotle both thought, although in very different ways, that individual instances of a thing must relate to universals that exist apart from the particular, individual instance. Plato envisioned a world of forms with universals that exist apart from the world of matter in which particular things are instantiated. That the ideal world of forms could be known through abstract reflection. Aristotle thought the universal form exists only when it is instantiated in an individual thing and that the universal form can only be known through empirical experience of individual things. Both for Plato and Aristotle, the individual thing "participated" in its universal nature, and the relationship between the particular and the universal allows for an evaluation of the individual thing's virtues. We can say, not just that this is a glass of wine, but that this is an *excellent* glass of wine; not just that this is a person, but that this is an *excellent* person.

Christian Platonists relocated the world of forms into the mind of God. Aquinas reworked both Christian Platonism and Aristotle into the relationships between *esse* and existence and potency and act. For a thing

---

13. Wippel, "Essence and Existence," 390–91.

14. Mahoney, "Sense, Intellect, and Imagination," 606.

15. Mahoney, "Sense, Intellect, and Imagination," 608.

16. Mahoney, "Sense, Intellect, and Imagination," 609.

17. Mahoney, "Sense, Intellect, and Imagination," 610.

to participate in its universal nature, then, is to participate in God. Since humans as creating things participate in God, we can receive illumination from him, or develop analogical concepts, which give us true knowledge of him, as the knowledge of a particular thing gives some knowledge of its form.

This book's perspective is that, granting that the details of Aristotle's cosmology should never have been asserted as dogma, and for all the incredible technological and scientific progress humanity has enjoyed since the Enlightenment, and for all the undeniable benefits that have accrued to ordinary people from the overthrow of old monarchies and the rise of political liberalism, the loss of transcendence found in Greek thinkers such as Plato and Aristotle, and in the early Christian tradition, has set us on the path of nihilism.[18] We can correct the tradition without abandoning it. Later chapters will provide philosophical and theological arguments for these claims. But first, we must ask, what *was* the cause of the sudden elision of metaphysics and God from Western legal and political thought between the Middle Ages and today? Why did the Enlightenment lead to today's secular age?

In 1210, the teaching of Aristotle's works at the University of Paris was prohibited.[19] This prohibition eventually was ignored. Theologians at Paris made critical use of Aristotle in relation to received sources of authority in scripture and the church fathers, while a newly established faculty of arts explored Aristotle's texts as sources apart from the theological tradition.[20] Fear that Aristotle's ideas undermined sacred teaching, however, along with broader disputes about clerical control over the curriculum, led to the condemnation issued by the Bishop of Paris, Stephen Trempier, in 1277.[21] The condemnation related to 219 philosophical and theological theses being debated by both the theology and arts faculties at Paris and placed Aquinas' synthesis under suspicion.[22] John Duns Scotus' criticism of Aquinas therefore was both intellectually motivated and responsive to the politics of the condemnation.[23]

---

18. Cf. Hunter and Nedelisky, *Science and the Good*.

19. Dod, "Aristoteles Latinus," 71.

20. Lohr, "The Medieval Interpretation of Aristotle," 80–98.

21. Kuksewicz, "Criticisms of Aristotelian Psychology and the Augustinian-Aristotelian Synthesis," 31; Thijssen, "Condemnation of 1277."

22. Thijssen, "Condemnation of 1277."

23. Kuksewicz, "Criticisms of Aristotelian Psychology and the Augustinian-Aristotelian Synthesis," 626.

Scotus believed that the emphasis on analogy and mediation in Aquinas leads inevitably skepticism and fideism. If we cannot obtain direct knowledge of God, Scotus argued, we cannot have certain knowledge, and if we cannot have certain knowledge, at best we can make claims about God on faith unsupported by any reasons, or we can give up on claiming any knowledge about God. Scotus sought to overcome this problem by asserting that "being" must be a univocal rather than an equivocal term.[24]

According to Scotus, "God is not only conceived in a concept that is analogous to a concept of a creature—that is, in a concept that is entirely different from one that is applied to a creature—but also in a concept that is univocal to him and to a creature."[25] Scotus defined "univocal" to mean a concept for which "its unity is sufficient for a contradiction to arise when it is affirmed and denied of the same thing."[26] Without a univocal concept common to creatures and God, the human mind, Scotus argued, cannot know anything about God.[27] Human knowledge of God, then, begins with knowledge of lower things and proceeds to a concept of the "highest" things.[28] According to Scotus, "[u]nder the concept of a creature there is no concept or species representing something that is proper to God alone and entirely different from what applies to creatures."[29]

It seems, then, that Scotus imagined God as, in essence, like other beings in the universe. God is then on a kind of continuum as the "highest" being in existence. This, of course, is not the classical Christian understanding of God and creation. A good statement of the classical view comes from Gregory of Nyssa's second book *Against Eunomius*: "The barrier which separates uncreated nature from created being is great and impenetrable."[30]

---

24. Ashworth, "Medieval Theories of Analogy."

25. John Duns Scotus, *Ordinatio* 1.3, ¶ 26.

26. Scotus, *Ordinatio* 1.3, ¶ 26.

27. Scotus, *Ordinatio* 1.3, ¶ 35. Scotus states that "a concept that is not univocal to the object shining out in the phantasm, but entirely different and prior and related to it by analogy, cannot arise by virtue of the agent and the phantasms. Therefore such a different concept, which is supposed to be analogous, will never occur naturally in the intellect. . . . And so it will be impossible to have some concept of God in the natural way, which is false." He later says that "every inquiry about God assumes that the intellect has an identical, univocal concept that it receives from creatures." *Ordinatio* 1.3, ¶ 39.

28. Scotus, *Ordinatio* 1.3, ¶ 61.

29. Scotus, *Ordinatio* 1.3., ¶ 62.

30. Gregory of Nyssa, *Contra Eunomium II*, ¶¶ 69–70. Gregory continues:

There is intractable debate, however, about whether Scouts intended his concept of the univocity of being as merely semantic or as an actual statement about God's nature. In the section of his *Ordinatio* we have been quoting, Scotus goes on to say that "being (*ens*) is univocal for all concepts. For concepts that are not absolutely simple it is univocal, and of them it is predicated *in quid*.[31] For absolutely simple concepts it is univocal, but as something that can be determined or denominated—not, however, as said *in quid* of them, for that includes a contradiction."[32] This kind of statement supports the view that Scotus meant the concept of univocity only semantically. If that is the case, however, it is difficult to see what work univocity does beyond analogy. It is difficult to see how a concept is univocal, rather than analogical, if the being signified by the concept, to use Gregory of Nyssa's words, resides apart from created being behind a "great and impenetrable" barrier.

Even if Scotus only meant claims about the univocity of being semantically, his concept of univocity sat at the headwaters of an intellectual stream that would accelerate into the Enlightenment and that persists today: in the thought of many moderns, "God" is reduced to part of the furniture of the universe. If "God" is part of the universe, a cause *within* the universe, it is easy to question how "God" serves as an explanation for anything. As the natural sciences begin to uncover more and more about the deep history of the cosmos, it appears that

---

One is finite, the other infinite; the one is confined within its proper measure as the wisdom of its Maker determined, the limit of the other is infinity. The one stretches out in measurable extension, being bounded by time and space, the other transcends any notion of measure, eluding investigation however far one casts the mind. In this life one may perceive both a beginning and an end of what exists, but the Blessedness transcending creation approaches neither beginning nor end, but is by nature beyond the meaning of both, always remaining the same and self-consistent, with no measurable progress from one state of life to another. It does not come to life by partaking of the life of another, which might lead to the thought of the beginning and end of that participation, but what it actually is, is life acting in itself; it becomes neither greater nor less by addition or subtraction. There is no room for increase by growth in the infinite, and what is by nature invulnerable cannot suffer what we conceive as diminution.

31. *In quid* is a term that answers the question *"Quid est"* (What is it?). Wolters, *The Transcendentals and Their Function in the Metaphysics of Duns Scotus*, 79. Scotus' use of this common scholastic term can be confusing. See Langston, *Scotus and Ockham on the Univocal Concept of Being*, 105 n. 1. Langston suggests that, for Scotus, "being" is predicated of something "if a metaphysical reality that corresponds to 'being' is found in the thing as an essential component." Langston, *Scotus and Ockham*, 106 n. 2.

32. Scotus, *Ordinatio* 1.3, ¶ 150.

science will finally explain everything through natural laws, without the hypothesis of a great God-creature stirring the primordial soup.

If God is part of the furniture of the universe, as God is for many today, the basis for the classical concept of a natural law as the ideal source of positive law collapses. The "laws of nature" are a brute fact, an "is," without reference to any higher source of an "ought."[33] It is not surprising, then, that the stream of late medieval scholastic theology that dramatically broke from the Christian-Aristotelian-Platonic synthesis, starting with Scotus, began to view—or at least to speak of—the natural law in terms of God's *arbitrary commands* rather than in terms of God's perfect, transcendent being.

Scotus has often been cited as the source of the voluntaristic notion that "Things are good because God wills them and not vice versa, so moral truth is not accessible to natural reason."[34] Scotus' moral theory did, in fact, emphasize the will, but he also emphasized God's inherent goodness. Scotus considered whether there are two kinds of justice in God, one relating to God's own goodness and one relating to how God relates to creatures: "the whole definition of justice . . . insofar as it is applicable to God, could be reduced to two sorts, the first of which would be called rectitude of the will with respect to what is due to divine goodness; the other, rectitude of will with respect to what the exigencies of the creature demand."[35] This raises the question whether God is *constrained* to act in a certain way towards creatures, which would compromise God's freedom and omnipotence. Scotus concluded that

> [J]ustice properly speaking represents a habitual state of rectitude of will, and hence as a habit it inclines one in a quasi-natural manner to another or to oneself as quasi-other. Now, the divine will does not have any rectitude that would incline it deterministically to anything other than its own goodness as a quasi-other (recall that the divine will is related to any other object only contingently, so that as will it has the capacity to will either this or its opposite). From this it follows that there is no justice in God except that which inclines him to render to his own goodness that which is its due.
>
> Thus there is also but one act, conceptually and in reality, to which this habit of justice inclines this will.[36]

33. For further discussion of the "is/ought" problem, see chapter 7.3.
34. Quinton, "British Philosophy."
35. Scotus, *Ordinatio* IV., dist. 46.
36. Scotus, *Ordinatio* IV., dist. 46, 187.

God's absolute freedom means that he can act with regard to creatures in any way he chooses even if that action contradicts what justice contingently would require towards the creature: God's "primary act [of justice towards himself] does not look to any [created] object or secondary act, because insofar as it looks to such his justice does not incline his will in any necessary manner."[37]

Scotus related the freedom of God's will with respect to justice to the distinction between God's absolute and ordained power. According to Scotus, "[i]n every agent acting intelligently and voluntarily that can act in conformity with an upright or just law but does not have to do so of necessity, one can distinguish between its ordained power and its absolute power."[38] The ordained power is the ability to act in accordance with an upright or just law. If an agent can act "beyond or against such a law . . . its absolute power exceeds its ordained power."[39] Scotus tied this to the legal concepts of acting *de facto*, according to absolute power, or *de jure*, according to ordained power.[40] If an agent has no ability to change or control the ordained law, the agent's absolute power cannot exceed its ordained power.[41] However, Scotus said,

> [W]henever the law and its rectitude are in the power of the agent, so that the law is right only because it has been established, then the agent can freely order things otherwise than this right law dictates and still can act orderly, because he can establish another right or just law according to which he may act orderly.[42]

In other words, if the agent has the power to change the ordained law, the agent can render licit an action that otherwise would have been illicit. Scotus suggested that this is the case for a ruler who can change the positive law that governs his subjects.

---

37. Scotus, *Ordinatio* IV., dist 46, 188.

38. Scotus, *Ordinatio* I, dist. 44, 191.

39. Scotus, *Ordinatio* I, dist. 44, 191.

40. Scotus, Ordinatio I, dist. 44, 191. This use of the distinction between *de facto* and *de jure* authority shows that the word "absolute" in relation to the power under discussion is confusing. No human agent ever really has "absolute" power. A human agent's power is always contingent on the force that agent can muster, the psychological persuasion the agent can conjure, and so on. A general may possess *de facto* authority to control the state because he controls the army, even if the law locates *de jure* authority in the prime minister, but the general can lose his *de facto* authority if someone else mounts a stronger army.

41. Scotus, *Ordinatio* I, dist. 44, 191–92.

42. Scotus, *Ordinatio* I, dist. 44, 192.

The qualification that the agent's absolute power exceeds its ordained power only when the law is "right only because it has been established" seems important. Aquinas, in his treatment of the relationship between the natural law and positive law, noted that the positive law can never fully instantiate the natural law in any particular time or place, and that even when the positive law is generally consistent with the natural law, there are many ways the positive law can be configured according to practical reason.[43] The positive law, then, is always contingent and to some degree malleable.

But for Aquinas, a dictate of the positive law would never be right *only* because it has been established by some governing authority. The positive law is only right and just insofar as it is in accordance with the natural law. Or, as Aquinas quoted Augustine, "an unjust law is no law." Scotus seems to allow for the possibility that the positive law could be "right" *only* because the sovereign has the power to enact it, without any necessary regard for the natural law.

This is clear in Scotus' discussion of the relationship between the absolute and ordained power in God. "God," Scotus said,

> insofar as he is able to act in accord with those right laws he set up previously, is said to act according to his ordained power; but insofar as he is able to do many things that are not in accord with, but go beyond, these preestablished laws, God is said to act according to his absolute power. For God can do anything that is not self-contradictory or act in any way that does not include a contradiction (and there are many such ways he could act); and then he is said to be acting according to his absolute power.[44]

It is not self-contradictory for God to change any law, "because no law is right except insofar as the divine will accepts it as established."[45] Therefore, Scotus said, "God can act otherwise than is prescribed not only by a particular order, but also by a universal order or law of justice, and in so doing he could still act ordainedly, because what God could do by his absolute power that is either beyond or runs counter to the present order, he could do ordainedly."[46]

In this discussion of absolute and ordained power, it seems that Scotus must deny any concept of natural law. His discussion of the natural

43. See discussion in Opderbeck, *Law and Theology*.
44. Scotus, *Ordinatio* I, dist. 44, 192.
45. Scotus, *Ordinatio* I, dist. 44, 192.
46. Scotus, *Ordinatio* I, dist. 44, 193.

law in relation to the Ten Commandments, however, is more subtle than a denial of natural law in favor of voluntarism *tout court*.[47] The problem addressed here is a *locus classicus* for debates between natural lawyers and divine command theorists: the fact that in the Old Testament God at times commanded people to do things that contradict some of the Ten Commandments. For example, God commanded Abraham to sacrifice Isaac (violating the seventh commandment against murder); enabled the Israelites to plunder the Egyptians during the exodus (violating the ninth commandment against theft); and commanded Joshua to kill the Canaanites and take their land (violating the ninth commandment and, perhaps, the seventh commandment against murder).

A common response to this problem, Scotus notes, is that, while the Ten Commandments do belong to the natural law, God may provide temporary dispensations from the Commandments in specific circumstances where other concerns of the natural law require it.[48] Scotus rejectsed this move because he considered a "dispensation" from a command the same as a revocation of the command rather than a clarification of the general rule to apply to a contingent circumstance.[49] Scotus also rejected the idea that the Commandments are dictated by the natural law, because in that case, God's will would be "necessarily determined in an unqualified sense in regard to willing things other than himself," which in Scotus' view would compromise the divine freedom.[50]

Scotus' solution was to distinguish between the first and second tables of the Commandments. The first table, the first five commandments, "regard God immediately as their object."[51] The worship and love of God alone is an immutable rule of the natural law because God is God. The second table, the second five commandments, are contingent rules for human relationships. Rules against murder, adultery, theft, bearing false witness, and coveting are contingent, and God can change them, although, "speaking broadly," all the commandments "fall under the law of nature.[52] As Allan Wolter argued, then, it is unfair to say Scotus denied

47. Scotus, *Ordinatio* III, suppl., dist. 37, 198–207.

48. Scotus, *Ordinatio* III, suppl., dist. 37, 200.

49. Scotus, *Ordinatio* III, suppl., dist. 37, 200.

50. Scotus, *Ordinatio* III, suppl., dist. 37, 201.

51. Scotus, *Ordinatio* III, suppl., dist. 37, 202.

52. Scotus, *Ordinatio* III, suppl., dist. 37, 204. Scotus was even more specific than this: "To put all we have said together, first we deny that all the commandments of the second table pertain strictly to the law of nature; second, we admit that the first two

the reality of the natural law. Scotus was addressing a set of questions about natural law and contingency that were common in scholastic treatments of the subject.[53] However, Scotus supplied a novel solution that reinforced a trend towards voluntarism. Combined with Scotus' idea of the univocity of being, we can see the danger of reducing God to a large, arbitrary power operating within the universe, rather than understanding God as the transcendent source of goodness. This was certainly not Scotus' intent, and his concerns about recognizing the divine freedom were vitally important. Nevertheless, his emphasis on will univocally conceived rather than on transcendent goodness will carry through into modern concepts of law, including into the modern problem of neurolaw.

William of Ockham adopted Scotus' theory of univocity. For the scholastics, drawing on Aristotle, a common test of the language of analogy was the notion of "health." The example they often used was that an animal could be called "healthy" and urine or food could be called "healthy." Those who argued for analogy said "healthy" cannot mean precisely the same thing in each case. As applied to urine, "healthy" is an analogy, meaning the quality of the animal's urine suggests the animal is healthy overall. Applied to food, "healthy" is also an analogy, meaning the food is of good quality and conducive to the animal's health. Ockham disagreed that this use was analogical. "Formally speaking," he said, "'health' taken in the first manner [as applied to 'animal', 'food' and 'urine'] is only one and the same *word*; taken in the same manner it is one and the same *concept*."[54] "It is the same," Ockham said, "with being (*ens*)."[55]

For this reason, Ockham said, "[t]here is a concept, common to God and creatures, which can be predicated of them in the manner of an essence and the first mode of intrinsic (*per se*) predication."[56] This concept, according to Ockham, "is univocal to God and creatures without there being a composition in God Himself."[57] Nevertheless, like Scotus, Ockham qualified the concept of univocity: "nothing that

---

commandments belong strictly to the law of nature; third, there is some doubt about the third commandment of the first table; fourth, we concede that all the commandments fall under the law of nature, speaking broadly."

53. Wolter, *Duns Scotus on the Will and Morality*, 22–23.

54. Ockham, *Reportatio*, III, Q. viii, 109.

55. Ockham, *Reportatio*, III, Q. viii.

56. Ockham, *Ordinatio*, D.II., Q. ix, P *sqq*, 102.

57. Ockham, *Ordinatio*, D.II., Q. ix, P *sqq*, 105.

exists in a creature," he said, "whether it be essential or accidental, has perfect similitude with something which really exists in God. It is this strict univocation and no other that the saints and authors deny is found between God and creatures."[58] And, like Scotus, Ockham suggested that univocity might come in degrees, and that although a univocal term suggests similarity, the subjects of the term (creatures and God) might be even more dissimilar than similar—a concept not far removed from Aquinas' approach to analogy.[59]

While Ockham's approach to the concept of univocity was similar to Scotus', Ockham's ethical theory seems more extreme. Ockham emphasized the priority of the will, including the absolute power of God to ordain whatever God wills, over the intrinsic properties of being. For Ockham, the liberty of indifference was "the power to will, to nil, or to do nothing with respect to any object."[60] Although Ockham still wrote in the context of the Aristotelian stream of scholasticism, in contrast to others in that tradition, he denied that reason determines the will's action.[61] The liberty of indifference, in relation to God's absolute freedom, means that God could command *anything at all* and we would be obligated to define the command as good. Ockham attempted to preserve the relationship between natural law and positive ethical commands but, as Marilyn Mc-Cord Adams notes,

> Ockham's moral theory does inherit difficulties kindred to those confronting authoritarian divine command theories. For right reason infers from divine natural excellence that God ought to be loved above all and for God's own sake; suitable informed right reason, that divine commands are a secondary ethical norm. But according to Ockham, divine liberty of indifference means God could forbid us to love or even command us to hate him. Likewise, God could command the opposite of what right reason dictates, whether in general or in particular.[62]

Ockham's voluntarist approach to divine commands and the natural law influenced some important later thinkers in the natural law tradition.[63]

---

58. Ockham, *Ordinatio*, D.II., Q. ix, P *sqq*, 106.

59. Ockham, *Reportatio*, III, Q. viii, 106–8.

60. Adams, "Ockham on Will, Nature, and Morality," 245.

61. Adams, "Ockham on Will, Nature, and Morality," 254.

62. Adams, "Ockham on Will, Nature, and Morality," 266.

63. See Oakley, "Medieval Theories of Natural Law."

As Francis Oakley has argued, the condemnations at the University of Paris "marked the beginning of a theological reaction that was to vindicate the freedom and omnipotence of God at the expense of the ultimate intelligibility of the world, and Ockham . . . was the classic product of this reaction."[64] And, Oakley suggested, "the voluntaristic interpretation of the natural law tends to carry over into a positivist interpretation of law in general."[65]

3. Grotius and Hobbes

At the turn of the ages towards modernity, we can see this influence in one of the great early modern natural law jurists, whose ideas still underpin international law today, Hugo Grotius. In his prologue to his masterpiece *On the Law of War and Peace*, Grotius stated that, while one source of law lies in nature, there is "another source of law besides the source in nature, that is, the free will of God."[66] The commands of scripture, including those of the Ten Commandments, according to Grotius, derive only from God's will, not from the law of nature, although they are consistent with the law of nature.[67] The law of nature has a cause in God, Grotius said, but the "law of nations" is based in "common consent."[68] Because the laws of nature, the divine commands, and the laws of nations are so conceptually distinct, Grotius suggested that the study of law could theoretically proceed "even if we should concede that which cannot be conceded without the utmost wickedness: that there is no God, or that the affairs of men are of no concern to Him."[69] As Charles Taylor notes in his classic book *A Secular Age*, "Grotius' derivation of Natural Law doesn't follow the path of an Aristotelian-Thomist definition of the ends of human nature."[70] Instead, Grotius' vision "proceeds almost geomet-

---

64. Oakley, "Medieval Theories of Natural Law: William of Ockham and the Significance of the Voluntarist Tradition," 81–82.

65. Oakley, "Medieval Theories of Natural Law: William of Ockham and the Significance of the Voluntarist Tradition," 83.

66. Grotius, *The Law of War and Peace*, Prologue, 4.

67. Grotius, *The Law of War and Peace*, Prologue, 15.

68. Grotius, *The Law of War and Peace*, Prologue, 12.

69. Grotius, *The Law of War and Peace*, Prologue, 4.

70. Taylor, *A Secular Age*, 126.

rico" from general observations about humanity's sociabilitiy—a framing that is entirely immanent and pragmatic.[71]

These sorts of ideas resonate in one of the true founders of legal positivism, Thomas Hobbes. Hobbes denied there were any universals and attributed them only to perception: "whatsoever accidents or qualities our senses make us think there be in the world, they are not there, but are seemings and apparitions only."[72] Human beings ascribe names to things, which makes us think the qualities of those things are universal, but the universal qualities are merely conceptual markers attached to names, not real qualities.[73] There is no self-evident knowledge, nor can truth be ascertained only through reasoning. Scientific knowledge can only be obtained through evidence ascertained through the senses.[74] "Good" and "evil" are only words we attach to sensations of pleasure or pain:

> Every man, for his own part, calleth that which pleaseth, and is delightful to himself, GOOD; and that EVIL which displeaseth him: insomuch that while every man differeth from other in constitution, they differ also one from another concerning the common distinction of good and evil. Nor is there any such thing as . . . simply good. For even the goodness which we attribute to God Almighty, is his goodness to us. And as we call good and evil the things that please and displease; so call we goodness and badness, the qualities or powers whereby they do it.[75]

Based on this reduction of "good" and "evil" to sensations of pain or pleasure, Hobbes then described various virtues and vices in terms of various emotional "passions."[76] These passions, Hobbes said, proceed "from the action of external objects upon the brain, or some internal substance of the head" and then proceed from the brain to the "heart."[77] The various passions in different people often conflict, and each individual is compelled to seek only his own good.[78] This produces a natural state of war, in which each person, in his own liberty, exercises his natural desire

71. Taylor, *A Secular Age*, 126

72. Hobbes, *The Elements of Law*, 3.10.

73. Hobbes, *The Elements of Law*, 5.1–5.

74. Hobbes, *The Elements of Law*, 6.

75. Hobbes, *The Elements of Law*, 7.3.

76. Hobbes, *The Elements of Law*, 9.

77. Hobbes, *The Elements of Law*, 10.1.

78. Hobbes, *The Elements of Law*, 13.3–6.

of self-preservation against the other.[79] This natural state of war, however, ultimately will result in self-destruction, since no person can maintain power for long. Reason therefore dictates *that every man divest himself of the right he hath to all things by nature.*[80] The mutual divestment of rights between different people in order to preserve peace is a form of contract.[81] A breach of the social contract is an injury that is unjust.[82] "The names of just, unjust, justice, injustice," then, "are equivocal and signify diversely."[83]

From his concept of social contract and the injustice of injury that comes from breach of the social contract, Hobbes derived a number of maxims he defines as laws of nature, such as "[t]hat every man do help and endeavor to accommodate each other, as far as may be without danger of their persons, and loss of their means, to maintain and defend themselves."[84] These maxims, however, seem to hang in mid-air. Indeed, Hobbes subsequently said that "consent and covenant may so alter the cases, which in the law of nature may be put, by changing the circumstances, that that which was reason before, may afterwards be against it; and yet is reason still the law."[85] In other words, there is no natural law or law of reason above specific circumstances that guides particular applications of the natural law in those specific circumstances. The specific circumstances determine the law of reason. This led Hobbes to conclude that "[t]he sum of virtue is to be sociable with them that will be sociable, and formidable with them that will not. And the same is the sum of the law of nature . . . ."[86]

There is much to commend in figures such as Scotus, Ockham, Grotius, and Hobbes. Scotus and Ockham tried to articulate God's divine freedom against what seemed like a principle of necessity that supervened on God.[87] Grotius and Hobbes tried to articulate minimal theories of law

79. Hobbes, *The Elements of Law*, 14:11–12.

80. Hobbes, *The Elements of Law*, 15.2 (emphasis in original).

81. Hobbes, *The Elements of Law*, 15.8.

82. Hobbes, *The Elements of Law*, 16.2.

83. Hobbes, *The Elements of Law*, 16.4.

84. Hobbes, *The Elements of Law*, 16.8 and 17.

85. Hobbes, *The Elements of Law*, 17.11.

86. Hobbes, *The Elements of Law*, 17.15.

87. Indeed, as Oliver O'Donovan has noted, the distinction between creator and creation requires us to maintain that in God's divine freedom *this* creation is not necessary, but rather is contingent on God's free decision. O'Donovan, *Resurrection and Moral Order*, 39. As O'Donovan notes, "although we may perhaps dare to speak, by way of analogy and hesitantly, of a divine love that 'had' to express itself in creation,

against the backdrop of decades of war between putatively Christian nations and parties. Grotius' ideas remain important to the relations between nations today, and Hobbes' ideas helped inform democratic constitutionalism, a sanguine development in global history, even though Hobbes himself believed the social contract must be overseen by an absolute monarch.[88] But, at the same time, by the time we get to Hobbes' theory of law, something vital has been lost.

Political philosopher Jean Bethke Elshtain suggests that the rule of law was ultimately weakened by nominalism and voluntarism. In her Gifford lectures, Elshtain noted how the nominalistic sense of will, power, justice, and law has informed Western concepts of political sovereignty since the late Middle Ages:

> *If* there is a vital move in theology, law and ethics with nominalism, it is this: An emphasis on the primacy of will over intellect is lodged as the gravamen of understandings of power and authority—a seismic shift from realist emphases. Within medieval realism, even as Jesus, the Mediator, helps us to "rise to meet him," as Augustine puts it, so an enduring fabric and structure of unchanging law forges a connection between God and human beings. Human reason has access to it and can come to know and embrace the law freely. The grounding of ethics lies in law. There is an element of predictability here: You can "take it to the bank," as we nowadays say.[89]

Elshtain connects this nominalist tendency with legal positivism:

> By contrast, the rise of a command-obedience account of law, what in modernity came to be called legal positivism, turned, at

---

as soon as we go beyond that to suggest that it had to create this world and not some other one, we say in effect that the 'creation' is not a creation at all, but an emanation, a reflection of the inner law of God's being, sharing its necessity and thus, in some sense, sharing its divinity." *Resurrection and Moral Order*, 39. But insofar as God *has* willed to create *this* world, O'Donovan further argues, "there is no reason why this proper theological concern should not be fully accommodated within a teleological and generic understanding of created order." *Resurrection and Moral Order*, 39. Therefore the *source* of "justice" is indeed ineffable, since it lies in the being and will of God. But though it is ineffable, it is not bereft of human apprehension, if we, too, are God's creatures.

88. For a good discussion of how later Whig constitutionalists struggled to deal with Grotius and Hobbes, see Ward, *The Politics of Liberty in England and Revolutionary America*, 95–98 (noting that Grotius and Hobbes "offered secularizing and, in Hobbes' case, emphatically individualistic models of political theory" that appealed to the Whigs, but that "those models also contained dangerous absolutist tendencies").

89. Elshtain, *Sovereignty*, 50–51.

least in its early foundations, on the theory of a willful supreme being who might as well have created things differently than he did—and might yet do so by undoing what he has done. . . . Remaining on the trail of the will in theology and politics—the voluntarist tendency—earthly sovereignty is to social, political, and religious life as God's sovereignty is to the emergence of law and dominion in the first instance. [90]

As God's being was elided from the equations of law and justice, first the absolute human sovereign, and then autonomous self, and then the irrational self, and finally the mercilessly deterministic brain, began to take God's place. As John Milbank observes,

> In the thought of the nominalists . . . the Trinity loses its significance as a prime location for discussing will and understanding in God and the relationship of God to the world. No longer is the world participatorily enfolded within the divine expressive Logos, but instead a bare divine unity starkly confronts the other distinct unities which he has ordained. . . . This dominance of logic and of the *potentia absoluta* is finally brought to a peak by Hobbes: "The right of Nature, whereby God reigneth over men, and punisheth those that break his Lawes, is to be derived, not from his creating them, as if he required obedience as of gratitude for his benefits; but from his Irresistible Power."[91]

We can see in Hobbes the progression down from the Greek, Roman, and Christian natural law traditions to the lineaments of contemporary neurolaw—even to the prominence given to the brain. In the following chapter we will see how this flattened view of the law came to dominate Anglo-American jurisprudence starting in the nineteenth century through today's neurolaw project.

90. Elshtain, *Sovereignty*, 51.

91. Milbank, *Theology and Social Theory*, 15–16 (quoting Thomas Hobbes, *Leviathan*). Hobbes' nominalist and voluntarist views concerning law, power, and sovereignty were, of course, hotly contested in their own time and formed the substrate of ideas that led to the English Civil War (1642–51). See Hill, *The World Turned Upside Down*. A notable contrast to Hobbes was Sir Edward Coke, Chief Justice of the Court of Common Pleas in the early seventeenth century, who decided the famous *Bonham's Case*, 77 Eng. Rep. 107 (1610), which suggested the practice of judicial review. As Coke stated in his opinion, "it appears in our books, that in many cases, the common law will controul Acts of Parliament, and sometimes adjudge them to be utterly void: for when an Act of Parliament is against common right and reason, or repugnant, or impossible to be performed, the common law will controul it, and adjudge such Act to be void." For a comparison of Coke and Hobbes see Stoner, *Common Law and Liberal Theory*.

3

The Path of Reductive Neurolaw

REDUCTIVE NEUROLAW SCHOLARS ARGUE that neuroscience completely rewrites the concept of "law" because it destroys any meaningful concept of intentionality. They want to replace any notion of autonomous general legal principles with neurobiology. Law, like everything else, could be fully explained by science.

For these reductive neurolaw scholars, neuroscience suggests that "the brain is a physical entity governed by the principles and rules of the physical world," and that "brain determines mind."[1] Contemporary neuroscience thereby claims to elide the soul and the mind—what many neuroscientists call "the ghost in the machine."[2] All of the faculties attributed in medieval Christian theology to the "sensitive soul" (locomotion, appetite, sensation, and emotion), as well as the intellectual faculties attributed to the human "rational soul," these scientists suggest, can or will be accounted for by brain functions.[3] As Martha Farah of the University of Pennsylvania's Center for Neuroscience & Society puts it, "as neuroscience begins to reveal the mechanisms of personality, character, and even sense of spirituality dualism becomes strained. If these are all features of the machine, why have a ghost at all? By raising questions like this, it seems likely that neuroscience will pose a far more fundamental challenge

1. Garland, *Neuroscience and the Law.*

2. See Garland, *Neuroscience and the Law.* For the origin of the term "ghost in the machine," see Ryle, *The Concept of Mind.*

3. See Murphy, *Bodies and Souls, or Spirited Bodies,* 55–69.

to religion than evolutionary biology."[4] Not just religion, but law as well, can be reduced to neuroscience. Farah notes with some understatement that "[t]he idea that behaviour is determined by physical causes is hard to reconcile with the intuitive notions of free will and moral agency on which our legal systems are based."[5]

1. Law, Freedom, and Neuroscience

Indeed, "free will" is an illusion, many neurolaw scholars argue. Among their most compelling bits of evidence for this claim are studies, based on the pioneering work of Benjamin Libet, suggesting that the brain signals the body to engage in actions before we become consciously aware of the action we will take.[6] This "precognition" suggests that our actions are automatic responses to stimuli and that our conscious "decisions" are really merely *ex post* determinations not to "veto" what the brain has already signaled its readiness to do. We have, at best, "free won't" rather than "free will."[7] Therefore, "according to neuroscience, no one person is more or less responsible than any other for actions. We are all part of a deterministic system that someday, in theory, we will completely understand."[8] The notion of "responsibility" is only a "social construct," law is an instrumentalist tool useful for engineering of the society we are constructing, and the society we are constructing ultimately is reducible to the evolutionary history embedded in our brains.

David Eagleman, Director of the Initiative for Neuroscience and the Law at the Baylor College of Medicine, is a leading proponent of this view.[9] Eagleman states the issue for neurolaw as follows: "the crux of the question is whether all of your actions are fundamentally on autopilot or whether there is some little bit that is 'free' to choose, independent of the rules of biology."[10]

Eagleman offers a seemingly mundane example: the everyday ac-tivity of driving home from work and opening the front door of one's

---

4. Farah, "Neuroethics."

5. Farah, "Neuroethics."

6. Garland, *Neuroscience and the Law*, 56.

7. Garland, *Neuroscience and the Law*, 56

8. Garland, *Neuroscience and the Law*, 68.

9. See https://scilaw.org/.

10. Eagleman, *Incognito*, 166.

home.[11] Most of us will realize, if we reflect on these actions once we are comfortably seated on the couch after a long day, that we drove home on mental auto-pilot and that we opened the door without thinking about the location of the doorknob. If our route had been changed because of road construction, or if our significant other had installed a new door with a different type of opener, things would have been different: these new facts would have required greater attentiveness. For Eagleman, this means that the conscious aspect of returning home from work is only a "little bit" of the story. Once we become habituated to the routine, it becomes automatic.[12] The same is true, he argues, for all our actions, including what we mistakenly attribute to intentionality.

In a recent interview, Eagleman acknowledged that his view of neurobiology undermines libertarian notions of personal autonomy and free will.[13] Asked whether neuroscience completely erodes or at least challenges the notion of individual autonomy, he replied, "I'm afraid it does," "you are your biology," and "what I'm pretty certain about now is that to whatever extent we have free will it is only a bit player in what actually happens in people's lives."[14]

Eagleman asserts that "[t]he unique patterns of neurobiology inside each of our heads cannot qualify as *choices*; these are the cards we're dealt."[15] He suggests that "it is difficult to find the gap into which to slip free will—the uncaused causer—because there seems to be no part of the machinery that does not follow in a causal relationship from the other parts."[16] He argues that concepts of "blame" should be replaced with "science" and that "[b]lameworthiness should be removed from the legal argot."[17] Blameworthiness is merely a "backward-looking concept that demands the impossible task of untangling the hopelessly complex web

11. Eagleman, *Incognito*, 166.

12. Eagleman, *Incognito*, 166.

13. See http://www.youtube.com/watch?v=wSQY7zHk5y8.

14. Eagleman, http://www.youtube.com/watch?v=wSQY7zHk5y8. Of course, he does not explain how his views about biological determinism are consistent with his description of first-person phenomenological qualia ("I'm afraid. . ." "I'm pretty certain . . "). And just moments before offering that grim response, he suggests that bio-feedback treatments for criminals would provide them with a "libertarian" way to "help themselves."

15. Eagleman, "The Brain on Trial."

16. Eagleman, "The Brain on Trial."

17. Eagleman, "The Brain on Trial."

of genetics and environment that constructs the trajectory of a human life."[18]

Eagleman's near-mechanistic view of human nature is reflected in his bold and ultimately frightening vision of the legal system. Since people do not really possess moral agency, the question for the law is not whether the accused is to *blame* for his or her conduct, but rather whether there is something "different" about the person's neurobiology that led the person to act in a certain way.[19] We should think about criminal conduct "[i]n the same way we think about any other physical process, such as diabetes or lung disease."[20]

Eagleman admits that, at present, only in relatively rare cases can we assert with confidence that a person's anti-social conduct was caused by an identifiable brain condition, such as a tumor, but this, he claims, is merely a problem of technology.[21] In principle, he suggests, science will one day be able to measure biological states with a degree of comprehensiveness and granularity that will permit a full diagnosis of criminal conduct. Culpability, he argues, should not "be determined by the limits of current technology."[22] In place of traditional legal concepts of fault and blame, Eagleman proposes a "forward-looking" system in which criminals would receive bio-feedback treatments designed to retrain their brains towards "pro-social behavior."[23]

How does Eagleman define what "pro-social" should mean in a world of neurobiological determinism? He speaks of "social contracts," "society's needs," and what we can "hope for" as "a society that respects individual rights and freedom of thought."[24] All of these concepts, of course, presuppose the very "folk" concepts of freedom, autonomy, and intentionality that Eagleman's neuroscience supposedly deconstructs. Yet for Eagleman, these concepts are merely artifacts of evolution. "A meaningful theory of human biology," he argues

> Cannot be reduced to chemistry and physics, but instead must be understood in its own vocabulary of evolution, competition,

18. Eagleman, "The Brain on Trial."
19. Eagleman, *Incognito*, 174–77.
20. Eagleman, *Incognito*, 170.
21. Eagleman, *Incognito*, 175–76.
22. Eagleman, *Incognito*, 176.
23. Eagleman, *Incognito*, 176.
24. Eagleman, *Incognito*, 176.

reward, desire, reputation, avarice, friendship, trust, hunger, and so on—in the same way that traffic flow will be understood not in the vocabulary of screws and spark plugs, but instead in terms of speed limits, rush hours, road rage, and people wanting to get home to their families as soon as possible when their workday is over.[25]

Instead of assuming people ordinarily possess a degree of agency that allows them to choose whether to abide by the law, Eagleman argues that "criminals should always be treated as incapable of having acted otherwise."[26]

The role of the legal system would then shift from assigning blame based on agency to changing the law-breaker's brain state in order to produce more desirable behavior. This would be accomplished by a "prefrontal workout," consisting of cognitive biofeedback.[27] A person's sentence—their prescribed prefrontal workout regimen—would depend on the degree to which the person's biology is "modifiable," based on some as-yet-undiscovered measure of neuroplasticity.[28] The concept of variable neuroplasticity is important, Eagleman observes, because contrary to the ideals of developed democracies, all people are *not* created equal: "[w]hile admirable, the notion [of human equality] is simply not true."[29] People vary widely, both in nature and in nurture.[30] With this truth in hand, we could "tailor sentencing and rehabilitation" to the individual's specific neurobiological make-up.[31]

If neurolaw is truly to fulfill its promise, why *doesn't* an ardent believer such as David Eagleman go all-in for lobotomies, chemical castrations, and other more direct biological interventions? "The ethical problem," Eagleman suggests, "pivots on how much a state should be able to change its citizens."[32] This is a "landmark problem" in neuroscience: "as we come to understand the brain, how can we keep governments from meddling with it?"[33] One of Eagleman's concerns is that legal advances of

25. Eagleman, *Incognito*, 218–19.
26. Eagleman, *Incognito*, 177.
27. Eagleman, *Incognito*, 182–86.
28. Eagleman, *Incognito*, 188–89.
29. Eagleman, *Incognito*, 189.
30. Eagleman, *Incognito*, 187.
31. Eagleman, *Incognito*, 188.
32. Eagleman, *Incognito*, 182.
33. Eagleman, *Incognito*, 182.

recent years, such as civil rights legislation, should not be compromised: "[o]ur social policies work to cement into place the most enlightened ideas of humanity and to surmount the basest facets of human nature."[34]

2. Law and Science

The drive to make the law "scientific" is not in the first instance the result of any empirical observations of evolutionary biology or neuroscience. Rather, it is rooted in the broader intellectual movement towards legal positivism and instrumentalism. In his insightful book *Law as a Means to an End*, Brian Tamanaha describes the shift in Anglo-American law towards legal instrumentalism starting in the nineteenth century.[35] Tamanaha traces how "law" in the West became unmoored from any transcendent source and began to occupy the place of a "science." He explains that

> Science is oriented toward uncovering causal relations, effects and functions, formulated in terms of principles or laws. Non-instrumental views portrayed law *as* an immanent ordering (of the universe or of the community). Under a scientific view, law would come instead to be seen as the *source* of social order—to produce social order is the function or purpose or end of law. In turn, this new perspective, over time, would open up questions about the efficiency and utility of law in carrying out its functions. The subtle but fundamental difference can be put thus: law *is* order, versus law *maintains* order.[36]

Tamanaha notes that in the Anglo-American legal tradition, historically, "law was not seen as an empty vessel that could be filled in with whatever content might be desired by law makers to serve whatever end was desired."[37] There were various theories of legal legitimacy, including "natural law, principle and reason, or customs from time immemorial," all of which finally located law in some transcendent source.[38] But, according to Tamanaha, a variety of intellectual currents, including Spenserian social Darwinism, laisez faire economics, and Benthamite

34. Eagleman, *Incognito*, 186.
35. Tamanaha, *Law as a Means to an End*.
36. Tamanaha, *Law as a Means to an End*, 21.
37. Tamanaha, *Law as a Means to an End*, 35.
38. Tamanaha, *Law as a Means to an End*, 35.

utilitarianism, contributed to the rise of "legal positivism" throughout the nineteenth century.[39] Legal positivism is a form of "command" theory of law, in which the law is simply whatever the authority with the power to enforce it says it is.[40] Legal positivism is readily twinned with legal instrumentalism, which understands the law as a tool for achieving ends that are essentially infinitely malleable.[41] The law becomes severed from any transcendent source beyond the chosen instrumental ends instantiated in the will of whoever has the power to enforce the law. As Isaak Dore suggests, "[l]egal positivism thus stands as the main philosophical rival to natural law theory."[42]

This notion that law is reducible to power and will is reflected in Justice Oliver Wendell Holmes, Jr.'s influential essay *The Path of the Law*, delivered at the opening of Boston University Law School and published in the *Harvard Law Review* in 1897.[43] Holmes' essay is so important that it occupies the opening slot in David Kennedy and William Fishers' compilation of *The Canon of American Legal Thought*.[44]

Holmes opens his essay with the claim that "[w]hen we study law we are not studying a mystery but a well-known profession."[45] From the study of precedent—the "oracles of the law"—Holmes argued, the law student can discern the nature of legal duties.[46] A legal duty is not a moral idea, but rather "is nothing but a prediction that if a man does or omits certain things he will be made to suffer in this or that way by judgment of the court."[47] The law exists to deter the "bad man," for "[a] man who cares nothing for an ethical rule which is believed and practiced by his neighbor is likely nevertheless to care a good deal to avoid being made to pay money, and will want to keep out of jail if he can."[48] Therefore, Holmes told the newly matriculated Boston University law students, "[i]f you want to know the law and nothing else, you must look at it as a bad man, who cares only for the material consequences which such

---

39. Tamanaha, *Law as a Means to an End*, 35–41.

40. Tamanaha, *Law as a Means to an End*, 43.

41. Tamanaha, *Law as a Means to an End*, 43.

42. Dore, *The Epistemological Foundations of Law*, 19.

43. Holmes, "The Path of the Law."

44. Kennedy and Fisher, *The Canon of American Legal Thought*.

45. Holmes, "The Path of the Law," 457.

46. Holmes, "The Path of the Law," 457.

47. Holmes, "The Path of the Law," 458.

48. Holmes, "The Path of the Law," 459.

knowledge enables him to predict, not as a good one, who finds his reasons for conduct, whether inside the law or outside of it, in the vaguer sanctions of conscience."[49]

The law *in esse*, for Holmes, had nothing to do with morality. Indeed, only "confusion of thought" could result from any equation of law and morality.[50] Instead, Holmes wondered aloud "whether it would not be a gain if every word of moral significance could be banished from the law altogether, and other words adopted which should convey legal ideas uncolored by anything outside the law."[51] If this were possible, Holmes mused, judges might better understand their role as social engineers.[52] Indeed, Holmes looked "forward to a time when the part played by history in the explanation of [legal] dogma shall be very small, and instead of ingenious research we shall spend our energy on a study of the ends sought to be attained and the reasons for desiring them."[53]

A key "step towards that ideal" for Holmes was "that every lawyer ought to seek an understanding of economics."[54] Holmes concluded his germinal essay with a nod to the form of practical reason that underwrote his philosophy: "Read the works of the great German jurists," Holmes advised, "and see how much more the world is governed to-day by Kant than by Bonaparte."[55] There were no choices for Holmes other than the seemingly opposite poles of rational freedom and dictatorial tyranny.

There is a profound irony here that seems to escape neurolaw scholars such as David Eagleman: Justice Holmes wrote the infamous U.S. Supreme Court opinion in *Buck v. Bell,* a 1927 case that upheld the forced sterilization of "mentally retarded" persons.[56] In that case, Holmes wrote that

> We have seen more than once that the public welfare may call upon the best citizens for their lives. It would be strange if it could not call upon those who already sap the strength of the State for these lesser sacrifices, often not felt to be such by those

49. Holmes, "The Path of the Law," 459.

50. Holmes, "The Path of the Law," 460.

51. Holmes, "The Path of the Law," 464.

52. Holmes, "The Path of the Law," 469 (stating "I think that the judges have failed adequately to recognize their duty of weighing the considerations of social advantage").

53. Holmes, "The Path of the Law," 474.

54. Holmes, "The Path of the Law," 474.

55. Holmes, "The Path of the Law," 478.

56. *Buck v. Bell*, 274 U.S. 200 (1927).

concerned, to prevent our being swamped with incompetence. It is better for all the world, if instead of waiting to execute degenerate offspring for crime, or to let them starve for their imbecility, society can prevent those who are manifestly unfit from continuing their kind. The principle that sustains compulsory vaccination is broad enough to cover cutting the Fallopian tubes.[57]

The climactic line of Holmes' opinion in *Buck v. Bell* is widely regarded as one of the most embarrassing in the history of U.S. Supreme Court Jurisprudence: "Three generations of imbeciles are enough."[58]

3. From the Bad Man to Homo Economicus to Homo Irrationalis

After the horrors of World War II and the Holocaust, there was a renewed debate over the viability of natural law theories and the claims of the primary rival theory, legal positivism, encapsulated in arguments between H. L. A. Hart on the positivist side and Lon Fuller on the natural law side.[59] Related debates continued among Hart, Ronald Dworkin, and Fuller.[60] Fuller insisted on the connection between law and morality, but did not relate his theory to any classical concept of God or teleology.[61] Dworkin developed a naturalist theory of law rooted in natural rights of individuals or groups, but likewise without a reference to God or teleology, and, some commentators suggest, in a form that is "process-oriented and instrumental, rather than broadly or substantively ethical."[62] Today the "new" natural law theory of John Finnis is important in some pockets of the legal academy. We will discuss Finnis in chapter 8. For now, we note that Finnis also purports to eschew any notion of teleology or any

57. *Buck v. Bell*, 274 U.S. at 207.

58. *Buck v. Bell*, 274 U.S. at 207.

59. See Dore, *The Epistemological Foundations of Law*, chapter 10; Fuller, "Positivism and Fidelity to Law"; *The Morality of Law*; Hart, "Book Review"; *The Concept of Law*.

60. Dore, *The Epistemological Foundations of Law*, 670–710; Dworkin, "The Elusive Morality of Law"; Fuller, "A Reply to Professors Cohen and Dworkin."

61. Dore, *The Epistemological Foundations of Law*, 576.

62. Dore, *The Epistemological Foundations of Law*, 553. See Dworkin, *Taking Rights Seriously*; *Law's Empire*.

reference to God.[63] Arguments about natural law therefore remain alive in contemporary political theory and in the legal academy, but they are decidedly *modern* arguments, seemingly committed to a-theistic epistemology and metaphysics.

Meanwhile, the flow of legal scholarship, at least in the United States, has largely left natural law theories behind. In the contemporary history of American legal thought, the conjoining of legal positivism and legal instrumentalism has tended to break into two sometimes contradictory streams: the law and economics movement, and critical legal studies ("CLS").[64] Law and economics seeks to explain legal rules in terms of microeconomic principles, offering what it presents as pragmatic solutions shorn of metaphysical speculation.[65] CLS, drawing on Marxian and postmodern analysis, seeks to explain legal rules by deconstructing the power relations behind the rules.[66] CLS can be critical, indeed hostile, to law and economics, but in some ways they are natural bedfellows. It is law and economics, after all, that supplies the notion of "capture," which shows how most regulatory requirements result from the influence of power industries that influence ("capture") the regulators.

But law and economics, following Holmes's naturalistic bent, purports to offer a "scientific" analysis of legal rules that can supply an objective basis for policymaking.[67] Perhaps for this reason, over the past twenty-five years or so, law and economics has been a reigning paradigm for legal scholarship, while CLS has declined, except among pockets of diehard adherents (often among dispossessed groups such as racial minorities, women, and the LGBT community). To be sure, there are other very important paradigms in the legal academy that eschew the positivism behind both law and economics and CLS, notably deontological approaches informed in one way or another by John Rawls.[68] Nevertheless,

63. Finnis, *Natural Law and Natural Rights*, 52. Finnis further purports to offer a natural law theory "without needing to advert to the question of God's existence or nature or will." *Natural Law and Natural Rights*, 48–49.

64. See Kennedy, *The Canon of American Legal Thought*, at 7. See also Fitzpatrick and Hunt, "Introduction to Critical Legal Studies."

65. See Dore, *The Epistemological Foundations of Law*, 905–9.

66. See Dore, *The Epistemological Foundations of Law*, 857–84.

67. Hackney, *Under Cover of Science*.

68. Rawls, *A Theory of Justice*. It is beyond the scope of this Book to offer a critique of Rawlsian legal theory. In short, critics argue that Rawlsians cannot articulate a reason why anyone *ought* to honor the original position and the veil of ignorance, if cutting the veil and betraying the original position would make an individual actor

law and economics continues to represent a default "scientific" posture for many legal scholars.[69]

In recent years, however, the law and economics movement has witnessed a significant shift occasioned by the rise of behavioral economics.[70] Classical microeconomics assumes rational utility-maximizing actors who act on perfect information, a model that even neoclassical economists admit almost never obtains in the real world.[71] Behavioral economics, in contrast, assumes that people do things for reasons that are often irrational or sub-rational.[72] This assumption is informed by empirical behavioral psychology studies.[73] And behavioral economics has spawned a robust new sub-discipline of behavioral law and economics.

---

better off. A defender of Rawls might argue that the original position ought to be honored because it protects the rights of all citizens and thereby promotes the aggregate well-being of everyone. This sounds, however, like a utilitarian argument and not a deontological one. Utilitarian arguments fail for the same reason: why *ought* any individual actor care about aggregate social welfare? Who says maximizing aggregate social welfare is "good" if reaching that goal decreases individual welfare for some? The question of what comprises "the good" is begged. For a general introduction to the "original position" in Rawls' thought, see Freeman, "Original Position." For a classic critique of Rawls, see Nozick, *Anarchy, State and Utopia.*

69. Kennedy and Fisher divide American legal thought into eight schools: "Legal Realism, Legal Process, Law and Economics, Law and Society, Critical Legal Studies, Modern Liberalism, Feminist Legal Thought, and Critical Race Theory." *The Canon of American Legal Thought*, 7. Law and Economics and Law and Society, however, are in fact both branches of Legal Realism, with Law and Economics and Law and Society representing sociology and other social sciences apart from economics. See Tamanaha, *Law as a Means to an End*, 123–26. Likewise, Feminist Legal Thought and Critical Race Theory are branches of Critical Legal Studies. Tamanaha, *Law as a Means to an End*, 120–23. Legal Process and Modern Liberalism represent the pragmatist and Rawlsian influences.

70. See, e.g., Jolls et al., "A Behavioral Approach to Law and Economics"; Korobkin and Ulen, "Law and Behavioral Science"; Korobkin, "What Comes After Victory for Behavioral Law and Economics?" (stating that "[t]he battle to separate the economic analysis of legal rules and institutions from the straightjacket of strict rational choice assumptions has been won by the proponents of 'behavioral law and economics'").

71. See Jolls et al., "A Behavioral Approach to Law and Economics"; Korobkin and Ulen, "Law and Behavioral Science."

72. See Jolls et al., "A Behavioral Approach to Law and Economics" (stating that "Economic analysis of law usually proceeds under the assumptions of neoclassical economics. But empirical evidence gives much reason to doubt these assumptions; people exhibit bounded rationality, bounded self-interest, and bounded willpower").

73. See Jolls et al., "A Behavioral Approach to Law and Economics"; see also Wright and Ginsburg, "Behavioral Law and Economics: Its Origins, Fatal Flaws, and Implications for Liberty" (noting that "[e]merging close on the heels of behavioral economics over the past thirty years has been the 'behavioral law and economics' movement, which explores the legal and policy implications of cognitive biases").

Behavioral law and economics scholarship can offer useful and interesting insights concerning the limitations of rational choice theory for legal analysis. Critics have argued, however, that the experiments upon which behavioral economics is based are not transposable to real-world market situations.[74] Here reductive neurolaw enters the stage. The supposedly harder science of neurobiology—"harder" precisely because it is a *natural* science rather than a *social* science—might confirm the behavioral economists' insight that human beings are finally not rational beings. Neurolaw thereby promises the fulfillment of Holmes' dream.

Neurolaw, then, seems to represent the culmination of the modern debate about whether the concept of natural law as a transcendent source of norms towards which positive law can aspire has finally been supplanted by a modern understanding of nature without transcendence. Behavioral law and economics shows that the explanation we thought we had in classical utility maximizing law and economics—an explanation that ultimately invoked the concept of *rational* behavior and therefore a standard of reason—is a fiction. Neurolaw shows that the *real* explanation is in our neurochemistry, driving the concept of law even further from any source outside the self. Presumably this would move the concept of law even deeper into human subjectivity. In the end, however, it dissolves subjectivity as well. It does not result in any movement back out towards a source for the self or for the self in relation to other selves, because what is outside is only the random walk of evolution, which is merely a contingent fact and not a thing of any ontological substance. Although this result seems nihilistic, reductive neuroscientists tell us it is the only plausible view in our scientific age. The next three chapters show why this is not so.

---

74. Ginsburg, "Behavioral Law and Economics," 1044–52.

4

Method in Theology and Science

M Y ARGUMENT IN THIS book is that the loss of transcendence in our concept of law, leading to reductive neurolaw, is at heart a theological problem. God has been replaced by "science" not only because of the epochal changes of the Reformation, the growth of empirical natural science, and devastating wars, but most basically because "God" was gradually reduced to a piece of furniture in the universe, which could be discarded in favor of an apparent pragmatic settlement. Neurolaw is attractive to many contemporary thinkers because it appears finally to supply the bridge between natural science, ethics, and law that premodern thinkers believed ultimately must refer to a transcendent source in God. One axis of the theological problem we have already highlighted is that relating to universals and the relationship between God's being and God's will. Another related axis is the relationship between theology and natural science.

This chapter supplies a methodological perspective for my arguments about law, science, and human nature. As Jeffrey Stout and others have noted, modern theology, particularly when it attempts to engage the natural sciences, always entails a significant amount of methodological "throat clearing."[1] In this sense, the book is a sustained argument against

---

1. Stout said that "[p]reoccupation with method is like clearing your throat: it can go on for only so long before you lose your audience." Stout, *Ethics After Babel,* 163. Similarly, although William Placher argued that theologians should "abandon their preoccupation with method and get on with the business of doing theology," he acknowledged the need to discuss method. Placher, *Unapologetic Theology,* 7. Placher

reductionism in both the natural sciences and the humanities, with a specific application to law.

The questions I am asking in this book about human agency, law, and jurisprudence in light of contemporary knowledge about neuroscience and human evolution imply more basic questions about the relationship between theology and the natural sciences, or even more fundamentally, about the relationship between "faith" and "reason." Some aspects of this chapter present background concerning debates in theology and science that have also been treated elsewhere, as the footnotes suggest. I am also making some methodological moves, however, that I do not believe have been fully explored in the theology and science literature. In particular, I try to argue for the priority of theology without falling into the trap of fideism. My view is that problems of the sort I am trying to address in this book entail metaphysical truths that imply and *require* theology as a given framework. "Natural science," if it is to operate from an epistemologically stable base, already presumes a doctrine of creation. Therefore, "natural science" is a subdivision of "philosophy," which is always related to and contained within "theology."[2] This kind of methodological perspective, I think, recovers important insights from theology that were lost, or at least flattened, in modernity. This perspective informs arguments made later in the book about the sources of law and the role law might play in how we think of human nature.

This kind of posture, however, raises significant issues in light of the history of the natural sciences in relation to Christian theology. From the Galileo affair to contemporary "scientific creationism" and "intelligent design" arguments, Christians have too often advanced claims in the name of theology that ironically undermine the essential Christian conviction that creation is a contingent reality with an inherent stability, rationality, and consistency resulting from God's continual sustenance of the created order. In response to this extreme response, many modern "theology and science" scholars propose models that seem to relegate theology to the

---

acknowledged the irony: "Prolegomena to Prolegomena! Worse and Worse!" Similarly, David Kelsey has noted that "in today's methodologically hyper-self-conscious world of technical academic theology," any kind of "broadly methodological judgment" will prove controversial and should be identified. Kelsey, *Eccentric Existence*.

2. See Aquinas, *ST* I.6, Reply 1 and 2 (stating that "[s]acred doctrine derives its principles not from any human knowledge, but from the divine knowledge, through which, as through the highest wisdom, all our knowledge is set in order. . . . The principles of other sciences either are evident and cannot be proved, or are proved by natural reason through some other science").

background or that significantly modify the orthodox conception of God as the transcendent creator and sustainer of all things.[3] The method I wish to follow seeks to avoid these twin dangers by proposing a robust doctrine of God and creation that leads to an equally robust anthropology and epistemology. While such a method cannot convince skeptics who require basic belief in God to be justified on supposedly neutral terms, I hope it at least demonstrates that the Christian belief in God and creation is consistent with a meaningful concept of reason. In fact, after laying the methodological groundwork, I will argue that the Christian doctrines of God and creation supply far richer notions of human agency, reason, and law than any reductively materialist doctrine.

1. From Convergence to Conflict

The field of "science and religion" has become an important sub-discipline in modern theology.[4] This development parallels the rapid ascendancy of "science" as the paradigm of trustworthy authority in modernity and the related development of the "conflict" or "warfare" narrative of the relation between science and religion.[5] The rise of secularism is intimately related to the social and intellectual authority commanded by "science" in modernity.[6]

Theology in the Christian, Jewish, and Muslim traditions historically interacted fruitfully with the "science" of the day, at least prior to the seventeenth century. The Hebrew creation narratives in the biblical book of Genesis both absorb and distinguish the ancient Near Eastern cosmologies of Assyria, Babylon, and Egypt.[7] The church fathers adapted and transformed Platonic philosophy and cosmology, and medieval Muslim,

3. For a discussion of the Christian doctrine of creation, see, e.g., Fergusson, *Creation*; Swartz, *Creation*; McGrath, *The Foundations of Dialogue in Science & Religion*, 36–79; Pannenberg, *Toward a Theology of Nature*, 29–49; Hart, *The Beauty of the Infinite*, 249–318.

4. See, e.g., Muers and Higton, *Modern Theology: A Critical Introduction*, chapter 11; Harrison, *The Cambridge Companion to Science and Religion*; McGrath, *Science & Religion*.

5. See McGrath, *Science & Religion*, 9–11.

6. See, e.g., Taylor, *Sources of the Self*, chapter 19; *A Secular Age*, chapter 7; Gregory, *The Unintended Reformation*, chapter 1; Israel, *Radical Enlightenment*; Brooke, "Science and Secularization."

7. Walton, *Ancient Near Eastern Thought and the Old Testament*; Hyers, *The Meaning of Creation*.

Christian, and Jewish theologians adapted the insights of Aristotle after the rediscovery of the Aristotelian corpus by Islamic scholars.[8]

In 1616, however, the Copernican view of heliocentrism, confirmed and popularized by Galileo, was condemned by the Catholic Church.[9] Galileo himself was condemned and his works were banned by Papal decree in 1633.[10] The Papal Decree of Condemnation asserted that

> The proposition that the Sun is the center of the world and does not move from its place is absurd and false philosophically and formally heretical, because it is expressly contrary to Holy Scripture.
>
> . . .
>
> The proposition that the Earth is not the center of the world and immovable but that it moves, and also with a diurnal motion, is equally absurd and false philosophically and theologically considered at least erroneous in faith.[11]

There is considerable scholarly debate about the circumstances of Galileo's condemnation. As Charles Hummel describes it, "Galileo's trial of 1633 was not the simple conflict between science and religion so commonly pictured. It was a complex power struggle of personal and professional pride, envy, and ambition, affected by pressures of bureaucratic politics."[12] Galileo's own acerbic personality, as well as the crisis of the Reformation, the Counter-Reformation, and the Thirty Years' War, are also often cited by defenders of the Church as contextual factors around Galileo's condemnation. Even after Galileo's condemnation, heliocentrism continued to be taught as a mathematical concept, and by 1835, the heliocentric texts of Copernicus and Galileo were removed from the Catholic Church's Index of Forbidden Books.[13] In 2000, Pope John

8. *See* Boersma, *Heavenly Participation*; Burrell, *Freedom and Creation in Three Traditions*; Lindberg, "The Fate of Science in Patristic and Medieval Christendom"; Cunningham, *Darwin's Pious Idea*, chapter 7.

9. *See* Hummel, *The Galileo Connection*; "Famous Trials: The Trial of Galileo" webpage, available at http://law2.umkc.edu/faculty/projects/ftrials/galileo/galileo.html.

10. Hummel, *The Galileo Connection*, 108–18; "The Trial of Galileo" webpage, text of Papal Condemnation, available at http://law2.umkc.edu/faculty/projects/ftrials/galileo/condemnation.html.

11. "The Trial of Galileo" webpage, text of Papal Condemnation, available at http://law2.umkc.edu/faculty/projects/ftrials/galileo/condemnation.html.

12. Hummel, *The Galileo Connection*, 116.

13. The Vatican Observatory Website, "The Galileo Affair," available at http://vaticanobservatory.org/index.php?option=com_content&view=article&id=197%3At

Paul II formally apologized for the Church's treatment of Galileo, along with apologies for historic mistreatment of Jews, the Crusades, and other matters.[14]

Notwithstanding these qualifications, the Galileo affair represents a touchstone event for the relationship between theology and science. The heliocentric cosmos challenged not only the interpretation of a few biblical passages, but also the broader Aristotelian cosmology that informed the medieval synthesis of "science" and theology.[15] When Newtonianism subsequently questioned Aristotelian causation and the sense of a great chain of being more broadly, Lyellian geology questioned the antiquity of the earth and the "days" of creation recorded in Genesis 1, and Darwinism questioned anthropocentric biology, theology faced an even more significant challenge.[16] At the same time, scientific methods of textual analysis, archeology, and historiography were being applied to the biblical texts in ways that questioned the fundamental integrity of the Bible.[17]

Nineteenth-century Christian thinkers reacted to the Newtonian, Lyellian, and Darwinian challenges inconsistently. During the ascendency of Newtonianism, many opted for a kind of mechanistic deism that was at odds with the Christian view of a God who is intimately providentially involved with creation.[18] In Christian theology's first encounters with Darwinism, notwithstanding the perhaps exaggerated accounts of the clash between Samuel Wilberforce and Thomas Henry Huxley, the majority responded with cautious appraisal and appropriation of both Lyell and Darwin, while working with notions of providence that attempted to accommodate both the biblical picture and Newton.[19] Their

---

he-galileo-affair&catid=89%3Ahistory-of-astronomy&Itemid=242&lang=en.

14. The theological basis for these apologies is set forth in the International Theological Commission's December 1999 document *Memory and Reconciliation: The Church and the Faults of the Past*, available at http://www.vatican.va/roman_curia/congregations/cfaith/cti_documents/rc_con_cfaith_doc_20000307_memory-reconc-itc_en.html, approved by then-Cardinal Josef Ratzinger acting as Prefect of the Congregation for the Doctrine of the Faith.

15. See Hummel, *The Galileo Connection*, chapter 1.

16. See Muers and Higton, *Modern Theology*, chapter 11. As Conor Cunningham argues, it is not at all clear that any of these developments do, in fact, challenge all notions of a chain of being or of human uniqueness. Cunningham, *Darwin's Pious Idea*, 2–3. This perspective will be developed later in this chapter.

17. See Gignilliat, *A Brief History of Old Testament Criticism*.

18. See Taylor, *A Secular Age*, chapter 7.

19. From a Protestant perspective, for example, see Warfield, B. B. *Warfield*,

efforts sometimes led to theological aberrations, such as William Paley's "watchmaker" natural theology, but they nevertheless worked from a framework that assumed that the "book of scripture" and the "book of nature" spoke complementary truths.[20]

The fundamentalist-modernist controversy that erupted among American Protestants in the early twentieth century, however, ignited a tinderbox of conflict, highlighted in the infamous "Scopes Monkey Trial" of 1925 in Dayton, Tennessee.[21] Fundamentalists rejected Darwinian science *in toto*, and further rejected *in toto* the historical-critical inquiry of the biblical sources.[22] The rise of Protestant fundamentalism supported the development of "creation science," which asserts that the Bible can be read as an inerrant scientific text and that God literally created the universe in six days around 6,500 years ago.[23] In the view of "creation science," there is a clear conflict between theology and modern evolutionary science.

The fundamentalists who took up the mantle of defending the faith from the modernists in the early twentieth century typically were less flexible than predecessors, such as B. B. Warfield, who could cautiously incorporate at least some of the empirical data of the new natural sciences and the new biblical scholarship into his understanding of biblical inspiration and inerrancy. Significant portions of *The Fundamentals* were devoted to attacks on higher criticism and Darwinism that lacked any texture or nuance.[24] A line was drawn: any accommodation to Darwin's theory of evolution was a surrender of the essentials of Christian faith.

Evolution, Science, & Scripture. For a typical account of the Huxley-Wilberforce conflict as a watershed crisis moment for Christian theology, see Muers and Highton, *Modern Theology*, 212–15. For a more careful account of the Huxley-Wilberforce encounter, *see* Livingstone, "That Huxley Defeated Wilberforce in Their Debate over Evolution and Religion"; Lucas, "Wilberforce and Huxley: A Legendary Encounter." For an account that limits the immediate significance of the debate but underscores the genuine theological tensions felt by Wilberforce over the problem of human evolution, see James, "On Wilberforce and Huxley."

20. *See* McGrath, *Science & Religion*, 31; Henry, "Religion and the Scientific Revolution.".

21. McGrath, *Science & Religion*, 220–21.

22. See Marsden, *Understanding Fundamentalism and Evangelicalism*, chapter 6.

23. See Numbers, *The Creationists*; "Answers in Genesis" website, available at http://www.answersingenesis.org.

24. See, e.g., the following essays in Torrey and Dixon, *The Fundamentals*: Griffith Thomas, "Old Testament Criticism and New Testament Christianity"; Dyson Hague, "History of the Higher Criticism"; Franklin Johnson, "Fallacies of the Higher

The populist dynamism of the American evangelical movement, however, could not long permit evangelical fundamentalists to remain on the cultural sidelines. The period following World War II in particular witnessed a resurgence in world missions along with a new cultural visibility and prominence for American Evangelicals eager to retain the theological underpinnings of *The Fundamentals* while distancing themselves from the isolationism of post-Scopes fundamentalism. Evangelical leaders such as Carl Henry, J. I. Packer, Bernard Ramm, and Francis Schaeffer, and institutions such as Wheaton College, promoted political engagement and "the integration of faith and learning." Although they were not yet prepared to grant the validity of Darwinian evolution, neo evangelical intellectuals mostly accepted Lyellian geology and the mainstream scientific consensus about the vast age of the Earth. Ramm's 1954 book "The Christian View of Science and Scripture," which argued for the validity of "framework" or "day-age" interpretations of Genesis 1, was highly influential over the American Scientific Affiliation, a conservative evangelical organization devoted to finding harmony between their theology and the natural sciences.[25]

Not all who wished to identify as culturally engaged evangelicals, however, were willing to accept even Lyellian geology. In 1961, largely

---

Criticism,"; Henry Beach, "The Decadence of Darwinism"; George Frederick Wright, "The Passing of Evolution;" An Occupant in the Pew, "Evolutionism in the Pulpit." It should be noted that *The Fundamentals* contained a few notable examples of more careful thought about Christian faith and natural science, including James Orr's essay "Science and Christian Faith." Orr noted that, in the Bible, "[n]atural things are taken as they are given, and spoken of in simple, popular language, as we ourselves every day speak of them. The world it describes is the world men know and live in, and it is described as it appears, not as, in its recondite researches, science reveals its inner constitution to us. Wise expositors of the Scriptures, older and younger, have always recognized this, and have not attempted to force its language further." James Orr, "Science and Christian Faith." Orr further argued that "few are disquieted in reading their Bibles because it is made certain that the world is immensely older than the 6,000 years which the older chronology gave it. Geology is felt only to have expanded our ideas of the vastness and marvel of the Creator's operations through the aeons of time during which the world, with its teeming populations of fishes, birds, reptiles, mammals, was preparing for man's abode—when the mountains were being upheaved, the valleys being scooped out, and veins of precious metals being inlaid into the crust of the earth." James Orr, "Science and Christian Faith." Unfortunately the weight of essays in *The Fundamentals* did not follow Orr's measured approach. Nevertheless, even Orr insisted on the special, recent creation of Adam and Eve.

25. Ramm, *The Christian View of Science and Scripture*. For a discussion of the American Scientific Affiliation and the disputes between progressive creationists and young-earth creationists, see Numbers, *The Creationists*, 159–81.

in response to Ramm, Henry Morris and John Whitcomb published *The Genesis Flood*, a powerful apology for "scientific creationism."[26] Morris and Whitcomb believed that a "literal" reading of the Bible, including the conclusion drawn from biblical chronology that the earth is less than 10,000 years old, could be supported through the proper application of scientific methods. They promoted a "catastrophic" rather than "uniformitarian" view of geology, under which most of the features mainstream geologists attribute to long, gradual processes could instead be explained with reference to a worldwide deluge at the time of Noah. *The Genesis Flood* was an immediate sensation and remains a basic text for young-earth creationists today. Sociologically, it divided, and continues to divide, American evangelicals among those who insist upon young-earth creationism and some version of "flood geology" and those who do not. More importantly for Christian theology broadly considered, the young-earth creationist model promoted in *The Genesis Flood* supplied, and still supplies, much of the fuel for culture war debates over "science and religion" around the world. From the 1960s through the present, American courts, including the Supreme Court, have heard challenges to public school science curricula mounted by young-earth creationist or intelligent design ("ID") advocates, and presently the multi-million dollar "Creation Museum" in Kentucky does brisk business and underpins a vast young-earth creationist educational network popularized by the "Answers in Genesis" organization.[27]

ID attempts to demonstrate that evolution cannot account for at least some complex biological systems. It seeks scientific evidences for "design" in creation through statistical gaps and probability and information theory.[28] Although many ID proponents do not identify with scientific creationism's insistence on reading the book of Genesis literally, they likewise presume that the biblical revelation must somehow conform to and be confirmed by "science."[29] And because of this presumption, ID

---

26. Whitcomb and Morris, *The Genesis Flood*.

27. For significant case law, see *Epperson v. Arkansas*, 393 U.S. 97 (1968); *Edwards v. Aguillard*, 428 U.S. 578 (1987); *Kitzmiller v. Dover Area School District*, 400 F. Supp.2d 707 (2005). For the Creation Museum, see the Creation Museum website, available at http://creationmuseum.org/. For Answers in Genesis, see the Answers in Genesis website, https://answersingenesis.org/.

28. Dembski, *Intelligent Design*.

29. *See* Cunningham, *Darwin's Pious Idea*, 278–80.

advocates generally argue that the findings of evolutionary biology fundamentally conflict with Christian theology.[30]

The extraordinary cultural influence of "new atheists" such as Richard Dawkins represents another extreme node of this warfare thesis.[31] Darwinism is here elevated to an all-encompassing worldview. For example, David Sloan Wilson, Distinguished Professor of Biological Sciences and Anthropology at Binghamton University, argues that Darwinian evolution fully explains everything, including every aspect of human nature.[32] Anyone who thinks otherwise, including "intellectuals" who are not religious, is a kind of fundamentalist, an "academic creationist."[33] Religion, for these ultra-Darwinists, is like a pernicious virus that must be eradicated by science.[34]

In contrast—or apparent contrast—to these conflict models, many opt for an "independence" model in which "science" and "religion" occupy entirely separate, non-overlapping domains.[35] The late biologist Stephen Jay Gould introduced the concept of "nonoverlapping magisteria" (NOMA) that purported to separate scientific claims from moral truth.[36] This perspective is reflected, to a certain extent, in the U.S. National Academy of Sciences statement on the compatibility of science and religion:

30. Hence the double meaning in the title of one of William Dembski's recent books: *The End of Christianity: Finding a Good God in an Evil World*, in which Dembski argues that Christianity fails without a scientifically demonstrable chronology for the fall from Eden. Dembski's attempt to provide such a chronology is certainly far more sophisticated than that of creation science. He accepts the geological age of the earth and even the broad outlines of biological evolution (albeit punctuated in some way by infusions of divine "design" apart from the ordinary processes of nature), but he argues that the fall had retroactive effects because time can run forwards and backwards. Absent this sort of mathematical construction of the retroactive effects of time, however, it seems that Dembski would agree with the ultra-Darwinists that Christianity has been *scientifically* falsified.

31. See, e.g., Dawkins, *The God Delusion*. See also Cunningham, *Darwin's Pious Idea*, 272–75 ("Our Auntie Jean and Richard Dawkins").

32. Wilson, *Evolution for Everyone*.

33. Sloan Wilson, *Evolution for Everyone*, 3 (quoting The Nation, "The New Creationism: Biology under Attack," 1997).

34. Dawkins, *The God Delusion*.

35. McGrath, *Science & Religion*, 46–47.

36. Gould, "Nonoverlapping Magesteria." See the discussion of NOMA in Cunningham, *Darwin's Pious Idea*, 270–72.

Science and religion are based on different aspects of human experience. In science, explanations must be based on evidence drawn from examining the natural world. Scientifically based observations or experiments that conflict with an explanation eventually must lead to modification or even abandonment of that explanation. Religious faith, in contrast, does not depend only on empirical evidence, is not necessarily modified in the face of conflicting evidence, and typically involves supernatural forces or entities. Because they are not a part of nature, supernatural entities cannot be investigated by science. In this sense, science and religion are separate and address aspects of human understanding in different ways. Attempts to pit science and religion against each other create controversy where none needs to exist.[37]

"Independence" models, however, seem inevitably to devolve into "conflict," in which "faith and evidence" and "natural and supernatural" are put at odds, as the NAS statement above reflects.

2. Strong Integration: Process Theology

In contrast to these conflict models, the mainstream science and religion literature emphasizes "dialogue" between and/or "integration" of scientific and religious perspectives.[38] Strong integrationist models tend towards a willingness to reconfigure religious categories in ways that seem required by the natural sciences. Process theology, which tends to identify Godself as part of the developing and emerging cosmos, is a prime example of this sort of move.[39] For process theology, reality is fundamentally a dynamic process.[40] Rather than envisioning God as the transcendent source of the universe, for process theology, "God is not the exception to the dynamic nature of the universe, but rather the dynamic God-world relationship is the primary example of creaturely experience in its many expressions."[41] In this view, "[i]n our dynamic and ever-changing world, God is the

37. National Academy of Sciences website, "Evolution Resources," "Compatibility of Science and Religion," available at http://www.nationalacademies.org/evolution/Compatibility.html.

38. See McGrath, *Science and Religion*, 47–49.

39. See Cobb and Griffin, *Process Theology*.

40. See Epperly, *Process Theology*, 20.

41. Epperly, *Process Theology*, 21.

most dynamic and ever-changing reality; God's becoming embraces the eternal, temporal, and everlasting in an ever-creative, self-surpassing dialogue with the universe."[42]

Because God is a dynamic and evolving reality, process theology eschews the classical notion of God's perfections.[43] Process theologians view the claim that God is omniscient and omnipotent as remnants of Greek thought best left behind.[44] They argue that a God who is omniscient and omnipotent must be responsible for evil and that both scripture and Christian experience disclose God in relational terms.[45] They further argue that God's classical perfections would destroy the possibility of human creativity and creaturely freedom.[46] Many process theologians argue, in particular, that evolutionary theory elides the classical understanding of God's perfections:

> While some Christians believe that God has directed the course of the universe from the very beginning, determining every detail without creaturely input, and is guiding the universe toward a pre-determined goal, process theology imagines an open-ended universe, in which God's vision is also open-ended and subject to change in relationship to creaturely decision-making and accidental occurrences.[47]

A thread that ties these claims together within process theology is the integration of theology and science.[48] Indeed, "[p]rocess theology is firmly rooted in an evolutionary understanding of the universe."[49] Thus process theology also eschews the concept of creation *ex nihilo*, arguing that, instead, "[e]ven before the big bang, God was interacting with the primordial elements of this universe or another universe from which this universe may have emerged, as some cosmologists suggest. God has never been without a world, which provides opportunities for, and limitations of, the embodiment of God's creative vision."[50]

---

42. Epperly, *Process Theology.*
43. Epperly, *Process Theology*, 33–44.
44. Epperly, *Process Theology*, 34.
45. Epperly, *Process Theology*, 38–44.
46. Epperly, *Process Theology*, 83–91.
47. Epperly, *Process Theology*, 97.
48. Epperly, *Process Theology*, 92–102.
49. Epperly, *Process Theology*, 97.
50. Epperly, *Process Theology*, 98.

This vision of emerging reality also affects process theology's anthropology. Human beings are not metaphysically special but rather are "fully embedded in the evolutionary process."[51] Human beings are not impacted by any sort of "original" sin but rather have always partaken in a bilateral relationship of call-and-response with God.[52] In fact, "[t]o the surprise of many more traditional theologians, process theologians recognize that deviation from God's moment by moment vision is not always bad: it may inject new possibilities into the creative process."[53] Moreover, showing its debt to Hegel, process theology tends to identify the human "soul" not with particular individuals, but rather with human society extended over time.[54] The "soul" is "in every sense a part of nature, subject to the same conditions as all other natural entities."[55] Further, "the body, and specifically the brain, is the immediate environment of the soul."[56] Because of the embeddedness of the human person and specifically the human brain in the flux of evolutionary history, the human soul is intimately connected with the entire universe:

> The soul is, then, in immediate contact with some occasions of experience in the brain and with the mental poles of experiences of other souls. . . . Indirectly, but intimately, the soul also pre-hends the whole society that constitutes its body and still more indirectly, but still very importantly, the wider environment that is the whole world. At the same time, the soul contributes itself as an object for feeling by other souls, the contiguous occasions in the brain, and indirectly by the whole future world.[57]

51. Epperly, *Process Theology,* 99.

52. Epperly, *Process Theology,* 100–101.

53. Epperly, *Process Theology,*101.

54. See Cobb *A Christian Natural Theology Based on the Thought of Alfred North Whitehead.*

55. Cobb, *A Christian Natural Theology Based on the Thought of Alfred North Whitehead,* 19.

56. Cobb, *A Christian Natural Theology Based on the Thought of Alfred North Whitehead, 19.* See Cobb, 43–49 for Cobb's refinement of Whitehead's views on this point.

57. Cobb, *A Christian Natural Theology Based on the Thought of Alfred North Whitehead,* 23.

3. Presuppositionalism and Reformed Epistemology

Process theology entails a methodology that seems to privilege modern science as a broad epistemology. Other methods that involve some degree of conflict and some degree of consilience between theology and science challenge the epistemological grounds for what is sometimes called "scientism." As we have seen, this kind of move is employed in a crude form by the young-earth creationists. But it is also employed in a more sophisticated way by some theologians and philosophers in the Reformed tradition.

For example, Cornelius Van Til's "presuppositionalism" reflected a particular sort of adjustment between "faith" and "reason" within neo-Calvinist theology.[58] Van Til argued that all human knowledge claims are based on faith-based presuppositions. Because human beings are fundamentally sinful, their presuppositions are often wrong. A key function of scripture, in Van Til's system, was to provide a means of correcting sinful human presuppositions with divine revelation. Scripture supplied propositional content that must inform proper human reasoning. Among the basic propositional truths of scripture was that the universe is God's creation, not merely a product of chance.

Van Til's epistemology can lead to young-earth creationism, but that is not always the case. Indeed, one of the leading Reformed presuppositionalist thinkers today, who is a stalwart faculty member at Westminster Seminary in Philadelphia, is Vern Poythress, who argues in his book *Redeeming Science* that some version of evolutionary biology could be consistent with scripture, though he is also partial to certain kinds of intelligent design theories.[59] One of the subtleties here is that, while presuppositionalists such as Poythress insist on the propositional inerrancy of scripture, their epistemology precludes any claim that the propositional truth of scripture is self-evident to unaided reason. Thus, they refer to the "self-attestation" of scripture, which is related to the "illumination" of scripture by the Holy Spirit.[60]

A more sophisticated and formidable kind of presuppositionalism informs the "Reformed epistemology" of Alvin Plantinga, Nicholas

---

58. *See* Van Til, *The Defense of the Faith.*

59. Poythress, *Redeeming Science.*

60. See, e.g., Nicole and Michaels, *Inerrancy and Common Sense*; Silva, "Old Princeton, Westminster, and Inerrancy," 67–80 (stating that "I happen to believe that the essential historicity of Genesis 1–3 is a fundamental article of Christian orthodoxy").

Wolterstorff, and other notable American philosophical theologians. Plantinga contends that "knowledge" is a function of properly "warranted" belief, and that among the properly basic warrants are assumptions about the regularity and continuity of the universe along with the assumption that God exists.[61] In in his book *Warranted Christian Belief*, Plantinga emphasizes the internal witness of the Holy Spirit, which provides a form of epistemic certainty about the existence of God.[62] Plantinga argues that it is "[b]y faith—the whole process, involving the internal instigation of the Holy Spirit—something becomes *evident* (i.e., acquires warrant, has what it takes to be knowledge)."[63]

But Plantinga does not merely argue for a form of fideism. Rather, he suggests that the warrants of faith are shown to be sensible and reasonable in light of the entire context of the beliefs those warrants produce, and, indeed, that those beliefs make more sense than the possibility of atheism. This sounds like a form of coherentism, but Plantinga explicitly rejects "pure and unalloyed" coherentism as well as Bayesian coherentism.[64] Instead, Plantinga is partial to what he calls "BonJourian Coherentism," after the work of Laurence BonJour.[65] Plantinga suggests that BonJour's work presents a "chastened coherentism" that does not require either the foundationalist premises of "pure and unalloyed" coherentism or the mathematical foundations (with their own epistemic limits) of Bayesian coherentism.[66]

From this basis, Plantinga suggests that a better starting point is the question of "proper function."[67] The notion of "proper function," Plantinga says, "is inextricably involved with another: that of the *design plan* of the organ or organism in question—the way the thing in question is supposed to work, the way it works when it works properly, when it is subject to no dysfunction."[68] In *Warranted Christian Belief*, and in his

61. See Plantinga, *Warrant: The Current Debate*; *Warrant and Proper Function*; *Warranted Christian Belief*; *Where the Conflict Really Lies*.

62. Plantinga, *Warranted Christian Belief*, chapters 8 and 9.

63. Plantinga, *Warranted Christian Belief*, 265.

64. Plantinga, *Warrant: The Current Debate*, chapters 4, 6–7; for the "pure and unalloyed" comment, see 87. For a general discussion of coherentist models, see Olsson, "Coherentist Theories of Epistemic Justification."

65. Plantinga, *Warrant, the Current Debate*, chapter 5.

66. Plantinga, *Warrant, the Current Debate*, chapter 4.

67. Plantinga, *Warrant, the Current Debate*, 213.

68. Plantinga, *Warrant, the Current Debate*, 213.

more popularly accessible work on faith and science, Plantinga attempts to show how these conditions are met concerning what he considers the core beliefs of Christian faith, and addresses what he considers possible "defeaters" to his account of the warrants for Christian belief.[69]

In Plantinga's lexicon, "[a] defeater for a belief A is another belief B such that once you come to accept B, you can no longer continue to accept A without falling into irrationality."[70] In particular, Plantinga takes on arguments by prominent atheists such as Richard Dawkins and Daniel Dennett, who argue that evolution and theism are incompatible because there is a lack of evidence for design in the universe.[71] Plantinga suggests that "classical theists" generally believe statements about divine action and providence such as those found in the Heidleberg Catechism:

> Providence is the almighty and ever present power of God by which he upholds, as with his hand, heaven and earth and all creatures, and so rules them leaf and blade, rain and drought, fruitful years and lean years, food and drink, health and sickness, prosperity and poverty—all things, in fact, come to us not by chance but from his fatherly hand.[72]

This picture of divine action and providence, Plantinga suggests, is disrupted by Newtonian and Laplacian science, but is no longer problematic in light of quantum mechanics.[73] Given his presuppositional approach and his theological views about divine action, Plantinga also expresses support for fine tuning arguments and, at least to some extent, for intelligent design theory.[74] He suggests that the evidence of fine tuning in the universe and the discourse of intelligent design are consistent with the "design plan" of human noetic capabilities, while the atheistic belief that all of this apparent design arose through chance is highly implausible.[75] The best Dawkins and Dennett can do, Plantinga suggests, is show that the development of life by chance is not entirely impossible, while theism

69. See Plantinga, *Warranted Christian Belief*, Parts III and IV; *Where the Conflict Really Lies*; Dennett and Plantinga, *Science and Religion*.

70. Plantinga, *Warranted Christian Belief*, preface, xiii.

71. See Plantinga, *Where the Conflict Really Lies*, chapters 1 and 2; Dennett and Plantinga, *Science and Religion*.

72. Heidelberg Catechism, Question 27; Plantinga, *Where the Conflict Really Lies*, 65.

73. Plantinga, *Where the Conflict Really Lies*, chapters 3 and 4.

74. Plantinga, *Where the Conflict Really Lies*, chapters 7 and 8.

75. Plantinga, *Where the Conflict Really Lies*, chapters 7 and 8.

can do far better by showing a more complete and plausible picture of how theistic beliefs are warranted. But, as Plantinga acknowledges, his arguments do not represent an effort to prove the truth of Christian belief on Christian grounds. He agrees that "[e]verything [in his arguments] really depends on the *truth* of Christian belief," but hopes that he can at least refute "the common suggestion that Christian belief, whether true or not, is intellectually unacceptable."[76]

4. Dialogue and Critical Realism

Many proponents of "dialogue" models between science and religion identify themselves as "critical realists," and this may be the dominant paradigm in the contemporary "religion and science" literature, at least among conservative scholars.[77] A critical realist approach recognizes that all human knowing is mediated through human thought and language forms, including both scientific and theological knowing—and thus it is "critical."[78] Nevertheless, critical realists assert that there is a reality extrinsic to human thought and language that is capable of sustained investigation, and that human beings are capable of making progress towards fuller understanding of that extrinsic reality.[79] The theological realities that theologians attempt to investigate and the natural realities that scientists attempt to investigate must each be approached with tools appropriate to their respective domains.[80] As Alister McGrath argues, "[b]oth the scientific and religious communities can be thought of as attempting to wrestle with the ambiguities of experience, and offering what are accepted as the 'best possible explanations' for what is observed."[81]

McGrath develops his model of critical realism in science and theology in significant part from the philosophical contributions of

76. Plantinga, *Warranted Christian Belief*, preface, xiii.

77. See, e.g., McGrath, *Science & Religion*, 78–79, 82–83. McGrath identifies Thomas F. Torrance, Ian Barbour, Arthur Peacocke, and John Polkinghorne as well as himself, as critical realists. Portions of this section appear in my paper "Deconstructing Jefferson's Candle."

78. See McGrath, *Science & Religion*, 78–89, 82–83.

79. McGrath, *Science & Religion*, 78–89, 82–83.

80. *See* McGrath, *A Scientific Theology: Reality*, 226.

81. McGrath, *The Foundations of Dialogue in Science & Religion*.

Roy Bhaskar and Michael Polanyi.[82] For critical realists in the tradition of Bhaskar, society is *both* a preexisting given *and* a product of human activity.[83] Individuals do not create society, but they do continually reproduce and transform society.[84] Society is neither a reified structure that exists apart from human activity nor an entirely voluntary creation of individuals.[85] Bhaskar likens this "transformational model of social activity" to a sculptor who creates something out of the materials and tools available to her.[86] The result is that society emerges from, but is not reducible to, the choices of individuals.[87] Society is "a complex totality subject to change both in its components and their interrelations."[88]

Critical realists recognize that knowledge has both social and physical dimensions.[89] There is a reality external to human perception,

82. McGrath, *A Scientific Theology: Reality*, 226.

83. See generally Bhaskar, *The Possibility of Naturalism*.

84. Bhaskar, *The Possibility of Naturalism*, 36.

85. Bhaskar, *The Possibility of Naturalism*, 39 (stating that "society must be regarded as an ensemble of structures, practices and conventions which individuals reproduce or transform, but which would not exist unless they did so").

86. Bhaskar, *The Possibility of Naturalism*, 37.

87. Bhaskar, *The Possibility of Naturalism*, 37–44.

88. Bhaskar, *The Possibility of Naturalism* 41. In many respects, critical realism's transformational model of society sounds like the New Chicago School's model of law and norms. The difference is that for cyberlaw scholars in the New Chicago School tradition, the architectural "code" that makes up online spaces is entirely socially constructed—whether code-infrastructure is "open" or "closed" is entirely contingent on the individuals who participate in the digital commons. See Part II, *supra*. In contrast, in the critical realist view, "culture," "code," and "infrastructure" are not entirely the voluntary creations of autonomous individuals. Bhaskar's treatment of language and grammar is intriguing here. The rules of grammar, Bhaskar observes, are not infinitely malleable—they impose real, given limits on our speech. Bhaskar, *The Possibility of Naturalism*, 36. The rules of grammar, however, do not determine what we say; meaning is not reducible to the rules of grammar.

89. Roy Bhaskar states that:
Any adequate philosophy of science must find a way of grappling with this central paradox of science: that men in their social activity produce knowledge which is a social product much like any other, which is no more independent of its production and the men who produce it than motor cars, armchairs or books, which has its own craftsmen, technicians, publicists, standards and skills and which is no less subject to change than any other commodity. This is one side of "knowledge." The other is that knowledge is "of" things which are not produced by men at all: the specific gravity of mercury, the process of electrolysis, the mechanism of light propagation. None of these "objects of knowledge" depend on human activity. If men ceased to exist sound would

language, and cognition.[90] Human perception, language, and cognition, however, limit our direct epistemic access to reality.[91] Human perception of reality is a "transitive" dimension because it is subject to change based on human language, history, and culture.[92] Reality itself, however, is "intransitive."[93] According to Bhaskar, reality is stratified and can be conceived as three layered: empirical (observable by human), actual (existing in time and space), and real ("transfactual and enduring more than our perception of it").[94]

Bhaskar thus emphasized the social aspects of human knowledge without reducing all of reality to a human construction. An important aspect of Bhaskar's social theory of knowledge is his rejection of "methodological individualism"—the notion that societies are reducible to individuals.[95] A "social atomism" in which the analysis of societies can be reduced to the preferences of individuals will never adequately explain social action.[96] But neither is society merely the result of collective pressures on individuals, or a simple dialectic between these two poles. Rather, society has a dual character: social groups provide the ground through which individuals reproduce and sometimes transform society. A level of reality can emerge from a more basic level without being reducible to the more basic level.[97]

Like Bhaskar, Michael Polanyi recognized that logical positivism fails because it relies on some unverifiable foundations. As Polanyi noted, "It is indeed logically impossible for the human mind to divest itself of all uncritically acquired foundations. For our minds cannot unfold at all

---

continue to travel and heavy bodies fall to the earth in exactly the same way, though ex hypothesi there would be no-one to know it.

Bhaskar, *The Possibility of Naturalism*, 21.

90. See Archer et al., *Critical Realism*, ix–xiii (noting that "critical realism claims to be able to combine and reconcile *ontological realism, epistemological relativism*, and *judgmental rationality*.") (emphasis in original).

91. Bhaskar, *The Possibility of Naturalism*, 21.

92. Bhaskar, *The Possibility of Naturalism*, 21.

93. Bhaskar, *The Possibility of Naturalism*, 21.

94. Bhaskar, *The Possibility of Naturalism*, 21–62.

95. Bhaskar, *The Possibility of Naturalism*, 21–62.

96. Bhaskar, *The Possibility of Naturalism*, 21–62.

97. Bhaskar, *The Possibility of Naturalism*, 113 (stating that "the operations of the higher level cannot be accounted for solely by the laws governing the lower-order level in which we might say the higher-order level is 'rooted' and from which we might say it was 'emergent'").

except by embracing a definite idiom of beliefs, which will determine the scope of our entire subsequent fiducial development."[98] The notion of positivism itself, then, depends on an idiomatic structure that is neither verifiable nor self-evident.

Polanyi also emphasized the communal nature of scientific practice and the "tacit" knowledge involved in such communal information transfers. As he noted, "[t]he transmission of beliefs in society is mostly not by precept, but by example. . . . The whole practice of research and verification is transmitted by example and its standards are upheld by a continuous interplay with criticism within the scientific community."[99] Thus, scientific knowledge is a set of socially constructed analogical models that are developed through practices acquired and implemented in unique social networks.[100]

Finally, Polanyi realized that the social networks through which scientific practices are transferred, like all social networks, incorporate elements of social control. One of the principal means of control over scientific information networks is peer review. Polanyi observed that scientific journal referees "are the chief Influentials, the unofficial governors of the scientific community. By their advice they can either delay or accelerate the growth of a new line of research."[101] Nevertheless,

98. Polanyi, *Scientific Thought and Social Reality*, 76.

99. Polanyi, *Scientific Thought and Social Reality*, 61.

100. Polanyi explains this concern at the beginning of one of his key works, *The Tacit Dimension*. Describing the denial of independent science under communism, Polanyi says "I was struck by the fact that this denial of the very existence of independent scientific thought came from a socialist theory which derived its tremendous persuasive power from its claim to scientific certainty. The scientific outlook appeared to have produced a mechanical conception of man and history in which there was no place for science itself." *The Tacit Dimension*, 3. Polanyi's views, of course, were not entirely unique; they fit nicely into a constellation of contemporary philosophers of science who deconstructed the positivism that emerged following the collapse of Baconian science, including figures such as Thomas Kuhn, Imre Lakatos, and to some extent Paul Feyerabend. See Feyerabend, *Against Method*; Lakatos, *The Methodology of Scientific Research Programmes*.

101. Polanyi, *Scientific Thought and Social Reality*, 20. Polanyi stated that:
The referees advising scientific journals may also encourage those lines of research which they consider to be particularly promising, while discouraging other lines of which they have a low opinion. The dominant powers in this respect are, however, exercised by referees advising on scientific appointments, on the allocation of special subsidies, and on the award of distinctions. Advice on these points, which often involve major issues of the policy of science, is usually asked from and tendered by a small number of senior scientists who are universally recognized as being the most eminent in a particular branch.

within this social matrix, science can make genuine progress in understanding.

Similarly, theology, critical realists argue, seeks to interpret experienced reality within the context of a traditioned community.[102] In this respect, many critical realists are sympathetic to Alasdair MacIntyre's account of the role of community and tradition in the shaping of philosophical inquiry.[103] For Christians, of course, the central experienced reality that requires theological interpretation is the incarnation, death, and resurrection of Christ, and the interpretive community is the church.[104] Christian theology and doctrine develop as the Christian community reflects on this central experience. Just as in the natural sciences, massive paradigm shifts in the understanding of theology and doctrine should be rare, but some degree of revision must always remain a possibility because the reality that lies behind the experience is only ever partially understood.

This emphasis on the event of revelation in Christ among many Christian critical realists is not surprising, as many of them (including, notably, Alister McGrath), are connected to Karl Barth through the work of Thomas Torrance.[105] Barth, consistent with his understanding of revelation and philosophy, resisted any systematic definition of God:

> The equation of God's Word and God's Son makes it radically impossible to say anything doctrinaire in understanding the Word of God. In this equation, and in it alone, a real and effective barrier is set up against what is made of proclamation according to the Roman Catholic view and of Holy Scripture according to the later form of older Protestantism, namely, a fixed sum of revealed propositions which can be systematized like the sections of a corpus of law. The only system in Holy Scripture and proclamation is revelation, i.e., Jesus Christ.[106]

They are the chief Influentials, the unofficial governors of the scientific community. By their advice they can either delay or accelerate the growth of a new line of research.

Cf. Smolin, *The Trouble with Physics.*

102. McGrath, *The Foundations of Science & Religion*, 160–64.

103. McGrath, *The Foundations of Science & Religion*, 160–63 (citing MacIntyre, *Whose Justice? Which Rationality?*).

104. See Torrance, *Reality & Evangelical Theology*, 84–120.

105. See McGrath, *The Foundations of Science & Religion*, 34 (citing Torrance, *Theological Science*).

106. Barth, *Church Dogmatics*, I.1.§5.2.

But Barth—who, after all, over the course of thirty-five years wrote a *Church Dogmatics* comprised of about six million words of dense text—did not mean we can say nothing truthful about God. After resisting what he understood as the Catholic and scholastic Reformation's too-neat methods of systematization, Barth emphasized the importance of words and speech:

> Now the converse is also true, of course, namely that God's Son is God's Word. Thus God does reveal Himself in statements, through the medium of speech, and indeed of human speech. His word is always this or that word spoken by the prophets and apostles and proclaimed in the Church. The personal character of God's Word is not, then, to be played off against its verbal or spiritual character. It is not at all true that this second aspect under which we must understand it implies its irrationality and thus cancels out the first aspect under which we must understand it.[107]

Barth's concern throughout his discussion of the Word in volume I of the *Church Dogmatics* was to preserve the freedom and integrity of theology against Enlightenment rationalism.[108] Barth was particularly concerned with the way rationalism gave rise to nineteenth-century liberal Protestant thought, with its demythologizing program. Barth also resisted how rationalism underwrote both Protestant fundamentalism and the scholastic Thomism of much nineteenth-century Catholic thought. Torrance worked from these basic Barthian premises to modify Barth's famous "*nein*" to natural theology with a qualified "yes."

The critical realist approach to theology and science results in a paradigm in which the disciplines of theology and natural science remain distinct but can contribute to each other at higher levels. McGrath summarizes his version of this program as follows:

1. The natural sciences and the religions are quite distinct in terms of their methodologies and subject matters. It is quite improper to attempt to limit them, for example, by suggesting that the sciences have to do with the physical world and the religions with a distinct

---

107. Barth, *Church Dogmatics*, I.1.§5.2.

108. For discussion of the influences and sources of Barth's theology, see, e.g., Webster, "Introducing Barth"; McCormack, *Orthodox and Modern*; Hunsinger, *Evangelical, Catholic and Reformed*; *Reading Barth with Charity*.

spiritual world. The distinction between "science" and "religion" concerns more than subject-matter.

2. At points, despite their clear differences, those working in the fields of science and religion find themselves facing similar issues, especially in relation to issues of representation and conceptualization. At point after point, those interested in science and religion find themselves facing very similar questions, and even adopting similar approaches in the answers that they offer.

3. At points of major importance, the methods and theories of the natural sciences are genuinely illuminating to those concerned with religious matters. Equally, there are points where religious beliefs and approaches cast considerable light on issues of scientific method. The investigation of these convergences is mutually enlightening and significant.[109]

5. Fides et Ratio?

It is useful to compare McGrath's critical realism with Pope John Paul II's views on faith and science. The comparison demonstrates some residue of the old Protestant-Catholic debates about the effectiveness of human reason after the fall. But the comparison also highlights ways in which both branches of the Western church converge on the centrality of the doctrine of creation as the ground of the possibility of "science."

The Roman Catholic approach to faith and science, exemplified in the Pontifical Academy of the Sciences, is sometimes said to represent a "dialogue" approach.[110] There is of course not only one "Roman Catholic approach" to the relation between theology and science, and many Catholics working in this field would identify themselves as critical realists or assume the posture of critical realism without identifying it.[111] Indeed,

---

109. McGrath, *The Foundations of Science & Religion*, 34.

110. McGrath, *The Foundations of Science & Religion*, 47–48; Pontifical Academy of the Sciences website, available at http://www.casinapioiv.va/content/accademia/en.html.

111. See, e.g., Haught, *Making Sense of Evolution*; Heller, *Creative Tension*. Haught argues as follows:

Christian theology, I firmly believe, cannot responsibly take refuge in pre-Darwinian understandings of these concepts [of design, descent, and diversity]. Instead, it must look for theological reflection broad enough to assimilate

Pope John Paul II famously stated that "[s]cience can purify religion from error and superstition; religion can purify science from idolatry and false absolutes. Each can draw the other into a wider world, a world in which both can flourish."[112]

This oft-quoted statement of John Paul II was part of a longer letter to Jerry Coyne, Director of the Vatican Observatory, in preparation for a study week celebrating the three hundredth anniversary of Newton's *Philosophiae Naturalis Principia Mathematica*.[113] The pope stressed in that letter that the model he envisioned was one of dialogue rather than integration.[114]

Theologians, the pope noted, can utilize the best science of their times to help them understand and articulate theological truths, but science cannot simply dictate terms to theology:

> Now this is a point of delicate importance, and it has to be carefully qualified. Theology is not to incorporate indifferently each new philosophical or scientific theory. As these findings become part of the intellectual culture of the time, however, theologians must understand them and test their value in bringing out from Christian belief some of the possibilities which have not yet been realized. . . . Theologians might well ask, with respect to contemporary science, philosophy and the other areas of human knowing, if they have accomplished this extraordinarily difficult process as well as did these medieval masters.[115]

Likewise, the pope stated, the practice of natural science is neither to be equated with theology nor isolated from it:

> For science develops best when its concepts and conclusions are integrated into the broader human culture and its concerns for ultimate meaning and value. Scientists cannot, therefore, hold

---

all that is new in scientific research without in any way abandoning the substance of Christian teaching. This theological task requires a deep respect for traditional creeds and biblical texts, but it also assumes that in the light of new experience and scientific research, constant reinterpretation of fundamental beliefs is essential to keep any religion alive and honest. This is especially the case with Christianity after Darwin.

Haught, *Making Sense of Evolution*, xvii.

112. John Paul II to Rev. George V. Coyne, S.J., June 1, 1988.

113. John Paul II to Rev. George V. Coyne, S.J, June 1, 1988.

114. John Paul II to Rev. George V. Coyne, S.J., June 1, 1988.

115. John Paul II to Rev. George V. Coyne, S.J, June 1, 1988.

themselves entirely aloof from the sorts of issues dealt with by philosophers and theologians.[116]

The Catholic "dialogue" approach, at least on some readings of it, already assumes that all investigation of truth is theological. The possibility of "natural reason" is given precisely because of prior theological claims about the gift of created human nature and its capacity to participate in the truth of God. In his introductory discussion of the relation between theology and philosophy, *Fides et Ratio*, for example, John Paul II states that all knowledge, whether derived from philosophy or faith, depends first on God, who makes knowledge possible by grace. "Underlying all the Church's thinking," John Paul II said, "is the awareness that she is the bearer of a message which has its origin in God himself (cf. 2 Cor 4:1-2)."[117] The church did not receive this message through its own power or abilities, nor was the message communicated through abstract intellectual means. Rather, John Paul II said, it stems from a personal encounter with God in Christ.

Therefore there is no question of philosophy superseding faith. There is no sharp division, in *Fides et Ratio*, between "nature" and "grace": all that pertains to "nature," to God's creative design, is also the gift of "grace," of God's ecstatic, self-giving love. Nevertheless, for John Paul II, "nature" involves empirical realities that are susceptible to human knowledge through a form of reasoning appropriate to the object. "Philosophy" possesses an inherent integrity, structure, and grammar. "The truth attained by philosophy and the truth of Revelation," John Paul II said, "are neither identical nor mutually exclusive":

> Philosophy and the sciences function within the order of natural reason; while faith, enlightened and guided by the Spirit, recognizes in the message of salvation the "fullness of grace and truth" (cf. *Jn* 1:14) which God has willed to reveal in history and definitively through his Son, Jesus Christ (cf. *1 Jn* 5:9; *Jn* 5:31–32).[118]

John Paul II therefore saw a positive role for "philosophy" as a complement to "faith." Indeed, for John Paul II, "natural reason," apart from revelation, is capable of showing that there is a God who created the universe. Nevertheless, it is finally our *faith* in God's creative

116. John Paul II to Rev. George V. Coyne, S.J, June 1, 1988.

117. John Paul II, "Fides et Ratio" ¶7.

118. John Paul II, "Fides et Ratio," ¶9.

goodness that establishes confidence in the capacities of "natural reason" to comprehend creation, and it is our faith in God's transcendence that establishes the proper bounds of reason. These themes of transcendence and participation as applied to the relation between theology and science are perhaps reflected more clearly in an introduction John Paul II wrote for a 2004 Pontifical Academy of Sciences report in the Academy's four hundredth anniversary, where he stated,

> I am more and more convinced that scientific truth, which is itself a participation in divine Truth, can help philosophy and theology to understand ever more fully the human person and God's Revelation about man, a Revelation that is completed and perfected in Jesus Christ.[119]

6. Postliberalism and Other Narrative Theologies

"Postliberal" theology represents an effort to move beyond classical theological liberalism through "a return to a premodern faith rooted in the faith community, while fully realizing the impossibility of a full return to premodern dogma."[120] Although postliberal theology is a diverse movement, "it always stresses the narrative of scripture along with the community of the church and its practices."[121] Postliberal theology has been described as non-foundationalist, intra-textual, socially centered, respectful of plurality and diversity, and inclined towards an ecumenical "generous orthodoxy."[122] In this respect, postliberal theology reflects the "linguistic turn" and the influence of philosophers such as Ludwig Wittgenstein, Alasdair MacIntyre, and Thomas Kuhn, along with theologians such as Augustine, Aquinas, and Barth.[123]

---

119. Address of John Paul II to the Members of the Pontifical Academy of Sciences, ACTA 17, 14–15.

120. Michener, *Postliberal Theology*, 2. George Lindbeck, who along with Hans Frei is one of the fathers of the "Yale School" of postliberal theology, summarized this ethos in the preface to the original edition of his classic *The Nature of Doctrine*: "The difficulties [with modern theology] cannot be solved by, for example, abandoning modern developments and returning to some form of preliberal orthodoxy. A third, a postliberal, way of conceiving religious doctrine is called for."

121. Michener, *Postliberal Theology*, 4.

122. Michener, *Postliberal Theology*, 4.

123. Michener, *Postliberal Theology*, chapter 2.

Because postliberal and related narrative theologies focus on the constitutive character of theological language—that is, because they reflect the linguistic turn in philosophy—they can seem disinterested in any sort of modern faith-and-science project. Nevertheless, some key figures in these movements have made contributions to conversations about natural theology, including Stanley Hauerwas and Sarah Coakley.

Stanley Hauerwas is an unlikely entrant in the faith-and-science conversation, but he gave the Gifford Lectures in 2001, which were published as *With the Grain of the Universe: The Church's Witness and Natural Theology*. Hauerwas' central theme in those lectures was that "natural theology divorced from a full doctrine of God cannot help but distort the character of God and, accordingly, of the world in which we find ourselves."[124] This claim resonates with much of what the radical orthodoxy thinkers—profiled in the next section—have to say about natural theology. Indeed, Hauerwas here quotes John Milbank's quip that "'the pathos of modern theology is its false humility,'" and notes that "I hope Milbank's warning about false humility explains why I cannot help but appear impolite, since I must maintain that the God who moves the sun and the stars is the same God who was incarnate of Jesus of Nazareth."[125] Hauerwas argues, with John Howard Yoder, that the cross is the center of reality and that "those who bear crosses work with the grain of the universe."[126] The cross, Hauerwas says, is central to God's being, and Christians cannot sidestep the cross in the interest of apologetics. Moreover, since the cross is central to God's being, it is also central to ecclesiology, "or the politics called church . . . ."[127]

Hauerwas then moves on to tackle the modern presumption that philosophy and other sciences stand alongside or above theology, rather than *under* the claims of *sacra doctrina* and theology. He argues that Aquinas understood "natural reason" and "revelation" as rational complements, not as "epistemological alternatives," such that "those who attempt in the name of Aquinas to develop a 'natural theology'—that is, a philosophical defense of 'theism' as a propaedeutic for any further 'confessional' claims one might want to make—are engaged in an enterprise

124. Hauerwas, *With the Grain of the Universe*, 15.
125. Hauerwas, *With the Grain of the Universe*, 16.
126. Hauerwas, *With the Grain of the Universe*, 9.
127. Hauerwas, *With the Grain of the Universe*, 16.

that Aquinas would not recognize."[128] Hauerwas cites as support for this view one of the "Reformed epistemologists" we mentioned in a previous section, Nicholas Wolterstorff. Aquinas, Hauerwas says, was engaged in a Trinitarian project "from beginning to end," imbued with the Aristotelian idea that we can only make sense of effects by trying to understand their causes.[129]

While Hauerwas seeks to retrieve the sense of holism and transcendence in pre-modern thought, he does not seek a naïve return to the Middle Ages. According to Hauerwas,

> The assumption that the Middle Ages represents a time when Christians "got it right" not only does an injustice to the complexity of the times and places so named, but also betrays the gospel requirement that even in a world that understands itself to be Christian, faithful witness is no less required for the truth that is Christ to be known. . . . The very attempt to tell the story of modernity as one of decline from a genuinely Christian world ironically underwrites the assumption that the story that Christianity *is* is inseparable from the story of Western culture.[130]

Hauerwas is also reluctant to offer a precise genealogy of modernity. He suggests the fact "[t]hat we live in an age in which the church is but another voluntary agency and theology, at best, one subject among others in the curriculum of universities is the result not just of mistakes in the thirteenth century but of the effect of innovations such as the clock that intellectuals (exactly because we are intellectuals) are prone to discount."[131] He ties this to a critique of what he takes as the Constantinian notion that Christian *belief* can be imposed as an intellectual system rather than received only through lived practices.

After this prolegomenon, Hauerwas profiles three previous Gifford lecturers, William James, Reinhold Niebuhr, and Karl Barth. For the purpose of this Book, the most interesting of these is Hauerwas' engagement of Barth, given the way in which Barth is also central to "critical realism" in theology and science. Hauerwas suggests that "Barth, in spite of his disavowal of natural theology, provides the resources necessary for developing an adequate theological metaphysics, or, in other words, a natural

---

128. Hauerwas, *With the Grain of the Universe*, 17. Hauerwas here is offering a critique of another of his favorite conversation partners, Alasdair MacIntyre.

129. Hauerwas, *With the Grain of the Universe*, 28.

130. Hauerwas, *With the Grain of the Universe*, 24.

131. Hauerwas, *With the Grain of the Universe*, 27.

theology," if "'natural theology' simply names how Christian convictions work to describe all that is God's good creation."[132]

One of the keys to Hauerwas' reading of Barth is Christology, and particularly the *humanity* of Christ as it relates to our humanity. Humans are distinct from the rest of creation because we can express our gratitude to God through knowledge and service, and we are capable of taking an active part in God's work of redemption through the building of culture.[133]

Another thinker in this group of postliberal theologians, though that label may not fit her precisely, is Sarah Coakley. In her 2012 Gifford Lectures, "Sacrifice Regained, Evolution, Cooperation and God," Coakley laid out a methodological and practical program for a revitalized natural theology. In those lectures, Coakley sometimes sounds like a critical realist and sometimes like a postliberal, so she serves as a useful bridge between these groups.

Coakley tries to show that current arguments in the philosophy of science, in particular the philosophy of biology about altruism and cooperation, are consonant with certain kinds of teleological perspectives on creation drawn from the Christian theological tradition. At the same time, she wishes to resist any suggestion that teleology is something superadded to nature by God or that evolution is a story about nature "getting better."[134] With Michael Polanyi and Simon Conway Morris, Coakley suggests that there might be some sort of "'irreducible structure' to evolutionary life itself," which invites philosophical and theological reflection.[135] She wishes to avoid the Kantian option in which God is a not a subject of reason but merely an "as if" that guarantees the moral law.[136] She also, however, wishes to avoid "*any* trace of the extrinsic God competing for space with the processes of His own creation."[137]

The path forward, Coakley believes, is in "neo-Aristotelian accounts of both biological processes and moral virtues," which ask about the purposes of phenomena such as cooperation and altruism.[138] Such neo-Aristotelian accounts, Coakley suggests, "cohere more illuminatingly"

132. Hauerwas, *With the Grain of the Universe*, 134.

133. Hauerwas, *With the Grain of the Universe* ,134.

134. Coakley, "Sacrifice Regained," Lecture 5, "Teleology Revisited: A New 'Ethico-Teleological Argument for God's Existence,'" 12.

135. Coakley, "Sacrifice Regained," Lecture 5, 12.

136. Coakley, "Sacrifice Regained," Lecture 5, 12–14.

137. Coakley, "Sacrifice Regained," Lecture 5, 18 (emphasis in original).

138. Coakley, "Sacrifice Regained," Lecture 5, 20.

with the phenomena of evolution than the kinds of consequentialism or emotivism that many evolutionary psychologists prefer.[139] Yet Coakley does not suggest that theology is only something that might provide some perhaps pleasant addendum to the magisterium of science. She notes that "[t]he era of a confident announcement of the existence of God based solely on de-contextualized rational argumentation . . . is one we now recognize as a mistaken philosophical 'blip'—it was a rearguard modernist attempt to beat Kant at his own game, to reassert the truth of 'theism' according to supposedly universalistic and a-historical canons of truth."[140] At the same time, however, she argues that "[t]he art of giving a reasoned, philosophically-and-scientifically-related, account of the 'hope that is in us' in a public space is a Christian *duty*, and it may take a great variety of forms."[141]

Coakley's methodological proposal entails six related "hallmarks": (1) "the rejection of 'flat-plane' foundationalism"; (2) "the resistance to non-realism and the fact/value split"; (3) "retrieving creation *ex nihilo*: God as Being"; (4) "the rejection of falsely-denuded 'deism' and 'theism'"; "(5) the alignment of will and reason in response to 'natural theology' arguments"; and (6) "the spiritual senses and the ascetic capacity to 'see' God in the world."[142] Coakley recognizes that "both evolutionary theory and Christian theology are founded in irreducible *narratives* of unfolding change and movement," such that neither are totally "objective" or free of context.[143] Nevertheless, Coakley eschews the claim that recognizing our dependence on context renders us incapable of reasoned claims about scientific and philosophical realism.[144] Such realism, Coakley suggests, requires a return to the theological notion of God as Being, which involves more careful attention to the question of divine action.[145] Coakley cites Aquinas as a key example of how to think about God's "relation" to

---

139. Coakley, "Sacrifice Regained," Lecture 5, 20.

140. Coakley, "Sacrifice Regained," Lecture 6, 5–6.

141. Coakley, "Sacrifice Regained," Lecture 6, 3. She states further that "this task is not about the soap-box, but it's not for the faint-hearted or defensive either. It has to be as philosophically and scientifically sophisticated as it is spiritually and theologically cogent; in short, it must not merely dazzle; it must truly invite and allure." Coakley, "Sacrifice Regained," Lecture 6, 4.

142. Coakley, "Sacrifice Regained," Lecture 6, 5–15.

143. Coakley, "Sacrifice Regained," Lecture 6, 5.

144. Coakley, "Sacrifice Regained," Lecture 6, 6.

145. Coakley, "Sacrifice Regained," Lecture 6, 8.

the world without engaging in onto-theology or constraining God within time as in open theism or process theology.[146] To avoid these mistakes, Coakley notes, it is essential to make specific *doctrinal* claims and not merely to argue for a generic kind of "theism."[147] In particular, the doctrine of the Trinity and careful attention to Christology are essential to Christian claims about divine action and the purposes of creation.[148] Finally, Coakley suggests that there is a necessary affective dimension to how (or whether) we "see" God in the world and that spiritual and ascetic practices can progressively enable us to see God better.[149]

Throughout her Gifford Lectures, Coakley focuses on the question of extraordinary altruism as an application of her method. She suggests that great moral figures such as Mother Theresa and Dietrich Bonhoeffer explode the usual game theoretic categories of "altruism" and "cooperation" in ways that suggest something beyond those categories.[150] Such examples, she suggest, have "seemingly passed beyond *mere* cultural evolution and become a manifestation of response to a transcendent realm of grace and 'supernormality'" and ultimately can best be explained with reference to Christology and the hope of the resurrection.[151]

7. Radical Orthodoxy's Critique of the Secular

Like postliberal theology, radical orthodoxy seems to bring resources to the faith and science conversation that have only recently entered the debate, for example in Conor Cunningham's *Darwin's Pious Idea*, Michael Hanby's *No God, No Science: Theology, Cosmology, Biology*, David Alcalde's *Cosmology without God?* and David Bentley Hart's *The Experience of God: Being, Consciousness, Bliss*. One of radical orthodoxy's core assertions is that *all truth claims are theological*—that narratives finally rooted in the being of the Triune God will ring true and narratives located elsewhere will ring hollow or worse will prove nihilistic.[152]

---

146. Coakley, "Sacrifice Regained," Lecture 6, 8–9.

147. Coakley, "Sacrifice Regained," Lecture 6, 10.

148. Coakley, "Sacrifice Regained," Lecture 6, 10–11.

149. Coakley, "Sacrifice Regained," Lecture 6, 11–13.

150. Coakley, "Sacrifice Regained," Lecture 6, Lecture 5, 18–20.

151. Coakley, "Sacrifice Regained," Lecture 6, 18; Lecture 6, 13.

152. See, e.g., Milbank, "Introduction, Suspending the Material: The Turn of Radical Orthodoxy," 3 (stating that "[t]he central theological framework of radical orthodoxy is 'participation' as developed by Plato and reworked by Christianity, because

In relation to the natural sciences, some thinkers influenced by radical orthodoxy (such as Cunningham, Hanby, Alcalde, and Hart) accept the basic empirical conclusions of the modern natural sciences, but argue that the natural sciences themselves make no sense except in relation to sound theologies of God, creation, and the human person. In contrast with many postliberal theologians, radical orthodoxy emphasizes a recovery and revitalization not only to the *language* of premodern faith but also of the *metaphysics* of the patristic Christian-Platonic synthesis.

Radical orthodoxy's intervention into the rhetoric of "theism" and "atheism" in the realms of epistemology and politics seems to offer a promising way beyond this looming collapse back into fundamentalism. At first blush, radical orthodoxy itself seems like a more sophisticated form of fundamentalism (and this is precisely what it is, some of its critics would argue). Radical orthodoxy insists that there is no neutral "secular" knowledge, that all arguments finally imply the metaphysics of being, and that the metaphysics of being are always theological. The question of God cannot be bracketed, set aside, or otherwise avoided. But the question of "God," for radical orthodoxy, is not a broad claim about "theism." It is, finally, the question of the Triune God revealed in Jesus Christ. This is the source of both the "radical" and the "orthodoxy" in "radical orthodoxy." "Theism" and "atheism" are then each seen as sides of the same heterodox or heretical coin. It is not that subjects such as mind, will, consciousness, and neuroscience can best be explained by the assumption of at least some god. It is that these phenomena finally *only* can be understood in connection with reference to the ecstatic relationality and unity of the *Triune* God, who gives creation as a gift of love, who creates the human person in his own image, and who in Christ redeems and fulfills the true nature of humanity.

It is not always clear, however, when these theological and philosophical claims might dictate or at least favor an empirical, propositional assertion at odds with the consensus of the modern natural sciences. As

any alternative configuration perforce reserves a territory independent of God. . . . Underpinning the present essays, therefore, is the idea that every discipline must be framed by a theological perspective; otherwise these disciplines will define a zone apart from God, grounded literally in nothing."); Cunningham, *Genealogy of Nihilism*; Oliver, "Introducing Radical Orthodoxy," 6 (noting that "Milbank's crucial point is that the secular is not simply the rolling back of a theological consensus to reveal a neutral territory where we all become equal players, but the replacement of a certain view of God and creation with a different view which still makes theological claims, that is, claims about origins, purpose and transcendence").

with the other varieties of Christian epistemology introduced above, one of the core tensions is whether the biblical narrative of "Adam and Eve" and the "fall" are in any sense "literal."[153] Can radical orthodoxy here offer only yet another kind of admixture of fideism and rationalism?

The founding charter for radical orthodoxy is John Milbank's *Theology and Social Theory*, which is a sustained critique of the presumed neutrality of the modern social sciences.[154] In a chapter on "Science, Power, and Reality," Milbank attempts to distinguish *social* science, which describes human behavior, from *natural* science.[155] Social science, Milbank argues, differs from natural science in that "human interaction in all its variety can only be narrated, and not explained/understood after the manner of natural science."[156] Milbank's critique of social science sounds like the longstanding argument in the broader academy about whether disciplines such as sociology, political science, economics, and psychology can truly be considered "scientific."[157] He adopts a phenomenological/narratival perspective on persons and cultures: "'Narrating,'" he says, "turns out to be a more basic category than either explanation or understanding: unlike either of these it does not assume particular facts or discrete meanings. Neither is it concerned with universal laws, nor universal truths of the spirit."[158] Narrative "is the final mode of comprehension of human society," and "[t]o understand or explain a social phenomenon is simply to narrate it . . . ."[159]

But this does not only apply to the *social* sciences. Even for the natural sciences, Milbank argues, "[a]s the phrase 'natural history' suggests, natural science does not rid itself of narrative, and indeed, it is just as possible to tell a story in which the characters are atoms, plants, animals, or quasars, as one where they are human beings."[160] The modern natural

153. See Tyson, "Can Modern Science Be Theologically Salvaged?" (Arguing that Cunningham's "mythologizing" of Adam and the fall separates theology and science in a way that causes insuperable dissonance.)

154. Milbank, *Theology and Social Theory*.

155. Milbank, *Theology and Social Theory*, 259–77.

156. Milbank, *Theology and Social Theory*, 259.

157. *See* Clarke and Primo, "Overcoming Physics Envy"; Gutting, "How Reliable Are the Social Sciences?"; Smith, *What is a Person?* chapter 5; King et al., *Designing Social Inquiry*.

158. Milbank, *Theology and Social Theory*, 267.

159. Milbank, *Theology and Social Theory*, 267.

160. Milbank, *Theology and Social Theory* 269.

sciences have largely lost this sense of narrative because of the influence of reductive positivism.[161] Citing Paul Feyerabend's *Against Method*, Milbank notes that the observation of "data" is never a merely neutral activity because the act of constructing the context of an observation already requires a theoretical structure.[162] All data is interpreted and there is no method without theory.

Therefore, for Milbank, scientific investigation always involves narrative. Milbank can then set aside as pretentious the claim of the modern social sciences to provide an objective, "scientific" account of society that atomizes social relations into discrete quantities, which always in the end implies relationships of competition and violence.[163] And, following Alasdair MacIntyre's account of traditioned inquiry, Milbank can offer an alternative narrative, that of Christian charity, in which human society is encompassed in an ontology of relational peace that begins with the ecstatic plenitude of the Triune God's self-giving in creation.[164]

It is unclear precisely how Milbank's account of the natural sciences in *Theology and Social Theory* contrasts with McGrath's critical realism. Milbank's references to the philosophy of science literature are extremely limited—in addition to Feyerabend, he refers only to Descartes, Kant, Whewell, Mill, Popper, and Lakatos (and that all in one sentence!).[165] Much of what Milbank says in *Theology and Social Theory* about the social and pre-empirical theoretical basis for the conduct and interpretation of experiments is entirely consistent with Polanyi's critically realist personalism, which Polanyi fleshes out it much greater detail. Perhaps there are two basic differences: (1) Milbank's narratival approach does not accord the sciences a methodologically separate space from theology, even at a pre-integrative level; and (2) Milbank's approach makes less space—although some space does seem to be given—for the alteration of the Christian theological narrative at a higher level of integration with discrete truths gleaned from the sciences. At a basic level, it is a difference between an analytic (critical realism) and phenomenological (narrative) frame of reference.[166]

161. Milbank, *Theology and Social Theory* 270.

162. Milbank, *Theology and Social Theory* 270–71, and note 13.

163. Milbank, *Theology and Social Theory,* 270–71, and note 13.

164. Milbank, *Theology and Social Theory,* chapters 11, 12, 13.

165. Milbank, *Theology and Social Theory,* 270–71.

166. My observations here in many ways mirror those made by Alister McGrath in his *A Scientific Theology: Reality,* 102–20.

A more sustained effort to address the natural sciences from a theologian associated with radical orthodoxy is Conor Cunningham's *Darwin's Pious Idea*. Cunningham does not offer an explicit methodology for "faith and science" in *Darwin's Pious Idea*. The book is primarily a critique of materialism and the extreme naturalism of contemporary ultra-Darwinists, blended with a critique of scientific creationism and intelligent design (ID) theory.[167] Cunningham seeks to demonstrate that each of these positions—materialism, extreme naturalism, scientific creationism, and ID theory—encode common philosophical presumptions that undermine belief not only in the God of traditional Christian theology, but also in the ability of human beings to conduct an enterprise such as "science."[168] In fact, Cunningham argues, materialism and extreme naturalism make it impossible to believe in "human beings" or even in "evolution" itself.[169] In contrast, Cunningham argues, "orthodox Christianity can offer an account of life and of nature that avoids such contemporary nihilism, and in so doing restore our commonsense world, and thus with it the possibility of beauty, truth, goodness, and lastly, our belief in evolution."[170] Thus Cunningham's implicit method is similar to Milbank's but also diverges from Milbank. Cunningham argues that reductive natural science is descendant of twisted theologies, particularly nominalism, and he adopts a metaphysical and phenomenological stance that seeks to demonstrate how Christianity not only "out narrates" but also is demonstrably true and necessary over materialism and naturalism even with respect to the nature and meaning of biological evolution.[171]

Cunningham's argument in *Darwin's Pious Idea* is "theological" throughout, but in the book's final chapter he makes a sustained move towards what the mainstream theology and science literature might call "integration."[172] In that chapter, he tackles what many consider to be the

167. Cunningham, *Darwin's Pious Idea*, xix.

168. Cunningham, *Darwin's Pious Idea*, xix.

169. Cunningham, *Darwin's Pious Idea*, xix.

170. Cunningham, *Darwin's Pious Idea*, xix.

171. Cunningham's references to nominalism in *Darwin's Pious Idea* are somewhat scattered and indirect. For example: "Why were they so against group selection? One can speculate that it was probably because it went against nominalist ontology." *Darwin's Pious Idea*, 40. It might be difficult for a reader not familiar with theological debates over nominalism to catch some of these references. They are far more direct and clear in Cunningham's *Genealogy of Nihilism*. See Cunningham, *Genealogy of Nihilism*, chapters 1 and 2.

172. See *Darwin's Pious Idea*, chapter 7.

central challenge proposed by biological evolution to Christianity: the meaning of "Adam" and the fall. For mainstream Christian scholars interested in relating some account of Adam and the fall to evolutionary biology, the most common approach is towards a neo-orthodox reading of the biblical text: the biblical story of Adam has no referent in natural history and is rather a story of "everyman."[173]

Cunningham seems to make a similar move at the outset of this chapter: he notes that "[m]any people believe there has been a cosmic Fall as a result of the 'sin' of the first humans, and death was a consequence of this supposed Fall."[174] Cunningham refers to patristic exegesis of the Genesis creation accounts, which was far more sophisticated than contemporary "creationist" readings, and which emphasized the typological and allegorical senses of the text.[175] In this reading, the biblical story of Adam and the fall is in fact the story not of a discrete moment in time that concerned a historical ancient human being who sinned, but rather it is the story of *Christ*.[176] The account of the "Garden" is not of a literal ideal state existing in the past, but rather is a form of eschatology as protology: human beings are made for union with God, yet we each experience disunion in our concrete circumstances. As Cunningham argues,

> Salvation is therefore true hominization, and thus real humanism: man becomes man only in Christ.
>
> A logical but sometimes overlooked consequence of this is that there is, in truth, only one Adam. By contrast, the entire idea of the Fall (original sin, etc.) is premised by the assumption that there could be more than one Adam. Yet Christ himself *is* the two trees in the Garden of Eden, while our sin and fallenness consist in every attempt, even as a possibility, to be human outside Christ. Genesis, we contend, is nothing less than a prophecy of the incarnation and passion of the Christ.[177]

The fall, then, is *felix culpa*: "[y]es, creation was intended to be perfect, and this eternal intention is its true nature; but God's foreknowledge

---

173. See, e.g., Migliore, *Faith Seeking Understanding*, 149–59; Enns, *The Evolution of Adam*.

174. Cunningham, *Darwin's Pious Idea*, 377.

175. Cunningham, *Darwin's Pious Idea*, 377–400.

176. Cunningham, *Darwin's Pious Idea*, 377–400.

177. Cunningham, *Darwin's Pious Idea*, 392.

of man's sin eschatologically ordered creation toward Christ and thus to perfection."[178]

Although this reading sounds neo-orthodox on the surface, Cunningham resists the kind of dualism that would render "Adam" and "the fall" merely in nominalist or Pelagian terms for a passing emotion that might be overcome through education or effort. The problem with such nominalist or Pelagian renderings is that they posit a stark dualism between "nature" and "grace" that cannot be maintained.[179] Following Henri de Lubac, Cunningham argues that there is no pure nature (*natura pura*), no space in which "nature" is not also already given as "grace."[180] Thus each "natural" human being also already participates in grace, in the "supernatural." And thus the participation of the entire human family in the sin of Adam, as well as the universal efficacy of the salvation made possible in Christ, are not merely individual instances of isolated experience, but involve the transcendence of human nature, which is given in creation.[181] The apex of creation, the concrete realization of nature-and-grace and natural-and-supernatural, is Christ.[182] It is only, then, in Christ that we are even capable of seeing "Adam."[183]

8. Towards an Integrated Methodological Perspective

I am unconvinced by approaches to "theology and science" that represent extremes, either in declaring a "war" between theology and science (as in materialistic atheism, young-earth creationism, and some forms of Reformed presuppositionalism) or in merging theology and science as in process theology. I am likewise unconvinced by "NOMA" approaches that cabin "theological" and "scientific" thought into discrete categories, usually resulting in the marginalization of theology. Integrative approaches represented by Alister McGrath's "critical realism" or John Paul II's "*fides et ratio*" are more compelling, and perhaps represent the best kind of analytic method. But such analytic methods, reflecting their debt to Anglo-American analytic philosophy, can leave us intellectually and

178. Cunningham, *Darwin's Pious Idea,* 399.
179. Cunningham, *Darwin's Pious Idea,* 399.
180. Cunningham, *Darwin's Pious Idea,* 399.
181. Cunningham, *Darwin's Pious Idea,* 399.
182. Cunningham, *Darwin's Pious Idea,* 399.
183. Cunningham, *Darwin's Pious Idea,* 399.

spiritually deracinated. The truth, we suspect, cannot so easily be broken into discrete analytic units, even if that sort of analytic process often yields important insights into our mental biases and limitations.

The strong integrationist program represented by process theology is in some ways appealing. It does take seriously the claims of the natural sciences. However, the way in which process theology tends to envision the "soul" as coincident with the universe itself as a conscious entity, perhaps as *the* conscious entity, finally strays far afield from the claims and methods of contemporary natural science. Although even some materialists explain will and consciousness as emergent properties of the lower-order realities of physical laws, they would not ascribe some super-added metaphysical status to those emergent properties.[184] It is unclear, then, whether process theology really *integrates* theology and science or whether process theology is at best *compatible* with some emergentist perspectives within the natural sciences.

Process theology also takes very seriously the problem of evil and the problem of creaturely freedom. Perhaps what the world religions have traditionally thought of as "God" is also an emergent property of the physical universe. Perhaps the physical universe itself is "alive," a growing consciousness in which we each, in our own small way, are a part, and which as a whole is expanding towards its own universal omega point. Perhaps the suffering of the world, our suffering, is neither meaningless nor tied up with an inscrutable and arbitrary Providence, but rather is the birth pang of a universal mind, a "God" if we wish to use that term, in the process of its own delivery, a new, whole, fresh, unblemished child.[185]

There is something compelling, of course, in the notion that human suffering is not without purpose, that our suffering is contributing to the birth of something better. But that might be little relief to the person who pauses to reflect on the fact that he or she will know nothing of this, will receive no *personal* justice or benefit aside from perhaps some present psychic comfort. Are we to suppose that the countless masses who have suffered great violence were just the compost that feeds the sprouting Great Emergent Mind, a science-fiction answer to the questions of Dostoyevsky's Grand Inquisitor?

Even the small present consolation of knowing that one is *at least* serving as compost requires some sense of certainty about the future's

184. See, e.g., Dennett, *Consciousness Explained.*
185. See, e.g., Nagel, *Mind and Cosmos.*

outcome. If emergence is the best hope, it is a frail hope, and really no hope at all. An emergent process by definition is uncertain. Emergence can only happen out of chaos. It is precisely the stochastic nature of the most basic level of physical reality—that of quantum physics—that might allow undetermined, supervenient realities to emerge. This is the difference between the Newtonian universe and the Einsteinian: Einstein (via Heisenberg) makes room for uncertainty. This uncertainty means that the universe's omega point might not be anything we would consider "good" at all. The emerging universal mind might be a fiery consuming monster. In fact, uncertainty means there can be *no* omega point. An omega point, a *final* end, would entail a *certain* end. The Canaanite Leviathan, the beast that emerges from of the primordial waters of chaos to swallow the world, cannot be tamed with hooks (cf. Job 41.) The Leviathan is without justice and without law.

Further, process theology's representation of the classical view of God's perfections in relation to creation *ex nihilo* and creaturely freedom tends towards parody and straw-man claims. It is unclear, for example, who comprises the Christians referenced by Epperly who "believe that God has directed the course of the universe from the very beginning, determining every detail without creaturely input."[186] In his *Guide for the Perplexed* on process theology, Epperly uses popular evangelical preacher Rick Warren's reference to God's providence in Warren's popular book *A Purpose Driven Life* as representative of the classical view.[187] To suggest that Warren lacks the sophistication of Gregory of Nyssa, Augustine, Aquinas, or Barth on these problems is more than an understatement, and Warren himself would not argue otherwise.

Among more significant representatives of the Christian tradition, perhaps some versions of Calvinism or Jansenism would frame this sort of statement, but orthodox Christian theology has always recognized creaturely freedom, and particularly human moral freedom, within the ambit of God's providence and in response to God's grace. Classical Christian orthodoxy is not deterministic fatalism. Indeed, the Second Council of Orange, though it condemned semi-Pelagianism, nevertheless held that human beings can participate or not participate in God's grace: "We not only do not believe that any are foreordained to evil by the power of God, but even state with utter abhorrence that if there are those who want to

---

186. Nagel, *Mind and Cosmos*, 97.

187. Epperly, *Process Theology*, 41–44 (citing Rick Warren, *A Purpose Driven Life*).

believe so evil a thing, they are anathema."[188] It seems, then, that process theology is overstating a case against a mythical opponent. In the end, the "God" of process theology, as well as its vision of the human "soul," tends to devolve into a kind of pantheistic spiritualism that ultimately vindicates neither contemporary science nor natural theology.

Critical realism as a model for interaction between theology and science seems far more promising than process theology. Unlike NOMA approaches, critical realism does not hermetically seal the boundary between "science" and "religion." Critical realism does not represent a Kantian move in which religious or moral feeling is cordoned off from "pure reason," and this is a genuine advance over the Kantian bent of much of the modern scientific establishment—as evidenced, for example, in the National Academies of Science statement on NOMA quoted previously. Moreover, critical realism creates genuine space for theological reform and development when certain theological claims plainly clash with reality. Without some space in which the observations of the natural sciences can influence theology, it is impossible to avoid the intellectual and moral disaster of fundamentalist systems such as young-earth creationism. Certainly, if we seek to be faithful to the spirit of the church fathers, we will want to do theology with a keen eye towards the creation as it is given to us.[189]

However, within critical realism, the interaction between the two disciplines of science and theology tends to be pictured as happening only at a higher level of integration. In this way, a kind of modest foundationalism underpins the entire project, even though many critical realists, including McGrath, strongly eschew foundationalism. This hidden modest foundationalism establishes the boundaries in which the theological and scientific disciplines do their own original work and in which any integrative work happens. But if the Christian confession truly is "realist," then there can be no autonomous space for a "science" that is not already "theological" in what it presumes about the nature of the universe, and there can be no neutral rule of correspondence that would adjudicate "between" theology and science.

Indeed, McGrath's own effort at constructing a natural theology is expressly non-foundationalist and presumes as a first principle "that the

---

188. Canons of the Second Council of Orange, available at http://www.fordham. edu/halsall/basis/orange.txt.

189. For a discussion of how some of the fathers interpreted biblical texts concerning creation, see Bouteneff, *Beginnings*.

logos through which the world was created is embedded in the structures of the created order, above all the human person, and incarnated in Christ."[190] Natural theology, for McGrath, is not an effort to obtain neutrally rational "proofs" of God's existence, but rather to demonstrate "that there is an accumulation of considerations which, though not constituting logical proof (how could experience *prove* anything in such a way?), is at the very least consistent with the existence of a creator God."[191] Nevertheless, two basic questions linger: (1) from the perspective of Christian theology itself, does critical realism envision a sufficiently *theological* account of "reason" that enables "natural science" in the first instance?; and (2) does critical realism propose an understanding of "nature" that resembles a kind of *natura pura*—a realm of pure nature that is not also already a realm of grace?

This reference to "nature" and "grace" highlights the potential distinction between McGrath's critical realism and some Roman Catholic perspectives: in particular, what should we make of the *analogia entis*? The subtle difference between this Roman Catholic vision as expressed by John Paul II and McGrath's more Reformed-oriented critical realism mirrors, in interesting ways, the dialogue between the two great Swiss theologians who continue to inform many of the differences between broadly Catholic and broadly Protestant approaches to natural theology: Barth and Balthasar.[192] The modified, qualified critically realist natural theology of Protestant thinkers such as T. F. Torrance and McGrath, who take their initial cues from Barth, is perhaps more cautious about the *analogia entis*, and therefore ends up with an integration of faith and reason only after a somewhat prolonged process of methodological separation.[193] A Catholic thinker such as John Paul II might more readily see analogical correspondences between God and nature.

Nevertheless, for a Catholic thinker such as John Paul II, even if, as Balthasar argued, "[n]ature cannot include grace at one moment and then exclude it the next," grace cannot be "necessarily derived" from nature, and the use of Aristotelian terminology to describe the movement of the creature towards the goal of the beatific vision as a sort

190. McGrath, *The Open Secret*.

191. McGrath, *The Open Secret*.

192. von Balthasar, *The Theology of Karl Barth*.

193. See Pryzwara, *Analogia Entis*. For an excellent discussion of how Barth developed his own thinking on the analogy of being, see McCormack, "Karl Barth's Version of an 'Analogy of Being.'"

of "natural" movement is only analogical.[194] Balthasar went so far as to argue that Barth's rejection of natural theology and the *analogia entis*, if properly understood, was consistent with the decrees of the First Vatican Council on natural knowledge of God, again if properly understood.[195] And, similarly, the Protestant critical realist McGrath approvingly refers to Erich Przywara's concept of the *analogia entis* as a model for the construction of natural theology.[196] If there are differences between critical realist and specifically Roman Catholic models for the interaction between theology and science, in many cases those differences may be passingly small.

These considerations suggest that a critical realist stance with an appropriately modulated understanding of the *analogia entis* could represent a robust, ecumenical way forward. Indeed, I think that is correct. Nevertheless, while the Protestant critical realist and Roman Catholic "*fides et ratio*" models present careful methodologies, they often are unclear on questions of particular application, not least in connection with areas of significant potential tension, such as the doctrines of divine sovereignty, human uniqueness, and the fall. I seek a method that does not suggest such basic truths could be overwritten by "natural" science.

In response to these problems, in the vein of Reformed presuppositionalism and Reformed epistemology, it is tempting seek to assert the epistemological primacy of *belief*, and specifically of belief in a God possessing the attributes of classical theism. From this primary belief, other primary beliefs may follow, including belief in the reliability of special revelation in the Bible as well as belief in the more general regularity of creation, or "general revelation," tempered by belief in sinful humanity's capacities for self-deception. If such theological beliefs are primary, then apparent conflicts between "science" and "faith" might be resolved by a model that admits a degree of conflict at these difficult tension points, even as it still tries to retain some confidence in "general revelation."

194. Balthasar, *The Theology of Karl Barth*, 267–75.

195. Balthasar, *The Theology of Karl Barth*, 309 (stating that "[i]t is really not possible to construct any genuine contradiction between Barth's statements in his anthropology about the capacity of human nature to know God within the concrete order of revelation (in *all* its conditions) and the statements of Vatican I"). For a recent discussion of the relationship between Barth and Balthasar, see Long, *Saving Karl Barth*.

196. McGrath, *The Open Secret*, 189.

The significant critique of this approach is that, while it might deliver an internally coherent worldview, it cannot guarantee that any such worldview actually corresponds to reality. It produces, at best, a chain of circular reasoning in which an antecedent is supposedly proven merely by showing its consistency with consequent propositions that assume the antecedent—in other words, it commits the fallacy of affirming the consequent. Sophisticated Reformed epistemologists such as Alvin Plantinga respond that they are not committing this fallacy because basic belief in God is known through revelation and faith, not through argument. The purpose of the argument is to show that there are no "defeaters," no fundamental logical inconsistencies, in holding the basic belief in God. But Plantinga also notes that in the Christian theological tradition faith is associated with a form of "certainty," and consistent with his Reformed heritage he understands that "certainty" to reside in the internal witness of the Holy Spirit and not in other kinds of proofs. Given the certain witness of the Holy Spirit, it is unclear why a Christian should be concerned about chains of reasoning that eliminate potential "defeaters." The certain testimony of the Holy Spirit should be indefeasible; if it is defeasible, it is not certain. Plantinga's response is that the apologetic exercise of removing potential defeaters is helpful to us in the human weakness and sin that can often obscure the Holy Spirit's witness.

An additional and perhaps more significant problem with Plantinga's approach is that, like naïve foundationalism, it can tend towards ontotheology. "Ontotheology," a term coined by Heidegger, is the notion that God is like any other being in the universe.[197] The problem of ontotheology is particularly acute in theology-and-science discourse precisely at the point addressed most directly by Plantinga: that of divine action and providence. Consider, for example, a typical statement of God's action in the Psalm 135: "He makes clouds rise from the ends of the earth; he sends lightning with the rain and brings out the wind from his storehouses."[198] It is an obvious mistake to conclude the God is literally sitting at the "ends of the earth" pushing around the storm clouds with a giant God-finger. The fact that we can understand the natural processes that give rise to thunderstorms—and that even Google Earth fails to reveal God pushing them around—does not falsify Psalm 135. When Psalm 135 says God

197. Regarding ontotheology, see Balthasar, *Theologic, Vol. 2: Truth of God*, 134–35, note 10, ; Westphal, *Overcoming Ontotheology*; Shindler, "Hans Urs von Balthasar, Metaphysics, and the Problem of Ontotheology."

198. Ps 135:7 (NIV).

causes the thunderstorms, we know this entails a kind of causation that differs from the natural causes of thunderstorms, and that these different levels of causality are not incompatible.

Aquinas spoke of these different levels of causality in Aristotelian terms as "primary" and "secondary."[199] Plantinga speaks of what he calls an "Aquinas/Calvin Model" of knowledge and warrant, but he does not seem to appreciate how Aquinas speaks of divine action or of the ways in which Aquinas and Calvin might relate or differ on this point.[200] And when Plantinga offers the Heidelberg Catechism as a statement of what Christian theists believe about God's action in creation, he does not seem to appreciate the subtle but significant debates about God's providence in relation to creaturely freedom that wound through both the Magisterial Reformation and the Catholic divisions over Jansenism and the very different perspectives of the eastern church. Plantinga's lack of depth on this difficult theological question seems to leave him without resources for thinking about divine action much beyond the flat perspectives of a kind of modern ontotheology. The same problem affects other points at which Plantinga, in some of his other work, significantly modifies the classical understanding of God's perfections that *was* (I would argue) shared by Aquinas and Calvin: that God *in esse* is simple and impassible.[201]

While Plantinga's contributions to epistemology and theology and science are helpful in demonstrating the priority of faith, then, they ironically fail to follow through with the Christian theological claim that God is the *transcendent* creator and cause of all that is, not a *part of* creation. However we try to conceive of and describe God's action in originating and sustaining the creation, or the possibility of miracles, or God's "emotional" connection to the creation, we must maintain the absolute *distinction* between God and creation, or else our project will collapse. For this reason, Plantinga's focus on "design" arguments ultimately is misplaced.

On the question of teleology and "design," Coakley's methodology holds greater promise because it explicitly refuses ontotheology and asserts the irreducible importance of the doctrines of Trinity, creation, incarnation, and resurrection. Indeed, I agree with every "hallmark" of Coakley's method. But Coakley's application of the method to "supernormal" altruism is problematic. The most significant problem is the issue

199. See generally, Aquinas, *Summa Contra Gentiles*, Book II; White, "Medieval Theories of Causation"; Burrell, *Freedom and Creation in Three Traditions*.

200. See Plantinga, *Warranted Christian Belief*, chapter 8.

201. See Plantinga, "Self-Profile," 36; *God, Freedom and Evil*.

of what "normal" or "supernormal" could mean in the context of evolution. As I will explore more fully in chapter 5.4, "normal" in evolutionary terms is only a statistical description, which changes not only over time but across fitness landscapes. The fact that there are some outliers—individuals who are extraordinarily altruistic in comparison to the mean (Mother Theresa), or extraordinarily selfish (Adolf Hitler)—is in itself neither remarkable nor particularly significant in relation to the total n of the sample size, which must include every human who ever has lived. But Coakley hints at what I believe is more significant: the more "normal" phenomenon of the law as an irreducibly transcendent and unique component of human "nature." As Coakley notes, there is a growing sense even among non-religious analytic philosophers that "balefully reductionistic moves in science, economics, public policy and the law" foreclose reasoned inquiry and argument, and a commitment to theoretic and ethical realism require some meaningful concept of "natural law."[202] I agree with Coakley that Aristotle and Aquinas, among others, are fruitful sources for bringing realism about natural law into conversation with evolutionary science, particularly, as Coakley suggests, in connection with neo-Aristotelian philosophy of science.[203] But my focus on "law," rather than on "supernormal" altruism, comports better with Coakley's (and Aquinas') own methodological preference for avoiding the use of theology as an outlier or afterthought. Theology best explains what is "normal," not only what is superadded to "nature."

In this regard, Milbank's approach in *Theology and Social Theory* is attractive for a number of reasons. First, it deflates the presumed historic warfare between "faith" and "science" by offering a holistic account of "reason" that is already embedded in the Christian tradition. There is no possibility of "conflict" between "faith" and "science" here because those terms simply have no meaning in isolation. There is, rather, a grand narrative of God's self-giving creative love, which allows for human beings as creatures to observe and study and delight in the creation. Second, it exposes the pretensions of reductive positivistic "science" as itself a kind of atheology, with pre-empirical theoretical commitments not derived from its own supposedly objective methods. Finally, it points toward a different form of apologetic in which the Christian narrative is offered in

---

202. Coakley, "Sacrifice Regained," Lecture 6, 7.
203. Coakley, "Sacrifice Regained," Lecture 6, 8.

the robust sense of a true *apologia* rather than as an "apology" before the bar of a totalizing modernity.[204]

A potential problem with Milbank's approach is evident in his reference to Feyerabend. Like other constructivist philosophers of science, Feyerabend was an anti-realist and a nominalist.[205] Milbank's theological project and the broader "radical orthodoxy," movement it spawned, of course, involves a sustained historical critique of the univocity of being, nominalism, and voluntarism.[206] While postmodern philosophers of science such as Feyerabend and Thomas Kuhn offer helpful resources concerning the social context of the natural sciences, their conclusions are finally incompatible with a realist participatory ontology grounded in the Christian doctrine of creation. It remains unclear how Milbank's "narrative" construal of the natural sciences in *Theology and Social Theory* can cohere with his and radical orthodoxy's other broad commitments.[207]

In this regard, while outside the peculiar milieu of conservative evangelical Protestantism and the American legal system it might be easy to dismiss young-earth creationism as a distracting sideshow, contemporary young-earth creationism presents a more subtle epistemological challenge for any Christian theologian who seeks to understand the catholic (that is, "universal" in the general sense) Christian tradition in relation to the modern natural sciences. Christian thinkers who reject young-earth creationism and accept the broad scientific consensus about the age of the universe and biological evolution usually insist that "evolution" is not the same thing as "evolution*ism*" or "scient*ism*"—that is, that the empirical truths of the natural sciences do not entail commitment to a worldview in which these empirical facts preclude the possibility of God and of some more or less traditional Christian theological claims about providence, the possibility of miracles, original sin, the inspiration of scripture, and so-on.[208] This argument is not often well examined by its proponents,

---

204. This apologetic theme is developed in Milbank's foreword to Davidson, *Imaginative Apologetics*. Interestingly, the chapter on faith and science in that volume was written by Alister McGrath.

205. See Oberheim, *Feyerabend's Philosophy*, 74–76 (noting that "Feyerabend's nominalism is a form of anti-realism about natural kinds").

206. See, e.g., Milbank, *Theology and Social Theory*, 13–18; see also Pickstock, "Duns Scotus: His Historical and Contemporary Significance."

207. A similar criticism of Milbank's early work is made by Alister McGrath in *A Scientific Theology: Reality*, 97–118.

208. See, e.g., Burnett, "What Is Scientism?"

but when it is carefully examined, it focuses on epistemology. Often the question is framed in terms of whether some form of positivism is true or whether, instead, some framework of belief must be prior to empiricism. The difficult problem is that savvy young-earth creationist advocates make precisely the same move. They further argue, however, that the literal inerrancy of the Bible is a valid and indeed essential aspect of this prior framework of epistemic belief.

Thus the immensely popular young-earth creationist apologists and Creation Museum founder Ken Hamm always begins his debates (which are often offered as spectacles for consumption by church and school groups) with epistemological arguments. "How do you *know* life arose through natural processes billions of years ago?" Hamm asks his interlocutor. "Were you there?" He concludes with the coup de grâce: "I know someone who *was* there, and he wrote about it in his book, and he says it *didn't* happen that way."[209] While this is phrased with the flair of a practiced showman, it does imply an epistemology that is not too far removed from seemingly more sophisticated postmodern and postliberal epistemologies. Indeed, Hamm does not hesitate to remind us that "there are no pre-theoretical facts" and that "all facts are interpreted." The essential point is that beliefs about God and revelation can and should come before, supply the parameters of, and establish the interpretive matrix for empirical observations. For Hamm, this means that the gap between "uniformitarian" science and young-earth creationism is at first more of a small shift in perception than a massive rejection of modern science.

We might not possess Hamm's rhetorical talents, but we might with some discomfort hear ourselves making the same kind of argument: which seems more likely, that what we have thought of for millennia as the human "mind" and "consciousness" and "will" are merely epiphenomena of a finally deterministic pattern of firing neurons, or that institutions like "the law" really represent the actions of free moral agents who are created in the image of and accountable to God? It is simply a matter of one's pre-empirical frame of reference. If we assume naturalism, then we will interpret the findings of the neurosciences as empirical confirmation of

---

209. See Ken Ham, "Were You There?" available at https://answersingenesis.org/the-word-of-god/were-you-there/. For a somewhat chilling video of Mr. Ham teaching children this mantra, see https://www.youtube.com/watch?v=OFmiLsm3aYM. Mr. Ham's recent debate with "Bill Nye the Science Guy," in which Mr. Ham focuses on his epistemological arguments, is available online at https://www.youtube.com/watch?v=_04SofYU7FI.

the intuition that matter is all there is. If we assume "theism," then we will minimize the findings of the neurosciences or find ways to accommodate them into a "theistic" framework. If we assume Christian orthodoxy, then we may simply explain "science" away as a narrative.

This line of thought inevitably comes back around to the question of *fides et ratio*: is the role of reason at most supportive of the inner witness of the faith prompted by the Holy Spirit, or can reason alone—"natural reason" in the language of the First Vatican Council—demonstrate the existence of the creator God? "Continental" and postliberal theologies that offer *phenomenological* perspectives on "faith and science" are helpful at this point, because such perspectives ask us what we mean by "reason." If "reason" entails the study of the whole structure of experience and consciousness, and cannot be reduced to the logic of propositional claims, then the supposed gap between the inner testimony of the Holy Spirit and other kinds of arguments may close.[210] "Faith" and "reason" then are not different ways of knowing. "Faith" always entails "reason" and "reason" always entails "faith."

In terms of "faith and science," a phenomenological approach would not break reality down into discrete units such as "evolution" and "the fall" and then seek to explain the apparent contradictions between those concepts through ever finer scholastic distinctions. Such an approach would take reality as a whole, as it presents itself to us, including the reality presented to us through revelation and the Holy Spirit, and recognize that it is both multifaceted and ultimately coherent. Indeed, the claim that creation is both "good" (implying that it is intelligible, beautiful, meaningful, and so on) and "fallen" (implying that it entails death, decay, and dissolution not inherent to its created goodness) reflects our common human experience of a world that is so often heartbreaking because its loveliness is glimpsed only through great pain.

Conor Cunningham's phenomenological reading of evolutionary biology, for example, is powerful, and his use of patristic sources to narrate the Christian vision as it is both protologically and eschatologically centered in Christ is compelling. There is some ambiguity, however, in

210. Advocates of the "Continental" philosophical tradition suggest that this is precisely the benefit Continental thought offers in relation to "analytic" or Anglo-American philosophy. *See* McCumber, *Time and Philosophy*; Critchley, *Continental Philosophy*. It is no coincidence that the radical orthodoxy thinkers I discuss in this book represent part of the "Continental" stream of philosophical theology, or that the "postliberal" theologians are partial to Wittgenstein, who is often seen as a sort of bridge between the analytic and Continental traditions.

the shape Cunningham provides that narrative at one of its most sensitive points: the question of "Adam." Cunningham does not intend to deny the reality of Adam. Nevertheless, most of Cunningham's patristic sources of biblical interpretation are Eastern, and most of the contemporary interpreters of those sources upon whom he draws are Eastern Orthodox.[211] Indeed, he quotes Orthodox scholar Peter Bouteneff, who argues (along with many contemporary historical-critical exegetes of all theological stripes) that "[n]either in Paul nor in the rest of the Bible is there a doctrine of original guilt, wherein all are proleptically guilty in Adam."[212] This seems a bit tendentious, as the understanding of "original sin"—and the reception of Augustine, notably in regard to "original sin"—remains one of the key sticking points between the Christian East and West.[213]

Cunningham makes an oblique reference to this difference in a footnote: "Yes, in the West, Fathers such as Augustine seem to emphasize the Fall, the advent of evil, and so on."[214] However, says Cunningham, "it is important to realize that Augustine, for example, developed his notion of original sin in a very particular context, namely, the Donatist

---

211. In particular, Bouteneff, *Beginnings*; Behr, *The Mystery of Christ*; Hart, *The Beauty of the Infinite*.

212. Behr, *The Mystery of Christ*, 383 (quoting Bouteneff, *Beginnings*, 41).

213. See Bouteneff, "Christ and Salvation," 94 (noting that "the transgression and the expulsion from Paradise narrated in Genesis 3 never engendered in the Christian East a doctrine of 'original guilt' or 'guilt in Adam.' . . . Likewise the early Genesis narratives did not produce in the Orthodox East a doctrine of total depravity, which would run counter to the conviction that human nature is at root good, even though distorted. The Paradise account, together with the other 'decline narratives' of Genesis 1–11, testify to the state of exile in which we currently find ourselves: at odds with God, with each other and with the created environment, and therefore in need of saving."); Ware, *The Orthodox Way*, 62 (stating that "[o]riginal sin is not to be interpreted in juridicial or quasi-biological terms, as if it were some physical 'taint' of guilt, transmitted through sexual intercourse. This picture, which normally passes for the Augustinian view, is unacceptable to Orthodoxy. The doctrine of original sin means rather that we are born into an environment where it is easy to do evil and hard to do good; easy to hurt others, and hard to heal their wounds; easy to arouse men's suspicions, and hard to win their trust"). Ware nonetheless states his understanding of "original sin" in ontological terms: "human beings, made in the image of the Trinitarian God, are interdependent and coinherent. No man is an island. We are 'members of one another' (Eph. 4:25), and so any action, performed by any member of the human race, inevitably affects all the other members. Even though we are not, in the strict sense, guilty of the sins of others, yet we are somehow always *involved*." Ibid.

214. Ware, *The Orthodox Way*, 513, note 38.

controversy, and the Pelagian one. So it was to this degree polemical."[215] But it is unclear whether this contextualization of Augustine can do all the work Cunningham assigns to it, at least not for the Western theological tradition.

As late as 1950, for example, Pope Pius XII's Encyclical *Humani Generis* responded to the developing science of human evolution with an insistence on a literal individual Adam, tied to a woodenly Augustinian doctrine of original sin.[216] Pope Pius XII seemed to tie this conclusion to what sounds like a fundamentalist-creationist reading of scripture:

> To return, however, to the new opinions mentioned above, a number of things are proposed or suggested by some even against the divine authorship of Sacred Scripture. For some go so far as to pervert the sense of the Vatican Council's definition that God is the author of Holy Scripture, and they put forward again the opinion, already often condemned, which asserts that immunity from error extends only to those parts of the Bible that treat of God or of moral and religious matters. They even wrongly speak of a human sense of the Scriptures, beneath which a divine sense, which they say is the only infallible meaning, lies hidden . . . .[217]

To be sure, the Catholic Catechism after the Second Vatican Council seems to sound a more cautious note concerning the different senses of scripture and its interpretation.[218] Pope Benedict XVI, in a set of homilies on the biblical creation texts, agreed with the patristic sources cited by Cunningham that "the biblical creation narratives represent another way of speaking about reality than that with which we are familiar from physics and biology."[219] These texts, Pope Benedict said, "do not depict the process of becoming or the mathematical structure of matter; instead, they say in different ways that there is only *one* God and that the universe is not the scene of a struggle among dark forces but rather the creation of his Word."[220] Concerning "original sin," Benedict took a "relational" approach to the doctrine.[221] For Benedict,

215. Cunningham, *Darwin's Pious Idea*.

216. Pope Pius XII, *Humani Generis*.

217. Pope Pius XII, *Humani Generis*, ¶¶22–23.

218. See *Catechism of the Catholic Church*, ¶¶101–41.

219. Benedict XVI, "In the Beginning," 25.

220. Pope Benedict XVI, "In the Beginning," 25.

221. Pope Benedict XVI, "In the Beginning," 73.

[t]o be truly a human being means to be related in love, to be of and be for. But sin means the damaging or destruction of relationality. Sin is a rejection of relationality because it wants to make the human being a god. Sin is loss of relationship, disturbance of relationship, and therefore it is not restricted to the individual. When I destroy a relationship then this event—sin—touches the other person involved in the relationship. Consequently sin is always an offense that touches others, that alters the world and damages it. To the extent that is true, when the network of human relationships is damaged from the very beginning, then every human being enters into a world that is marked by relational damage.[222]

This approach to original sin seems a far cry from the seeming biblical fundamentalism and Augustinian realism of *Humani Generis*. Nevertheless, the *Catechism* continues to affirm that the fall and original sin have a historical referent in time: "The account of the fall in *Genesis* 3 uses figurative language, but affirms a primeval event, a deed that took place *at the beginning of the history of man*. Revelation gives us the certainty of faith that the whole of human history is marked by the original fault freely committed by our first parents."[223]

This trepidation about the role of Adam is also evident in conservative evangelical and Reformed Protestant thought, even outside the confines of literalistic fundamentalism. For example, in a recent book on *Adam, the Fall, and Original Sin*, within a generally thoughtful collection of essays by evangelical and Reformed scholars, the author of a chapter on the science of human evolution felt compelled to publish pseudonymously, no doubt for fear of his position at an evangelical or Reformed school.[224] In a thoughtful essay in that same volume, Hans Madueme lays out the problem and offers some possible solutions.[225] Like Pope Pius in relation to Catholic theology, Madueme argues that a literal Adam and a literal fall are essential to Reformed orthodoxy.[226]

222. Pope Benedict XVI, *"In the Beginning,"* 73.

223. *Catechism of the Catholic Church,* ¶390.

224. See William Stone (a pseudonym), "Adam and Modern Science," in Madueme and Reeves, eds., *Adam, the Fall, and Original Sin*.

225. Madueme, "'The Most Vulnerable Part of the Whole Christian Account': Original Sin and Modern Science," in Madueme and Reeves, eds., *Adam, the Fall, and Original Sin*.

226. Madueme, "The Most Vulnerable Part of the Whole Christian Account."

Thus, it is unclear whether Cunningham's effort to employ a phenomenological method that exceeds the limits of both the ultra-Darwinists and the creationists succeeds. Perhaps it succeeds if one opts for an Eastern Orthodox account of the fall and original sin that draws primarily on some of the Eastern fathers, or for a neo-orthodox account that views Adam and the fall as entirely non-historical. But, it seems, the scientific understanding of biological evolution stands in considerable tension with the Western-Augustinian Christian tradition, as evidenced in documents such as *Humani Generis* and the *Catechism of the Catholic Church* as well as in contemporary conservative Reformed theologians who continue to insist that a "literal" Adam is essential to Christian theology.[227]

Perhaps another of Cunningham's comments towards the end of the final chapter of *Darwin's Pious Idea* hints at a solution, or at least at a way of managing some of these tensions: "We all stand before the law; such is the lot of man."[228] As Cunningham notes, "even if we know of laws, we don't think they are *the Law* but are rather somewhat arbitrary—cultural products, or fruits of evolution, and therefore relative."[229] Indeed, "in the Judeo-Christian tradition there was a time before the Law of Moses, a time before the Decalogue."[230] Yet, he continues, "from the time of Adam, there was prohibition."[231] Perhaps "the Law" is the "missing link" between Origen, Gregory of Nyssa, and Augustine, the methodological basis for narrating the true harmony of "faith" and "science." As Pope Benedict suggested, perhaps the loss of relational friendship occasioned by the fall is precisely the loss of the law, and perhaps Christ's fulfillment of the law is what enables us to overcome the ban of exclusion from our humanity and recover our participation in the law of love. "Law" might be the thread by which Christian theology "out-narrates" *and* out-argues reductive naturalism in a rich tapestry of human culture that participates in God's gracious gift of creation and redemption.

Traditional Christian (and Jewish and Islamic) theology asserts that God has revealed himself to specific individuals at unique moments in history, and that these moments of revelation can establish a new elect

---

227. See, e.g., Vandoodewaard, *The Quest for the Historical Adam*. As the title of Vandoodewaard's book suggests, he equates debates over the historical existence of Adam with debates over the "quest" for the historical of Jesus.

228. Cunningham, *Darwin's Pious Idea*, 414.

229. Cunningham, *Darwin's Pious Idea*, 414.

230. Cunningham, *Darwin's Pious Idea*, 414.

231. Cunningham, *Darwin's Pious Idea*, 414.

people and by extension a new relationship between God and humanity: the covenant with Noah, the call of Abraham, Moses at the burning bush and his receipt of the Torah, the anointing of David, the baptism of Jesus, the conversion of the apostle Paul. There was also such a moment of revelation to "Adam": when God disclosed to humanity the law of the two trees in the Garden. This act of God's self-disclosure, I argue, is an important part of what sets Adam apart from the broader stream of human biological evolution. Based on what we know about neural plasticity and epigenetic inheritance, we might even suggest that this encounter subtly but profoundly changed us *biologically*, even if Adam and his heirs undoubtedly remained embedded in the genetic flow among other contemporary *homo sapiens, homo neanderthalis*, and perhaps other species.[232]

As John Milbank notes in his most recent work, modernity tends to view "law" as Leviathan: a form of repression against our "true" animal nature.[233] Law can, of course, be repressive if it is not rooted in justice. But law as law is essential to freedom. Law sets the conditions *for* freedom. Indeed, the universe itself requires "law" as a condition of its existence. The "laws of nature" might represent the most basic potentials of being and existence.[234] We could even speak of a sort of "law" through which the most basic potentials of the being and existence of *God* can be expressed: the "law" of inner-Trinitarian relations. If each of the three persons of the Trinity is uniquely a "person," as orthodoxy holds, then there are "boundaries" to each of their personhood. Likewise, if each of the three persons of the Trinity interpenetrate each other and are of one substance, as orthodoxy also holds, then there is a "boundary" to their unity. This is, of course, an analogical use of the term "law," and we must not think of this sort of "law" as an imposition *upon* the being of God. Rather, these "laws" comprise a set of relationships that *proceed from* the being of God.[235] As such, they are an essential aspect of God's self-donation in creation, and comprise the most basic potentials of creation itself. At its

---

232. See, e.g., Merzenich, *Soft-Wired*; Heard and Martienssen, "Transgenerational Epigenetic Inheritance."

233. Milbank, *Beyond Secular Order*.

234. For a discussion of the "laws of nature," see chapter 6.2.

235. For a discussion of the procession of the Trinitarian persons and the being of God, see Balthasar, *Theo-Logic, Vol. 2*, Part III.A.2 ("Identity and Difference in God") (noting that "[t]he divine processions cannot, like those within a human mind, be accidental . . . since there is nothing accidental in God. They must therefore be identical with the real divine essence").

heart, this law is the law of ecstatic, self-giving *love*. The most basic law of "nature," and the most basic law of "politics," is the law of love.

The argument I am foreshadowing here could be considered a variant of the "moral argument" for God's existence.[236] I wish to distance myself somewhat from such arguments, however, in that they tend to argue from the phenomenon of an intuitive "moral sense" in humans to God's existence as the source of that intuition. My claim is more "Augustinian"—and, I would suggest, more fully "Thomistic"—than most contemporary versions of the moral argument. It is not so much our knowledge of objective moral truth that points toward God, but our knowledge that we are *separated* from the final, objective truth towards which our moral inclinations pull us: that is, towards God, who is love. Moreover, it is in understanding this lack that we truly begin to know *ourselves* both as *adamah* and as "in Adam."[237] One important way in which we can know our sense of lack in this regard is real comes from God's disclosure of the positive law in the divine command and in the uniquely human practice of formulating codes of positive law. This way of framing the moral claim, I argue, is more consistent with the historic, orthodox Christian tradition than many modern formulations. Indeed, it is precisely the claim made by St. Paul in his letter to the Romans:

> Therefore, just as through one man sin entered into the world, and death through sin, and so death spread to all men, because all sinned—for until the Law sin was in the world, but sin is not imputed when there is no law. Nevertheless death reigned from Adam until Moses, even over those who had not sinned in the likeness of the offense of Adam, who is a type of Him who was to come.[238]

But if the phenomenon of "law" can be reduced to neurobiology, as some neurolaw scholars argue, this story loses all purchase. If "law" is a phenomenon of human experience that shows how humans are related to a transcendent source, I can extend Cunningham's argument about why Christian theology and biological evolution are compatible, and indeed about why evolution is *impossible* without God. If "law" is merely an epiphenomenon of neurobiology, I have no argument. In the next chapter,

---

236. For a general discussion of such arguments, see Evans, "Moral Arguments for the Existence of God."

237. Cf. Rom 4:12.

238. Rom 5:12–14 (NASB).

I consider perspectives from paleoanthropology and neurobiology on the development of human agency and "mind" that could undermine my theological claims. I begin to argue in chapter 5, however, that efforts by scientists working in these disciplines to eliminate the concepts of transcendent agency that underpin traditional notions of "law" are unsupported and self-defeating.

5

Paleo-Law

Have We Always Been Human?

IN CHAPTERS 1 AND 2, we explored the slide away from transcendence that severed the links between God's being, the natural law, and the positive law. In chapter 3, we discussed the growth of contemporary neurolaw. In chapter 4, we framed a methodological perspective concerning theology and science from which the problem of neurolaw could begin to be addressed. In this chapter, we begin to apply that methodology to the phenomena of human evolution and the earliest development of positive law.

The earliest extant legal codes, like all positive law, address the problem of violence. Legal philosophy has long been vexed by the problem of violence. If "law" is merely the imposition of one person or group's will upon another person or group, then "law" is an empty term that merely signifies a kind of power maintained by violence. As we explored in chapter 1, the pre-modern approach is to refer to a concept of "natural" law rooted in a transcendent divine source.

As we saw in chapters 1–3, the debate about whether there is any sort of "natural" law—including whether the concept of "natural" law makes any difference or merely relocates the problem of violence from other humans to "nature" or "God"—is also longstanding. But it is only in the past hundred years or so that the modern natural sciences have begun to illuminate the even deeper antiquity and diversity of human evolution. If we wish to address the problem of "natural" law today, we must ask whether human evolutionary history undermines the kinds of founding myths (the Garden of Eden, the Atrahasis Epic, the Timaeus, and so-on) that supported claims about "natural" law made by many pre-modern writers. What can paleoanthropology and evolutionary neurobiology tell us about human "law"? Is "law" just an artifact of evolution's bloody flow?

This chapter reviews and critiques the narrative of human cultural evolution as told by some of its best-known narrators. It is important to understand this background narrative because it provides the "creation myth" for modern sociobiological and neurobiological ethical programs, including neurolaw. It also is important to understand the elements of this background narrative that any responsible theology must take as well-established conclusions about reality and to distinguish those elements from metaphysical conclusions that are not properly within the purview of the natural sciences.

1. The Evolution of "Human" Culture: The First and Last Human

Paleoanthropologists differ sharply about the nature and cause of the differences between *homo sapiens sapiens*—us—and the many human/hominid species that also form the human evolutionary tree.[1] Indeed, the ambiguity extends even to the use of the word "human."

The fascinating and beautifully produced book *The Last Human*, for example, offers photographs of forensic reconstructions based on fossil samples of twenty-two species of hominids dating back to over seven million years, as well as narratives of the possible lifeways of these creatures.[2] As the narratives proceed through the twenty-two species, the language subtly changes from "man-ape" to "apeman" to "man."

For the earliest species profiled, *Sahelanthropus tchadensis*, *Orrorin tugenensis*, and *Ardipithecus ramidus* and *kadabba*, the lifeway narrative evokes the "man-ape":

> On reaching the crown of a yellow-wood tree the man-ape began bending back branches. He softly hooted to himself for

---

1. For a good overview of the evidence for human evolution from a paleoanthropological perspective, see Tattersall, *The Fossil Trail*. For a discussion of the genetic evidence for human evolution, see Jones et al., *The Cambridge Encyclopedia of Human Evolution*, Part Seven: "Genetic Clues of Relatedness."

2. Sawyer and Deak, *The Last Human*.

there were no other man-apes in sight. Just when he felt the nest was right, he laid in it belly-up watching the sky darken, and waiting for the night. As the sun disappeared into the horizon, a small gust of wind licked up from the east. The light drizzle that began shortly after the wind died prompted the man-ape to break back small branches with leaves and cover his body. Feeling comfortable with his new blanket, he quickly fell asleep.[3]

A photo of the "man-ape" *Sahelanthropus tchadensis* suggests that the subject "contemplatively surveys the African landscape some seven million years ago."[4]

The Last Human, 32

The lifeway narratives shift to the term "man-ape" with *Australo-pithecus anamensis, Kenyanthropus platyops, and Australopithecus*

---

3. Sawye and Deak, *The Last Human*, 27.

4. Sawyer and Deak, *The Last Human*, 32.

afarensis, which lived in the African Great Rift Valley about four million years ago.[5] So, for example,

> Standing in the crook of a tree, a female man-ape reached up for unripe figs. Leaf monkeys jumped back and forth in the smaller branches of the tree crown dropping partly eaten figs on the man-ape below. One leaf monkey descended down to the man-ape's eye-level. Facing the man-ape, it chattered and squealed at her relentlessly. Harassed by the noise and debris, the man-ape descended the tree first. Remaining on two legs, she leisurely walked to another tree and picked the fruit from the lower branches.[6]

One of the species mentioned here, *Australopithecus afarensis,* is that of "Lucy," a famous and important specimen that exhibits the smaller braincase of an ape with a bipedal upright walking posture—a transitional form. A photograph of a reconstructed Lucy shows her, as the caption states, as she "searches desperately through the savannah for her missing three-year-old daughter."

The Last Human, 69

5. Sawyer and Deak, *The Last Human,* 46–47.
6. Sawyer and Deak, *The Last Human,* 63.

With two other Great Rift Valley species, *Paranthropus aethiopicus*, and *Australopithecus garhi*, both of which lived about two million years ago, the descriptor shifts to from "man-ape" to "apemen." Thus:

> With the evening quickly approaching, the apemen constructed nests from shrubs and herbs growing on the shaded woodland floor. Some of the youngsters made their nests in small trees above where the adults slept.
>
> Sitting up in her nest with the stick still in her hand, the apemen stared suspiciously at a small sapling within arm's reach. Cocking the stick with her right and bending the sapling with her left, she carefully inspected the foliage for snakes. When none were found, she put the stick down and stripped the sapling's bark. Getting at the underlying pith, she enjoyed a final bite before turning in for the night.[7]

A photograph of a reconstructed *Paranthropus aethiopicus* shows him looking contentedly in the direction of the camera, with what appears to be the hint of a smile. The caption tells us that, "[a]mused by the playfulness of his children, an adult *Paranthropus aethiopicus* watches protectively and lovingly."[8]

The Last Human, 83

7. Sawyer and Deak, *The Last Human*, 78.
8. Sawyer and Deak, *The Last Human*, 82.

With the introduction of the *Homo* genus the lifeway narratives drop the "ape" and use the terms "man" and "pygmy."[9] The narrative preceding *Homo rudolfensis* describes a wary encounter between men and baboons:

> A man, knee-high in water, was standing on two legs pulling plants out by the roots . . . . Five other men sat immobile below a patch of bush-willow trees, watching and trying to avoid the rain. A troop of baboons watched the men at a safe distance.[10]

A close-up of *Homo rudolfensis*, which lived near Lake Turkana about 1.9 million years ago, allows us to peer deep behind his eyes—dare we say into his soul? "Thoughts of tomorrow," the caption says, "underlie the intelligent gaze of *Homo rudolfensis*."[11]

The Last Human, 121

9. Sawyer and Deak, *The Last Human,* 113.
10. Sawyer and Deak, *The Last Human,* 115.
11. Sawyer and Deak, *The Last Human,* 120.

For *Homo habilis*, the terminology shifts to "pygmy," reflecting the problems paleoanthropologists have faced in classifying this species.[12] The narrative evokes a pygmy searching for food along the shore of a "grey-blue" lake "lined by the pink hues of hundreds of flamingoes": "Not discouraged by failure, the pygmy walked along the shore looking for other opportunities. Not finding any, he thought about all the food in the highland forest. It was early in the morning and the forest was close enough to make it there and back in a single day."[13] A photo reconstructing *Homo habilis*, which lived about 1.5 to 1.8 million years ago, suggests that "A brilliant African sky offers a visual wonder for a curious female *homo habilis*."[14]

The Last Human, 127

The title of "human" is first given with the introduction of *Paranthropus bosisei,* a stout species found in various African sites dating to 1.4 to 2.3 million years ago, and *Homo Ergaster, Homo georgicus, Homo erectus, Homo pekinensis,* and *Homo floresiensis,* with dates ranging from over 1 million years ago (*H. Ergaster*) to only hundreds or tens of thousands of years ago.[15] So:

12. Sawyer and Deak, *The Last Human,* 129.
13. Sawyer and Deak, *The Last Human,* 122.
14. Sawyer and Deak, *The Last Human,* 127.
15. Sawyer and Deak, *The Last Human,* 135.

A group of apemen, a gelada baboon troop, and two humans fed together on herbs and grasses along the shore, keeping a safe distance from the ramp-like hippo trails descending into the lake. With many of the grasses mature and turned to seed, the apemen concentrated on these, using their front teeth to strip the seeds from the tall tufts. Willing to brave their proximity to the hippo trail, the humans fed on the rootstocks of a small patch of sedges exposed by the receding shoreline. When an apeman came to feed next to them, the two humans became visibly uneasy, increasing their eye movements and averting a fixed gaze.[16]

And:

A shrill, squeaking cry caught the attention of two young men walking into the high veldt. They stopped, turned and looked around, but they saw nothing. Glancing at each other with quizzical looks they continued on their way.[17]

And yet more evocatively:

She didn't remember why, but at the time she was crying. Maybe she was sick or just hungry. The old woman held her in her arms, rocked her back and forth, and hummed. She placed some cherries in her hand. Eating them made here stop crying, and she felt better. Those were the earliest memories she had.[18]

The photographic reconstructions also become even more compelling. The caption explains, "After being separated from his group for several days, a young *Homo ergaster*, Nariokotome Boy, rejoices at seeing the familiar faces of his family."[19]

---

16. Sawyer and Deak, *The Last Human*, 131–32. One cannot help but notice the cadence of an old joke form: "A group of apemen, a gelada baboon troop, and two humans walk into a bar . . . ."

17. Sawyer and Deak, *The Last Human*, 139.

18. Sawyer and Deak, *The Last Human*, 149.

19. Sawyer and Deak, *The Last Human*, 147.

The Last Human, 147

And here Peking Man (*H. pekinensis*), which lived from 250,000 to 600,000 years ago, is pictured "Stalking his prey."[20]

The Last Human, 172

20. Sawyer and Deak, *The Last Human,* 173.

The broad outlines of the story told in *The Last Human* reflect the clear pattern of the evidence contained in fossils and genes: over millions of years, a variety of hominid forms flowered on the human evolutionary tree (or bush), many of which were evolutionary dead ends; moving forward in time towards the present, the morphology of some of these now-extinct species often appears closer to that of anatomically modern humans; and finally there remains one branch now occupied by only one species—us.

But where the narratives in *The Last Human* fill in cultural and mental landscapes of these creatures, which cannot be inferred so directly from bones, an emphasis on conscious awareness, agency, aesthetics, and values emerges that seems hard to justify. Note the adverbial phrases and richly anthropomorphic descriptions: "Feeling comfortable with his new blanket"; "contemplatively surveys"; "leisurely walked"; "searches desperately"; "enjoyed a final bite before turning in for the night"; "[a]mused by the playfulness of his children"; "watches protectively and lovingly"; "not discouraged by failure"; "curious"; "quizzical"; "thoughts of tomorrow"; "intelligent"; "earliest memories"; "rejoices." From these narratives, it seems that everything—every *one*—from *Sahelanthropus tchadensis* seven million years ago on—was capable of intentions, plans, memories, and even virtues such as courage, joy, and love.

In fact, no paleoanthropologist thinks our hominid forebears possessed these characteristics in the way we *homo sapiens sapiens* possess them. We may assume, with good reason, that things *like* what we now identify as "human" intentions, plans, memories, and virtues were present in varying degrees in our ancestors, if nothing else in virtue of the fact that they are ancestral to us. And we can observe in the archeological record the technologies employed by some of these ancestors, in the form of different kinds of stone toolkits. Yet there is no evidence that any of our distant hominid ancestors, or even our more recent early human forebears, possessed anything near the flower of what we now call "human culture." While the recovery of hominid/early human stone toolkits dating back millions of years is endlessly fascinating, modern chimps have been observed sharpened sticks and stone anvils as tools. Tool use itself therefore is not a distinguishing feature of humanity. The technology inherent in the Oldowan toolkit, dating back at least 2.6 million years, surpasses anything known to be used today by chimpanzees, but by upper paleolithic standards it was simple: a hammerstone was used to strike a stone core, which produced sharp flakes.[21]

The Acheulean toolkit, which appears in the archeological record about 1.76 million years ago, employed a two-stage technology, in which larger flakes stricken from the core were further refined by striking smaller flakes from their edges.[22] The resulting tool is called a "handaxe," which misleadingly conjures to mind something like a notched and grooved head attached to a wooden handle. In fact, the Acheulean handaxe is simply a large flaked stone that can be held in the hand.[23] The Acheulean toolkit remained unchanged for well over one million years, without being supplemented by other technologies.[24]

By about 400,000 to 200,000 years ago, the "prepared core technique" was developed, whereby a variety of flakes could be produced from a core with one strike.[25] This more precise technique facilitated the production of "points," which were attached to shafts in order to make spears, such as this point from Ethiopia dating from just over 100,000 years ago.[26]

The toolkits also diversified to include scrapers and awls for working hides and wood.[27] Still, the range of tools remained limited and there is no evidence of rapid innovation.

By the Upper Paleolithic (Europe) or Late Stone Age (Africa), however, there is evidence of far greater diversity and innovation. As the Smithsonian Institute's web resource notes,

> These toolkits are very diverse and reflect stronger cultural diversity than in earlier times. The pace of innovations rose.

21. Smithsonian Institute, "Early Stone Age Tools," available at http://humanorigins.si.edu/evidence/behavior/tools/early-tools.

22. Smithsonian Institute, "Early Stone Age Tools," available at http://humanorigins.si.edu/evidence/behavior/tools/early-tools.

23. Smithsonian Institute, "Early Stone Age Tools," available at http://humanorigins.si.edu/evidence/behavior/tools/early-tools.

24. Smithsonian Institute, "Early Stone Age Tools," available at http://humanorigins.si.edu/evidence/behavior/tools/early-tools.

25. Smithsonian Institute, "Middle Stone Age Tools," available at http://humanorigins.si.edu/evidence/behavior/tools/middle-tools.

26. Smithsonian Institute, "Middle Stone Age Tools," available at http://humanorigins.si.edu/evidence/behavior/tools/middle-tools.

27. Smithsonian Institute, "Middle Stone Age Tools," available at http://humanorigins.si.edu/evidence/behavior/tools/middle-tools.

Groups of *Homo sapiens* experimented with diverse raw materials (bone, ivory, and antler, as well as stone), the level of craftsmanship increased, and different groups sought their own distinct cultural identity and adopted their own ways of making things.[28]

At the same time, we begin to observe in the archeological record the first substantial evidence of symbolic art and spiritual/religious practices.

2. Language, Mind, and the Cultural Explosion

It seems, then, that most of the creatures profiled in *The Last Human*, for the vast majority of the millions of years over which those different species lived and died out, were capable, at best, of little more technology than modern chimpanzees, and were incapable of creating symbolic art or spiritual/religious artifacts. In evolutionary time, aside from some simple tools, what we call "human culture" appears suddenly and with little warning.

Indeed, most paleoanthropologists broadly agree that a "cultural explosion," a "big bang of human culture," occurred around 60,000 to 30,000 years ago.[29] As archeologist Steven Mithen notes, "with no apparent change in brain size, shape or anatomy in general—the cultural explosion occurred."[30] Similarly, paleoanthropologist Ian Tattersall, who curated the American Museum of History's Hall of Human Origins, argues that modern humans "are an altogether unprecedented presence on our planet."[31] Further, Tattersall says, the notion that "the long human story" represents "an extended and gradual struggle from primitiveness toward perfection" is simply false.[32] "The acquisition of the uniquely modern sensibility" reflected in the cultural explosion, Tattersall says, "was instead an abrupt and recent event."[33]

28. Smithsonian Institute, "Later Stone Age Tools," available at http://humanorigins.si.edu/evidence/behavior/tools/late-tools.

29. See Mithen, *The Prehistory of the Mind*, 151. As with all things in paleoanthropology, there are dissenters even from this widely held view. For a discussion of various views, see Bar-Yosef, "The Upper Paleolithic Revolution."

30. Mithen, *The Prehistory of the Mind*, 15.

31. Tattersall, *Masters of the Planet*, x.

32. Tattersall, *Masters of the Planet*, xi.

33. Tattersall, *Masters of the Planet*, xi.

Tattersall believes that our hominid predecessors generally did not possess the capacity for symbolic thought and had no robust sense of "self." For example, Tattersall describes *Homo heidelbergensis*, which lived between 600 and 200 thousand years ago, as follows:

> These were hardy, resourceful folk, who occupied and exploited a huge range of habitats throughout the Old World through the deployment of an amazing technological and cultural ingenuity. They were adroit hunters who pursued large game using sophisticated techniques, built shelters, controlled fire, understood the environments they inhabited with unprecedented subtlety, and produced admirable stone tools that at least occasionally they mounted into composite implements. Altogether, they lived more complex lives than any hominids had ever done before them.[34]

And yet, Tattersall observes, "throughout the period of *Homo heidelbergensis's* tenure no hominid produced anything, anywhere, that we can be sure was a symbolic object."[35] He therefore concludes that,

> If I had to wager a guess, it would be that the intelligence of these hominids, formidable as it may have been, was purely intuitive and non-declarative. They neither thought symbolically as we do, nor did they have language. As a result, we can't usefully think of them as a version of ourselves, certainly cognitively speaking.[36]

Although most paleoanthropologists agree that the fact of a "cultural explosion" is well documented, they disagree on what caused it. Tattersall suggests there are two leading theories: the theory of "mind" and the theory of "language." Tattersall himself falls into the "language" camp.

Tattersall acknowledges that "[t]he changeover of *Homo sapiens* from a nonsymbolic, nonlinguistic species to a symbolic, linguistic one is the most mind-boggling cognitive transformation that has ever happened to any organism."[37] He finds the theory of language compelling because language seems to bridge the "symbolic" and "intuitive" aspects of observed human nature and because language is a "communal

---

34. Tattersall, *Masters of the Planet*, 142.
35. Tattersall, *Masters of the Planet*, 142.
36. Tattersall, *Masters of the Planet*, 142–43.
37. Tattersall, *Masters of the Planet*, 220.

possession."[38] He takes these two aspects of human nature—symbolic and intuitive—to correspond to reason and emotion.[39]

Tattersall suggests that language first developed "in a small community of biologically prepared early *Homo sapiens* somewhere in Africa," perhaps first among children stretching their minds through play, though he acknowledges that "[t]he details of this transition will probably forever evade us . . . ."[40] Part of this "biological preparation," according to Tattersall, might have involved the brain's ability to make connections between higher areas—the cortex—"without passing through the older emotional centers below."[41] One of the first linguistic functions this might have facilitated, he suggests, was the ability to name objects. Another possibility he finds plausible is a significant increase in the brain's capacity for working memory, which facilitates executive functions such as "decision-making, goal forming, planning, and so-on."[42] In any event, he concludes, "it seems likely that a random modification of the already exapted brain, plus some children at play, led to the literal emergence of a phenomenon that changed the world."[43]

Steven Mithen, in contrast, is a prominent proponent of the "mind" school. Mithen argues that the cultural explosion "resulted in such a fundamental change in lifestyles that there can be little doubt that it derived from a major change in the nature of the mind."[44] Mithen draws on evolutionary psychologists who think of the "mind" not as a unified command center, but rather as a set of specialized modules that gradually developed in response to different environmental pressures. Instead of the common metaphor of a "computer" for the mind, Mithen employs the metaphor of a "Swiss army knife."[45] The key breakthrough for the cultural explosion, Mithen argues, must have been a new way of connecting the diverse modules of the early human mind so that they could communicate and coordinate with each other in new ways. Here he employs a different metaphor: the human mind became a "cathedral," with different "rooms"

---

38. Tattersall, *Masters of the Planet*, 220–21.

39. Tattersall, *Masters of the Planet*, 220.

40. Tattersall, *Masters of the Planet*, 220.

41. Tattersall, *Masters of the Planet*, 222–23.

42. Tattersall, *Masters of the Planet*, 224.

43. Tattersall, *Masters of the Planet*, 225.

44. Mithen, *The Prehistory of the Mind*, 215.

45. For a discussion of this metaphor as used by contemporary neuropsychologists, see Conor Cunningham, *Darwin's Pious Idea*, 197–201.

that can function seamlessly together. Like a visitor to a cathedral who might walk from the nave to the chapel to the altar, cognition could then flow across domains and make unified connections.

An early paleolithic person might have known "rock" in one domain that included making flake tools, "animal" in another domain that included scavenging carcasses for food, and "female" in yet another domain that included sex and reproduction—but these different cognitive modules might not have communicated with each other. An upper paleolithic person, in contrast, might have been able to make connections between "rock," "animal," and "female" in ways that gave rise to the symbolic "Venus" figurines found in the archeological record starting about 35,000 years ago, or the exquisite Lion Man figurine from Hohlenstein Cave in Germany, dating to about 30,000 years ago.[46]

Both Mithen and Tattersall, however, seem to recoil from the implications of their observations for any concept of transcendence, even as they exult in the transcendent beauty of something like the Lion Man figurine. At the conclusion of *The Prehistory of the Mind*, Mithen declares that "[t]he human mind is a product of human evolution, not supernatural creation. I have laid bare the evidence. I have specified the 'whats,' the 'whens' and the 'whys' for the evolution of the mind."[47] Mithen believes his explanations are complete and airtight. He seems to have no room for a concept of "why" beyond the biological, never mind a concept of causation that could encompass "evolution" as part of an act of "creation."

Similarly, in a strange coda to his *Masters of the Planet*, Tattersall reflects on universals and the bell curve.[48] He observes that,

> Yes, you can indeed find regularities in human behaviors, every one of them doubtless limited by basic commonalities in the structure of our controlling organs. But all such regularities are in reality statistical abstractions, and people are absolutely uniform in none of them. As a result, if any statistical phenomenon could be said to govern the human condition, it would be the "normal distribution" or the "bell curve." . . . In any human characteristic you might care to specify, physical or behavioral, you will find a bell curve. . . . For every saint, there is a sinner; for every philanthropist, a thief; for every genius, an idiot.[49]

46. Cook, "The Lion Man"; Curry, "The Cave Art Debate."
47. Mithen, *The Prehistory of the Mind*, 215.
48. Tattersall, *Masters of the Planet*, "Coda."
49. Tattersall, *Masters of the Planet*, 228–29.

These variations, he suggests mean there are no universals, but only variations along a curve.[50] Indeed, he claims, "apart from that basic ability we all share to re-create the world in the mind, perhaps the only other true 'human universal' we all show is cognitive dissonance."[51] This is quite a jarring "Coda" given Tattersall's exuberant claim in the previous chapter that human language, born in the play of children, represents a "communal possession" of humanity. It seems that Tattersall must toss aside his prior 220 pages of argument and resign himself to the fact that human existence can have no common meaning or purpose.

3. The Emergence and Reduction of Transcendence and "Law"

If Mithen and Tattersall's reservations about transcendence are correct, there can be no "law," or at least no possibility of the "rule of law." There may be cognitive connections that facilitate language and the production of cultural artifacts, but such signs must signify nothing beyond themselves. If there is nothing signified, there may be cultural and linguistic structures that encourage and enforce behaviors, but there cannot be "law."

Yet Tattersall strikes a hopeful note at the end of his Coda. Although humans have polluted the planet—a fact about which Tattersall does not hesitate to offer a negative value judgment rather than a placid observation about the normal distribution—there is hope, because "our rational abilities and our extravagant neophilia nonetheless remain beyond remarkable."[52] "From the very first stirrings of the human symbolic spirit," Tattersall assures us, "the technological and creative histories of humankind have revolved around an energetic exploration of the innovative potential released by our new way of processing information about the world."[53] Thus, "while the auguries appear indeed to be for no significant biological change in our species, culturally, the future is infinite."[54]

50. Tattersall, *Masters of the Planet*, 228–29.
51. Tattersall, *Masters of the Planet*, 228–29.
52. Tattersall, *Masters of the Planet*, 232.
53. Tattersall, *Masters of the Planet*, 232.
54. Tattersall, *Masters of the Planet*, 232.

How does Tattersall move from the confines of the normal distribution into an infinite future within a few paragraphs? How does he move from rejecting all universals to "*our* rational abilities," "*our* extravagant neophilia," "*the* human symbolic spirit," the "technological and creative histories of human*kind*," and "*our* new way of processing information about the world?"[55] He does not explain.

It seems that Mithen and Tattersall cannot accept the implications of their own evidence against reductive scientism. Mithen and Tattersall agree that something extraordinary happened around the cultural explosion. For all the language of intentionality, self-consciousness, symbolism, and memory that a book like *The Last Human* ascribes to our hominid forebears, Mithen and Tattersall argue that there has never been *anything* like these capacities as they present themselves in modern humans among any other creature known to have inhabited the earth. Purpose, meaning, and even beauty, joy, and hope keep bubbling up from the primordial ooze.

4. Law and Writing

The timeline for the species profiled in *The Last Human* concludes well before the cultural explosion. Even the cultural explosion is pre-historical, in the sense that there were no elaborate systems of writing or written records developed immediately during that time. The notion of positive law, however, by definition, entails a record.[56] We must look substantially later in human history, to the time of the first cities, to find such records.

The oldest law code discovered by archeologists is that of Ur-Nammu, ruler of the city of Ur during its third dynasty, which began in about 2050 B.C.[57] The tablet containing Ur-Nammu's laws dates to about three hundred years before Hammurabi created the code that was inscribed on a famous stele now on display in the Louvre.[58]

One side of the tablet containing Ur-Nammu's law code locates the origin of the laws in a creation myth. The chief gods An and Enlil

---

55. Tattersall, *Masters of the Planet*, 232 (emphasis added).

56. See Murphy, *The Philosophy of Positive Law*, 1–3 (discussing sources of positive law).

57. Kramer, *History Begins at Sumer*, 51–55.

58. Kramer, *History Begins at Sumer*. For a photograph and discussion of the Hammurabi stele, see the Louvre Museum website, available at http://www.louvre.fr/en/oeuvre-notices/law-code-hammurabi-king-babylon.

appointed the moon-god Nanna to rule over Ur, and Nanna in turn selected Ur-Nammu as their human representative. Ur-Nammu removed the "chislers" and "grabbers"—people who stole the citizen's oxen, sheep, and donkeys—from the city. He established a system of weights and measures and ensured equity for the poor and dispossessed. By his rule he ensured that "the orphan did not fall a prey to the wealthy," "the widow did not fall a prey to the powerful," and "the man of one shekel did not fall a prey to the man of one mina (sixty shekels)."[59]

The other side of the tablet lists Ur-Nammu's laws. The tablet is badly damaged and only five of the laws are readily discernible.[60] These show that the *lex talionis* already had been mitigated through a system of monetary payments. Thus, if a man cut off another man's foot with some sort of instrument (the text is unclear about what kind of instrument), he was liable for damages of 10 silver shekels; a severed nose required damages of 2/3 of a silver mina (40 silver shekels).[61]

Ur-Nammu certainly was not the first law-giver. Indeed, there are references dating about three hundred years before the Ur-Nammu law tablet to the legal reforms of Urukagina, ruler of this city of Lagash.[62] According to an inscription memorializing Urukagina, he "freed the inhabitants of Lagash from usury, burdensome controls, hunger, theft, murder, and seizure (of their property and persons). He established freedom (of a type). The widow and orphan were no longer at the mercy of the powerful: it was for them that Urukagina made his covenant with Ningirsu."[63] All of these references show that concepts of justice, the rule of law, and written law codes date at least to the foundations of the earliest Mesopotamian cities. Perhaps the inscribing of positive law is as old as writing itself.[64]

We know nothing of "law" prior to recorded history. But if Stephen Mithen's theory of mind is correct, the cognitive connections that facilitated art, science, and religion also would have facilitated concepts of "law"—and the lack of such connections would have meant that for early hominids/humans, there was no "law." And if Tattersall is correct,

---

59. Kramer, *History Begins at Sumer*, 54.

60. Kramer, *History Begins at Sumer*, 54.

61. Kramer, *History Begins at Sumer*, 55.

62. Kramer, *History Begins at Sumer*, 55.

63. http://history-world.org/reforms_of_urukagina.htm/.

64. The earliest written documents are Sumerian clay tablets that date to about 3400 B.C. See Haywood, *Historical Atlas of the Ancient World*, §1.07;

the acquisition of language would also have facilitated the concept of law, particularly positive law with its concrete expression in language.

The earliest small bands of hunter-gatherer hominid/humans, of course, would have operated according to sets of social "rules."[65] Social rules are not a uniquely human trait. Indeed, social ordering is a pervasive feature of the animal kingdom. Even insects, such as honey bees, can show intricate social ordering.[66] "Dumb" farm animals, such as the chickens I raise in my backyard, are socially strict creatures—hence the term "pecking order."[67] Other higher mammals, such as whales, dolphins, and elephants, display detailed social ordering with local cultural variations.[68] Modern chimpanzee bands possess elaborate cultural norms that regulate access to food, access to sex, access to affection, and even what we might anthropomorphically call "war" with other tribes.[69] Observations of chimpanzee and bonobo social ordering provide the raw material for many game-theoretic studies of human evolutionary psychology.[70]

But it seems clear that even the most socially "advanced" of the higher mammals do not possess concepts of social order closely akin to what we call "law." A dominant animal in the pack might perform a sort of "judicial" function by forcibly ending disputes, but there is nothing like a well-defined set of juridical procedures or principles. Most significantly, even these highest of social mammals appear to have no concept of binding abstract principles that would support a "rule of law." The "law" for them finally is, literally, the "law of the jungle"—chemistry, instinct, material and reproductive advantage, and force.

If we humans know a concept of "law" that refers the "legitimate" rule of law to abstract principles—indeed if we know even a concept of "legitimacy"—this requires a sort of cognitive capacity that only we humans, of all the creatures on earth, seem to possess. Could it be that the

65. For a discussion of the game theoretic analysis of social traits in evolutionary biology, see Ernst, "Game Theory in Evolutionary Biology," 304.

66. See Nature Web Focus: Honey Bees, available at http://www.nature.com/nature/focus/honeybee/ (noting that "Honeybees have fascinating social structure and advanced societies despite having brains that are five orders of magnitude smaller than humans").

67. See Percy, *The Field Guide to Chickens*, 39; Belanger, *The Complete Idiot's Guide to Raising Chickens*, 74.

68. See Wilson, *Sociobiology: The New Synthesis*, Part III.

69. See de Waal, *Chimpanzee Politics*; Boesch, *The Real Chimpanzee*, 102–4.

70. De Waal, *Chimpanzee Politics*.

same cognitive breakthroughs that facilitated the creative explosion in language art, technology, and religion also were necessary to the development of "law"? Indeed, could it be that an essential part of what marks us out as "human" is just this sense of transcendent "law"?

Such a notion resonates with the Bible's second creation narrative in Genesis 2. To be clear, we are not suggesting some kind of "concordist" reading in which Genesis 2 must in the literal sense conform to the upper paleolithic cultural explosion, much less to Mithen's intriguing but debatable views about the prehistory of the mind. The literal sense seems to be rooted in ancient Near Eastern mythological forms that cannot be correlated to any precise "historical" record. Yet all the senses of this text together do convey that God's institution of the "law of the Garden"—"do not eat of it"—represents something significant about the creation of the "human," the *adam*. To the *adam* and not to *Sahelanthropus tchadensis* or any of the other extinct species detailed in *The Last Human*, so it seems, God said "do not eat of it." Perhaps only the *adam* was cognitively prepared to hear this command. Indeed, it seems that no species of hominid/ human prior to the cultural explosion, at least, would have been prepared to hear.

5. Reductive Sociobiology

Reductive sociobiological and neurobiological orthodoxy demurs even from the modest claims of paleoanthropologists such as Mithen and Tattersall. David Sloan Wilson, for example, is clear in his evangelistic program for his version of evolutionism. "First," he says, "we must abandon the notion that some special quality was breathed into us by a higher power."[71] He claims that this does not demand an outright rejection of religious faith because, he says,—"*many* people manage to combine a vibrant religious faith with a fully naturalistic conception of the world."[72] But whatever he means here by "religious faith," there is no room in that faith for anything but the physical world. Sloan Wilson's epistemology is uncompromising: "[w]hat goes for knowledge of the physical world also goes for knowledge about ourselves. If something is wrong with your body, your mind, or society, it has a naturalistic explanation, just like [a] problem with your

71. Sloan Wilson, *Evolution for Everyone*, 68.
72. Sloan Wilson, *Evolution for Everyone*, 68.

car. Believing that we have special God-given abilities is like praying to your car on the side of the road."[73]

Sloan Wilson is not content merely to reduce "religious faith" to nature. He must include "culture" as well. "A common claim," even among non-religious people, he notes, "is that 'biology' sets broad limits to our behavior, such as eating and procreation, but that 'culture' determines what we do within the broad limits, such as making art rather than babies."[74] This high concept of "culture," he correctly observes, suggests that notwithstanding our evolutionary past we are free to choose our future destiny. To this claim that "culture" exerts some kind of downward causality Sloan Wilson cries, "Hubris, all hubris!"[75] Since whatever attributes make humans unique are merely "like an addition on to a vast multiroom mansion" over deep evolutionary time, "[i]t is sheer hubris to think that we can ignore all but the newest room."[76] Indeed, Sloan Wilson thinks claims that humans are "uniquely intelligent, moral, flexible, and capable of aesthetic appreciation" are mostly "self-congratulatory and suspect as factual claims."[77] He thinks it empirically established that "other species far surpass our intelligence for specific tasks and that traits associated with goodness can evolve in any species, given the right environmental conditions."[78]

Nevertheless, Sloan Wilson admits that humans possess a unique capacity to construct their own social environments, and indeed "evolutionary social constructivism" is the core of his moral and political philosophy.[79] The essential problem for morality, religion, and politics, in Sloan Wilson's scheme, is that "[s]ome individuals are driven to benefit themselves at the expense of others or their society as a whole."[80] To illustrate this problem, he surveys various game-theoretic models of altruism.

In a chapter titled "Love Thy Neighbor Microbe," for example, he describes a bacterial species, *Pseudomonas flourescens*, which creates a polymer mat that sticks the bacteria together in a colony.[81] The mat is

73. Sloan Wilson, *Evolution for Everyone*, 68.
74. Sloan Wilson, *Evolution for Everyone*, 69.
75. Sloan Wilson, *Evolution for Everyone*, 69.
76. Sloan Wilson, *Evolution for Everyone*, 70.
77. Sloan Wilson, *Evolution for Everyone*, 71.
78. Sloan Wilson, *Evolution for Everyone*, 71.
79. Sloan Wilson, *Evolution for Everyone*, 71.
80. Sloan Wilson, *Evolution for Everyone*, 13.
81. Sloan Wilson, *Evolution for Everyone*, 128–29.

biologically expensive to create, and eventually some mutant bacteria instead devote energy to reproduction. When the mutants begin to thrive, the mat collapses, and the colony disintegrates. "Thus," Sloan Wilson observes, "is the glue of civilization dissolved by sloth!" And such "examples of good and evil among microbes can be repeated without end because they are based on inescapable facts of social life."[82] All of this maps directly onto human behavior and human folk concepts of "good" and "evil." But, Sloan Wilson concludes, "[i]f the traits that we associate with goodness can evolve, then we can make them more common by providing the right environmental conditions. Far from denying the potential for change, evolutionary theory can provide a detailed recipe for change."[83]

Of course, the behavior of these bacteria has nothing to do with what most Christian theologians and philosophers traditionally have called "good" and "evil" because those categories relate to intentional states and transcendentals.[84] If the Platonic and Aristotelian philosophy and the Christian, Islamic, and Jewish traditions have anything to say about it, a microbe is neither "good" nor "evil" because microbes have no capacity for intentional participation in a "good" that is beyond themselves, nor can microbes intentionally deny "the good" and thereby abandon themselves to "evil." Microbes indeed do not have intentional "selves," or in the grammar of Christian theology, "souls." Even the Eastern/Buddhist traditions to which Sloan Wilson seems drawn—he seems to think the Dalai Lama would approve of his naturalist reductionism—locate "reality" in a transcendent realm, although finally in a very different way than in the West. But Sloan Wilson has already made his *a priori* commitment to absolute naturalism, so he has dismissed several thousand years of historical reflection on "good" and "evil" *tout court*. Here we must remark on Sloan-Wilson's cry of "Hubris, all hubris!" Yet what is "hubris" in a naturalistic game-theoretic world without transcendent virtues?

Similarly, Michael Graziano, Professor at Princeton University's Neuroscience Institute, denies any sense of the transcendent:

> When we say we are conscious, aware, self-aware, in conscious control of our actions, have a stream-of-consciousness understanding of ourselves, what we really mean, apparently,

---

82. Sloan Wilson, *Evolution for Everyone*, 129.

83. Sloan Wilson, *Evolution for Everyone*, 32.

84. This is discussed more fully in chapters 6 and 7.

is this: there is a system in the brain whose job is to construct models of intentionality of other people or of ourselves; and right or wrong, confabulated or not, the self-model, continuously updated, continuously refined, supplies the contents of our conscious mind.[85]

Since the author of this phenomenon is merely a system in the brain, Graziano says, "this sense of consciousness—a soul on a trajectory through waking life—is a perceptual illusion. It is a perceptual model that is at best a simplification and sometimes plain wrong."[86] All intentionality is reducible, for Graziano, to individual neurons.[87] And what seem like the products of self-reflexivity, awareness, and language—the sorts of cultural things Mithen and Tattersall argue radically distinguish modern humans from all other creatures—are merely "memes" that cause certain neurons to fire.[88] Graziano is particularly keen to apply his notion of neurobiology and memology to religion: "[b]elief after belief," he proclaims, "each component of a religion is ultimately present for one historical reason; the religion was better able to spread and survive because of it. Darwinian evolution selected for those traits."[89]

Notwithstanding Graziano's confidence in memology, the concept is highly problematic.[90] Nevertheless, there is something insightful about memology: it at least recognizes the phenomenon of "culture" as something that exists and exerts causality. The neurobiologist Graziano's memology does not mix well with the anthropologist Tattersall's rejection of universals (half-hearted though it turns out to be), nor can it be squared with evolutionary biologist Sloan Wilson's absolutist constructivism. If

85. Graziano, *God Soul Mind Brain*.

86. Graziano, *God Soul Mind Brain*, 65.

87. Graziano, *God Soul Mind Brain*, 97–101.

88. Graziano, *God Soul Mind Brain*, 150–58.

89. Graziano, *God Soul Mind Brain*, 160.

90. For a good critique of memology, see McGrath, *Dawkins' God*. No one has ever observed a "meme," nor by definition can "memes" ever discretely be observed because they are cultural phenomena and not encoded in biology like genes. Moreover, if memes can explain "belief after belief" in religion, they can do the same in science. This would mean there can be no "science" of archeology or paleontology that might offer insights into the development of human consciousness, awareness, language, or culture because the idea of something like "archeology" or "paleontology" is just a meme, as are any ideas of human consciousness, awareness, language, and culture. Memology itself must be merely a meme, as must the supposed explanatory power of Darwinian evolution.

cultural units replicate and spread akin to genes, then they have the capacity to become universals. A common cultural substrate might become as universal as a common biological substrate, and just as some common biological features demarcate a species, so might some common cultural features. Indeed, memologists commonly point to religion, belief in the "self" and in other "selves," and the "illusion" of free will as essentially universal units of human culture, notwithstanding their efforts to spread new and contrary memes to those notions.

This reference to the "illusion" of free will, however, highlights another problem for memology and materialism. If materialism is true, how can we speak of "culture," the "will," or the "mind" at all? There could not be any such entity as a cultural replicator, because "culture" must be more than the sum of the material that produces "culture." If Van Gogh's *Starry Night* is finally only described in terms of the matter that makes up the pigments and canvas arranged in patterns forced by the neurochemicals in Van Gogh's brain—neurochemicals that in their production, distribution, transmission, or reception apparently fell outside the normal distribution for *homo sapiens sapiens*, judging by Van Gogh's obvious mental illness—then there is nothing about *Starry Night* that could comprise "culture." "Culture," "pigments," "canvas," "patterns," "brain," "Van Gogh," "Starry Night," and so-on, would be signs without signifying anything *real*. In metaphysical terms, if materialism is true, neither memology nor any other theory of "culture" can be true. And since "law" is a persistent feature of human culture, if materialism is true, then there can be no metaphysical realism in the concept of "law." The next chapter shows why the claims of materialism and reductive neurolaw are almost certainly false.

6

Towards a Philosophical Critique of Neurolaw

CHAPTER 5 SURVEYED LITERATURE about the development of the human species, theories about the evolution of the human mind and cultural capacities, and the unique human capacity to formulate positive law as a cultural artifact. In chapter 5, we also began to see the resistance among paleoanthropologists and evolutionary sociobiologists to any recognition that human cultural capacities transcend their evolutionary history. In chapter 3, we saw how the rise of legal positivism starting in the nineteenth century finds its apotheosis in the emerging contemporary discipline of neurolaw. As chapter 3 suggests, advocates of reductive neurolaw draw inspiration from what they believe is the default view among neuroscientists and philosophers of mind who engage with the neurosciences about the mind-brand relations—in particular, that "mind" ultimately is only epiphenomenal.

Consistent with the methodology concerning theology and science in chapter 4, this chapter surveys a range of views in the philosophy of mind literature and evaluates arguments made for and against reductionism and eliminativism. This chapter suggests that arguments about the nature of the mind often are rooted in an outdated kind of logical positivism. This discussion will lead in chapter 7 to consideration of how fresh perspectives in the philosophy of science, including the "New Aristotelianism" concerning laws of nature, can help move the discussion forward and clarify our theological conclusions about law and human nature.

1. Mainline Positions in Philosophy of Mind and Their Misplaced Debt to Logical Positivism

While advocates of neurobiological or sociobiological reductionism often suggest that their views are the default posture for serious philosophers who have thought about these issues, at least outside the domain of the theologians, that is not the case. In his book *Beyond Reduction: Philosophy of Mind and Post-Reductionist Philosophy of Science*, philosopher Steven Horst charts the range of positions taken in the recent philosophical literature as follows:

TABLE 2.1. Table of Mainline Positions in Philosophy of Mind

	Reduction in natural science	Supervenience in natural science	Psychological reduction	Psychological supervenience	Positive EMC	Negative EMC	Normative reduction
Reductionists	Yes	Yes	Yes	Yes	Yes	Yes	Yes/No[a]
Eliminativists	Yes	Yes	No	No[b]	Yes	Yes	Yes
Dualists	Yes	Yes	No	No	Yes	Yes	No
Mysterians/ Nonreductive Materialists	Yes	Yes	No	Yes (mostly[c])	Yes	No	No

[a] Some reductionists, like the Positivists, took reducibility to be a normative condition, while others, like Oppenheim and Putnam, took it only as a hypothesis.
[b] For eliminativists, the failure of supervenience is a trivial consequence of the claim that there are no mental states to thus supervene.
[c] Davidson and other interpretivists either reject supervenience on the grounds that there are always multiple equally good intentional characterizations of a person's behavior, or hold to an odd version of it in which a physical description does not imply a unique mental description.

Hort's table categories the following issues he considers central to debates in the "mainline" philosophy of mind literature:

1. *Reduction in the natural sciences:* Is intertheoretic reducibility the rule among the natural sciences?

2. *Supervenience in the natural sciences:* Do the phenomena of special sciences like chemistry and biology supervene upon physical facts?

3. *Psychological reduction:* Can mental phenomena like consciousness and intentionality be reduced to facts in the natural sciences?

4. *Psychological supervenience:* Do mental phenomena supervene upon the facts of the natural sciences?

5. *Positive Epistemology-to-Metaphysics Connection (Positive EMC):* Does a reduction of A to B entail that A supervenes upon B?

6. *Negative Epistemology-to-Metaphysics Connection (Negative EMC):* Does the irreducibility of A to B entail that A does not supervene upon B?

7. *Normative Reductionism:* Does the irreducibility of a phenomenon A to facts statable in terms of the natural sciences imperil the scientific and ontological legitimacy of A?

As Horst's table suggests, the range of "mainline" views in the contemporary philosophy of mind include reductionists and nonreductive materialists who each believe in psychological supervenience but differ on psychological reduction; dualists who reject reduction; "mysterians" who, like nonreductive materialists, reject psychological reduction and accept psychological supervenience, but who think humans simply might not possess the capacity to know *why* mental states differ from physical states; and eliminativists who argue that supposed "mental states" are merely epiphenomenal.

Horst also notes the importance of the final element of his rubric, "normative reductionism." The metaphysical and epistemological issues here are central to this book and to my perspectives on the relationship between theology and science. Some philosophers who write about philosophy of mind argue that reality inherently is reducible to basic physical laws and that those physical laws can be known by humans. If something cannot be reduced to knowable physical laws, it is not a real entity. For these writers, this combination of reducibility and knowability delimits the scientific method, which is the only way we can know anything meaningful about reality. As Horst notes, this kind of thinking creates as sort of "crisis" mentality among reductionists and eliminativists: the task of reducing "folk" psychology to scientifically knowable laws is vitally urgent, because otherwise we will not know who we *really* are and will remain mired in the dark ages of religion and magic. As I suggested in chapters 2 and 3, a similar kind of crisis mentality informs the drive to transmute positive law into a "scientific" enterprise.

But as Horst also notes, normative reductionism is not the only view in the mainstream philosophy of mind literature. "Mysterians" and nonreductive materialists argue that at least some mental states entail real agency and freedom, and therefore are *not* fully reducible to physical laws. Philosophers in these camps will make different moves in metaphysics and epistemology than the reductionists and eliminativists, who think reality is circumscribed by knowable physical laws. Yet it is here, in how these questions of metaphysics and epistemology relate to physical laws— indeed, even to the question whether there *are* physical "laws," much less whether and how such "laws" can be known by humans—that, as Horst suggests, all the warring camps in the philosophy of mind literature seem hopelessly out of date. The literature on "laws of nature" is fascinating, complex, varied, and far from settled, but one thing is clear: almost no one writing in that field adopts the logical positivists' assumption that there must be a foundational, universal method that could identify and explicate those laws if they do exist.

2. Varieties of Dualism and Emergentism

Among the range of options in Horst's table, Christian theologians today tend to split into two camps: dualists and nonreductive emergentists.[1] Emergentism, perhaps mixed with a kind of dualism, is the theory of choice for thinkers who cannot accept the starker conclusions of neurobiological reductionism. As we will discuss in chapter 7, it also has become the theory of choice for theologians who want to avoid any form of anthropological dualism. In this section, we will discuss emergentism outside the confines of traditioned theological discourse.[2]

According to today's anti-dualists, Descartes proposed that "a person is a wholly immaterial substance possessing mental but no physical characteristics," and that this inner "person" somehow causes events in the physical body (for Descartes, famously, through the pineal gland).[3] Descartes was motivated towards such an extreme form of dualism because he did not think it possible for mechanistic processes

1. For the dualist perspective, see, e.g., Machuga, *In Defense of the Soul*; Cooper, *Body, Soul & Life Everlasting*; *Catechism of the Catholic Church*, ¶ ¶ 362–68. For emergentist perspectives, see, e.g., Green, *Body, Soul and Human Life*; Murphy, *Bodies and Souls, or Spirited Bodies?*; Hasker, *The Emergent Self*.

2. This formula of "traditioned theological discourse" is a bit clumsy, but I believe it is necessarily qualified, as I hope will become clear later in this section. In short, many supposedly atheistic emergentists end up with something like Spinoza's pantheism, Hegel's world-soul, or process theology's emerging God. It is really a new form of non-traditioned theology.

3. As E. J. Lowe observed, Descartes did not always consistently argue for such an extreme version of dualism, but it is nonetheless what is meant in contemporary discourse by "Cartesian dualism." Lowe, *An Introduction to the Philosophy of Mind*, 11.

to produce intelligent or apparently intelligent activities, such as thought and speech.[4]

Descartes' effort to explain the mind developed in the disenchanted cosmos of early modernity.[5] As suggested in chapter 2, the cosmic order of Ideas, in which "reason" involved a teleological participation in the good that draws the soul *towards* being and gives the universe intelligibility, was replaced by a cosmic order of mechanism, in which reason or rationality was located entirely in the internal representation of an external world of physical causes.[6] Contemporary physicalists understand the ways in which quantum mechanics changed Newtonian mechanism, but they agree with Descartes' most basic metaphysical assumption: that the participatory ontology of the Platonic/Aristotelian/scholastic world has no purchase on reality. The Cartesian notion of mind, for them, is a sort of vestigial appendage that does no real work.

If that were the sum of the equation, the reductivists and eliminativists surely would be right. The various arguments Descartes mounted in support of the disembodied mind or soul lack traction. His "conceivability" argument—that if it is possible to conceive of one's self as existing apart from a body, then this is in fact so—fails because it is possible to imagine all sorts of things that are not real states of affairs.[7] His "divisibility" argument—that the self is a simple and whole substance while the physical body is composed of parts and divisible—is question-begging.[8] Perhaps, as today's physicalists argue, the self is neither simple nor a substance, and there really is no such thing as a unified, persistent "self."[9] Further, Descartes' interactionist account of mental causation upon the physical violates empirical conservation laws.[10] The non-physical force of the Cartesian mind cannot alter the momentum of the physical vital spirits Descartes imagined were connected with bodily motion because

4. Lowe, *An Introduction to Philosophy of Mind*, 10–11.

5. See Taylor, *Sources of the Self*, 143–46.

6. Taylor, *Sources of the Self*, 143–46.

7. Lowe, *An Introduction to the Philosophy of Mind*, 1–13. Contemporary discussions of conceivability in relation to physicalism and consciousness often center of Frank Jackson's famous "There's Something about Mary" thought experiment. See Ludlow et al., *There's Something about Mary*.

8. See Lowe, *An Introduction to the Philosophy of Mind*, 13–15.

9. Lowe, *An Introduction to the Philosophy of Mind*, 13–15.

10. Lowe, *An Introduction to the Philosophy of Mind*, 25.

to alter momentum requires the addition of physical energy.[11] Nonreductive physicalists argue that their approach does not involve any of these problems because downward mental causation emerges from lower physical levels; there is no need to invoke new infusions of energy that would violate conservation laws.[12]

It is certainly not the case, however, that a very narrow form of Cartesian interactionist dualism is the only sort of dualism on offer in the current philosophical debate over the "mind-body" problem.[13] Horst mentions other more subtle forms of dualism in his catalog. Some important other philosophers, such as E.J. Lowe, opt for non-Cartesian dualist or idealist approaches to the mind-body problem.[14]

In his *Introduction to the Philosophy of Mind*, Lowe noted that good philosophers must "inform themselves as well as they can about a domain of empirical scientific inquiry before presuming to offer philosophical reflections about it."[15] But as science (by which Lowe means natural and physical science) "only aims to establish what *does* in fact exist, given the empirical evidence available to us," these sciences cannot in themselves "tell us what *could* or *could not* exist, much less what *must* exist, for these are matters which go beyond the scope of any empirical evidence."[16] Physicalism may or may not be true, but science alone cannot reach this determination. There is no *a priori* reason, then, to restrict the philosophical investigation of the mind-body problem to physicalist alternatives.[17]

Lowe argued that the problems with strong forms of Cartesian dualism can potentially be overcome by other ways of conceiving the causal interaction between mental and physical states.[18] Lowe stated the common causal closure argument in favor of reductive physicalism as follows:

11. Lowe, *An Introduction to the Philosophy of Mind*, 24–26.

12. Lowe, *An Introduction to the Philosophy of Mind*, 27–31.

13. See Lowe, *An Introduction to the Philosophy of Mind*, preface, which highlights some common physicalist alternatives. "Interactionist" dualism is the notion that the mind is separate from but interacts with and causes effects within the body.

14. For a brief overview of approaches to mind-body dualism, see Robinson, "Dualism."

15. Lowe, *An Introduction to the Philosophy of Mind*, 3.

16. Lowe, *An Introduction to the Philosophy of Mind*, 5.

17. Lowe, *An Introduction to the Philosophy of Mind*, 22–24.

18. Lowe, *An Introduction to the Philosophy of Mind*, 26.

1. At every time at which a physical state has a cause, it has a fully sufficient physical cause. (Call this premise *the principle of the causal closure of the physical*.)

2. Some physical states have mental states amongst their causes. (Call this premise *the principle of psychophysical causation*.)

3. When a physical state has a mental state amongst its causes, it is rarely if ever causally overdetermined by that mental state and some other physical state. (Call this premise *the principle of causal non-overdetermination*.)[19]

The principle of causal non-overdetermination "rules out the possibility that, whenever a mental state *M* is a cause of a physical state *P*, there is another physical state *Q* such that (a) *Q* is a cause of *P* and yet (b) even if one of the two states *M* and *Q* had not existed, the other would still have sufficed, in the circumstances, to cause *P* to exist."[20] The example Lowe refers to here is a common one in the law of Torts and in criminal law: a victim is shot simultaneously by two assailants, and the bullet from either gun would have been sufficient to cause death.[21] In such a case, there are independently sufficient causes for the victim's death, and both shooters are legally culpable. Premise (3) in the argument above, however, rules out the possibility of such independently sufficient causes with respect to mental states that are causes of physical states.[22] A mental state, according this argument, cannot comprise an independently sufficient cause of any physical state.

From these premises, physicalists reach the following conclusion:

4. At least some mental states are identical with certain physical states.[23]

In effect, with respect to causation of physical states, there is really only one shooter pulling the trigger.

Although this argument seems logically sound, as Lowe notes, some of its premises may be stated too broadly.[24] Most significantly, premise (1) can be stated in a weaker form:

19. Lowe, *An Introduction to the Philosophy of Mind*, 27.
20. Lowe, *An Introduction to the Philosophy of Mind*, 27.
21. Lowe, *An Introduction to the Philosophy of Mind*, 28.
22. Lowe, *An Introduction to the Philosophy of Mind*, 28.
23. Lowe, *An Introduction to the Philosophy of Mind*, 28.
24. Lowe, *An Introduction to the Philosophy of Mind*, 29.

(1*) Every physical state has a fully sufficient physical cause.[25]

Since causation is a transitive relation, the replacement of (1) by (1*) can support a theory of mind that avoids the physicalist conclusion (4).[26] If $S1$ is a fully sufficient cause of $S2$, and if $S2$ is a fully sufficient cause of $S3$, then $S1$ is also a fully sufficient cause of $S3$.[27] But this does not imply that $S3$ is causally overdetermined by $S1$ and $S2$. Lowe does not offer a specific example here, but we could return to the example of an accidental shooting that might be employed in Tort law. Assume A deceptively advises B that a weapon B is holding is a relatively harmless paintball gun, when the gun is in fact a high-powered rifle; and assume B shoots C with the gun in a paintball match and kills C. To use the terminology of Tort law, both A's deception and B's action in pulling the trigger are "actual causes" of C's death. C's death is not causally overdetermined by A and B's actions together; indeed, the "chain of causation" requires that *both* A and B's actions comprise actual causes of C's death. Questions of legal *liability*, of course, would remain. It might be that B did not breach any duty of care and thus was not "negligent" in relying on A's deceptive advice; or, it might be that B's reliance on A's advice was negligent, under the circumstances. But both A and B's conduct were in any event "actual causes" of C's death. But for B's pulling of the trigger, C would still be alive.[28]

Consider then that mental state M is not identical with a physical state but is a cause of physical state P; and that physical cause Q is a fully sufficient cause of M.[29] This would mean that both Q and M are causes of P. P is not in this case causally overdetermined by Q and M, and premise (3) is satisfied without implying premise (4).[30] But for M, P would not have obtained; if not M, not P. This is true even though Q also was a but-for cause of P.

---

25. Lowe, *An Introduction to the Philosophy of Mind*, 30.

26. Lowe, *An Introduction to the Philosophy of Mind*, 30; see also Lowe's discussion in his book *Personal Agency*.

27. Lowe, *Introduction to Philosophy of Mind*, 30.

28. For a discussion of multiple causation in tort law, see Johnson and Gunn, *Studies in American Tort Law*, chapter 7.

29. Lowe, *An Introduction to the Philosophy of Mind*, 30–31.

30. Lowe, *An Introduction to the Philosophy of Mind*, 30–31.

Lowe employs this version of (1*) to support an emergentist view of dualist interactionism.[31] In taking that approach, Lowe commits himself to the plausibility of the assumptions that otherwise underlie the argument: notably that every state has a "fully sufficient" physical cause, which obtains in both (1) and (1*). According to Lowe, emergentist views, including his own, "hold that mental states have come into existence as a result of the natural evolution of highly complex biological entities, rather than through any kind of divine intervention by a being who exists 'outside' the spacetime universe, such as God."[32] His concern is not to defend any sort of creationist account of the mind or soul, but simply to show that the causal closure of the physical does not rule out mental causation as a real cause of physical states.

But Lowe explicitly sets aside, for the purpose of evaluating this argument, the "not altogether uncontroversial" assumption in both (1) and (1*) "that there are no *uncaused* physical states."[33] This assumption, Lowe notes, raises the issue of "free will and determinism," as well as "cosmological and theological questions of whether there was a 'first' cause."[34] Lowe also brushes aside the argument that quantum indeterminacy undermines (1) and (1*) because, he argues, quantum indeterminacy obtains "on the atomic scale, rather than at the level of neural structure and function in the brain."[35]

Arguments like Lowe's seem to demonstrate that emergentism with downward supervenience is at least logically possible. Reductivists and eliminativists respond to emergentists by suggesting that it is just another unnecessary and damaging form of anti-scientific mysticism. Indeed, some thinkers who favor pansychism over some forms of emergence, such as Thomas Nagel, are "mysterians" who think the universe possesses mental properties that simply can never be fully explained by emergence. The title of Nagel's most recent book on this subject, *Mind and Cosmos*, suggests his affinity for some sort of Hegelian or Whiteheadian world-soul—a kind of process theology without even an effort to preserve some concept of "God." In short, emergentism invokes the gappiness. There seems to be no basis on which the issues between

---

31. Lowe, *An Introduction to the Philosophy of Mind*, 31, note 11.
32. Lowe, *An Introduction to the Philosophy of Mind*, 31.
33. Lowe, *An Introduction to the Philosophy of Mind*, 30.
34. Lowe, *An Introduction to the Philosophy of Mind*, 30.
35. Lowe, *An Introduction to the Philosophy of Mind*, 30.

reductionists-eliminativists and emergentists could ever be adjudicated, short of instantiating Laplace's Demon, which might not prove possible even if the reductionists and eliminativists are right about the causal closure of the physical.[36]

3. Beyond the Impasse? Pragmatist Cognitive Pluralism and Its Implications for Neurolaw

Philosophy must clarify theology, but what if the philosophers themselves lack clarity about their own project? As Horst notes, the positivist understanding of how "the natural sciences" work no longer operates in any area of the philosophy of science *except* for the philosophy of mind. According to Horst, "it might not be an overstatement to say that turn-of-the-millennium philosophy of mind is one of the last bastions of 1950's philosophy of science."[37] Horst suggests that "[t]he most important sea change in philosophy of science since the 1950s has been a rejection of this basic aprioristic approach to the study of science, and particularly a rejection of the imposition of canons of how science *ought* to proceed from sources outside of the sciences themselves."[38] Horst also suggests that an *a posteriori* analysis of the relationships between the sciences suggests that inter-science reductionism is not possible.[39]

Horst argues for a model of "cognitive pluralism" through which different sciences can conduct investigations appropriate to their own domains without reducing all those investigations to a supposedly foundational single science. This does not mean, Horst suggests, that there is no way to make inter-canonical connections between various sciences. But it does mean that the biological sciences, for example, are not ultimately encompassed by the domain of physics, and that physics is not ultimately encompassed by the domain of mathematics. It also means

---

36. For a discussion of this problem, see Horst, *Beyond Reductionism*, chapter 5.

37. Horst, *Beyond Reductionism*, chapter 5. Horst further notes that "[i]t is, alas, not the only, nor even the best-known such bastion. Reading well-compensated, mass-market books like E. O. Wilson's *Conciliance* or Francis Crick's *The Astonishing Hypothesis*, it is hard to escape the impression that the authors have not read any philosophy of science written since 1960." As we will see, the same is true for much of the current neurolaw literature.

38. Horst, *Beyond Reductionism*, chapter 5.

39. Horst, *Beyond Reductionism*, chapter 5.

that psychology is not ultimately encompassed by neuroscience—that cognitive psychology is not merely a "folk" discipline.

Horst's paradigm is helpful as a working or observational model of how the natural sciences actually operate—of what biologists and physicists and chemists and so on *think* they are doing in the lab. As with other forms of pragmatism, it is designed to make incremental progress on the immediate issues that philosophy thinks it can address, while setting aside questions that seem intractable—not least, big questions in metaphysics—and seeking modestly ambitious cross-disciplinary connections where possible. There are obvious parallels here between Horst's "cognitive pluralism" in the philosophy of science and the "critical realism" in theology and science described in chapter 4.

Indeed, contrary to Eagleman and Harris, some neurolaw scholars also adopt a form of pragmatism, something like Horst's cognitive pluralism, in which metaphysical questions are bracketed, excessive claims for reductionism are avoided, and positive law is studied at least "as if" humans are embodied responsible agents. For example, Stephen J. Morse, a law professor and Associate Director of the Center of Neuroscience & Society at the University of Pennsylvania, wonders "why so many enthusiasts seem to have extravagant expectations about the contributions of neuroscience to law, especially criminal law."[40] Morse suggests that

> Many people intensely dislike the concept and practice of retributive justice, thinking that they are prescientific and harsh. Their hope is that the new neuroscience will convince the law at last that determinism is true, no offender is genuinely responsible, and the only logical conclusion is that the law should adopt a consequentially based prediction/prevention system of social control guided by the knowledge of the neuroscientist-kings who will finally have supplanted the platonic philosopher-kings.[41]

Careful neurolaw scholars such as Morse recognize some of the problems with reductionism. As Morse notes, "the arguments and evidence that [reductive neurolaw scholars] use to convince others presuppose the folk-psychological view of the person. Brains do not convince each other, people do. Folk psychology presupposes only that human action will at

40. Morse, "The Status of NeuroLaw," 598.
41. Morse, "The Status of NeuroLaw," 598.

least be rationalizable by mental state explanations or will be response to reasons—including incentives—under the right conditions."[42]

Morse notes that "the legal view of the person does not hold that people must always reason or consistently behave rationally according to some preordained, normative notion of rationality."[43] Instead, he argues, the law requires only that people be *capable* of "minimal rationality according to predominantly conventional, socially constructed standards."[44] Such a notion of minimal rationality is important because law governs people, not machines:

> Machines may cause harm, but they cannot do wrong, and they cannot violate expectations about how people ought to live together. Machines do not deserve praise, blame, reward, punishment, concern, or respect because they exist or because of the results they may cause. Only people, intentional agents with the potential to act, can do wrong and violate expectations of what they owe each other.[45]

"If human beings were not rational creatures who could understand the good reasons for action and were not capable of conforming to legal requirements through intentional action or forbearance," Morse reminds us, "the law could not adequately guide action and would not be just."[46]

Nevertheless, Morse argues that, even if neuroscience destroys any concept of human free will, this would not matter one bit for legal doctrine.[47] Morse argues that "[c]riminal law doctrines are fully consistent with the truth of determinism or universal causation that allegedly undermines the foundations of responsibility. Even if determinism is true, some people act and some do not."[48]

In one sense, Morse is correct. A society could continue to employ legal doctrines that govern *behaviors* even if those behaviors are unfree. And even where legal doctrines govern *mental states*—such as the *mens rea* requirement in criminal law—the law could define those states with reference to the absence of certain kinds of constraints on action, such as

---

42. Morse, "The Status of NeuroLaw," 599.
43. Morse, "The Status of NeuroLaw," 600.
44. Morse, "The Status of NeuroLaw," 600.
45. Morse, "The Status of NeuroLaw," 600.
46. Morse, "The Status of NeuroLaw," 601.
47. Morse, "The Status of NeuroLaw," 605.
48. Morse, "The Status of NeuroLaw," 605.

unusual behavioral states defined as "insanity." But what Morse does not admit is that this would represent a *radically* different concept of "law" than what has historically obtained in Western culture. In particular, this conception would sever the notion of "law" from the notion of "justice." Why *ought* a society to enact laws that discourage some behaviors and encourage others? That is a question of justice. Without some concept of human freedom, there is no concept of justice, at least not in any sense familiar to our sense of "law."

Later in the same article, Morse seems to recognize this conundrum. He notes that "[d]espite our lack of understanding of the mind-brain-action relation, some scientists and philosophers question whether mental states have any causal effect, thus treating mental states as psychic appendixes that evolution has created but that have no genuine function."[49] This claim, he admits, is made by "serious, thoughtful people," and, if true, "would create a complete and revolutionary paradigm shift in the law of criminal responsibility and competence (and more widely)."[50] Nevertheless, Morse suggests, "given our current state of knowledge, there is little scientific or conceptual reason to accept" this broader critique.[51] It seems that Morse thinks some concept of supervenience might preserve a notion of intentionality that would underwrite some idea of rationality and justice in the law. And yet, Morse suggests that "[m]ost informed people are not dualists concerning the relation between the mind and the brain. That is, they no longer think our minds—or souls—are independent of our brains and bodies more generally and can somehow exert a causal influence over our bodies."[52]

A few bold philosophers and legal scholars have gone further than Morse and have more directly taken neurolaw to task for its reductionism of "mind" to "brain."[53] Michal Pardo and Dennis Patterson, in their article "Philosophical Foundations of Law and Neuroscience," observe that "[i]f anything unites the various problems and projects of neurolegalists, it is the belief that the mind and the brain are one. This belief has spread far beyond neurolegalists, for it is a pervasive feature of much of the current literature and research in neuroscience as well as more popular

49. Morse, "The Status of NeuroLaw," 610.

50. Morse, "The Status of NeuroLaw," 610.

51. Morse, "The Status of NeuroLaw," 610.

52. Morse, "The Status of NeuroLaw," 609.

53. See Nagel, *Mind & Cosmos*; Landesman, *Liebniz's Mill*; Ward, *More Than Matter*; Pardo and Patterson, "Philosophical Foundations of Law and Neuroscience."

writings."[54] Yet, Pardo and Patterson ask, "does it make sense to attribute to the brain psychological attributes normally attributed to persons? Can we intelligibly say that the brain thinks, perceives, feels pain, and decides? If we cannot, what are the implications for neuroscience and law?"[55]

Pardo and Patterson believe that the reduction of "mind" to "brain" is a category mistake. Nevertheless, they reject what they describe as the "Cartesian dualism" that posits the "mind" as a separate "substance" or "entity."[56] Instead, they opt for a phenomenological distinction between "behavior, reactions and responses of the living human being in the stream of life" and the "brain functions and activities" that relate to these behaviors, reactions, and responses. "This is the key," they claim, "to the mereological fallacy and the undoing of the reductive impulses of neurolegalists":

> Behavior is something only a human being (or other animal) can engage in. Brain functions and activities are not behaviors (and persons are not their brains). Yes, it is necessary that one have a brain in order to engage in behavior. But the reduction of a psychological attribute to a cortical attribute is a fallacious move from whole to part.[57]

A key aspect of Pardo and Patterson's critique is the interpretation of the relation between empirical observations of brain states and specific behaviors. For example, Pardo and Patterson criticize a "neuroeconomics" study of activity in different brain regions triggered by monetary offers in a ultimatum game.[58] The authors of the study concluded that different brain regions fire when the offer is perceived to be "unfair," and suggested that legal rules (presumably regarding information disclosures) could be tweaked to mitigate bad economic choices. Pardo and Patterson conclude that

---

54. Pardo and Patterson, "Philosophical Foundations of Law and Neuroscience," 1225.

55. Pardo and Patterson, "Philosophical Foundations of Law and Neuroscience," 1225.

56. Pardo and Patterson, "Philosophical Foundations of Law and Neuroscience," 1216.

57. Pardo and Patterson, "Philosophical Foundations of Law and Neuroscience," 1226.

58. Pardo and Patterson, "Philosophical Foundations of Law and Neuroscience," 1226.

The evidence does not support their interpretations. First, it makes no sense to say that the brain "decides," "reasons," or "adjudicates" anything. Second, all that the neuroscientific evidence shows with regard to the ultimatum game is what subjects' brains were doing while they (the subjects) were deciding whether to accept or reject the offer. Consider the following analogy. Suppose one's face turned red whenever he was angry. Now, suppose when faced with an unfair offer in the ultimatum game, his face turned red right before he rejected the offer. Surely we would not say that the person's face rejected the offer—why, then, conclude that his insula cortex did so because it too turned colors on an fMRI machine?[59]

But if Pardo and Patterson reject what they consider the Cartesian-dualist and reductionist accounts of the mind-brain relation, what do they offer instead? They propose that "[t]he mind is not an entity or substance at all (whether non-physical or physical). To have a mind is to possess a certain array of rational powers exhibited in thought, feeling, and action."[60] This concept, they suggest, is rooted in Aristotle. As they interpret Aristotle,

> the mind is not a part of the person that causally interacts with the person's body. It is just the mental powers, abilities, and capacities possessed by humans. Likewise, the ability to see is not a part of the eye that interacts with other parts of the physical eye. Under this conception, the question of the mind's location in the body makes no sense just as the location of eyesight within the eye makes no sense.[61]

They argue that this Aristotelian concept is "materialist/physicalist" in the sense that to lose the brain is also to lose the mind, but that it is nonreductive because "the mind is not identical with the brain."[62] And this means that, although neuroscience can contribute to law, it cannot overtake law.[63]

59. Pardo and Patterson, "Philosophical Foundations of Law and Neuroscience," 1238.

60. Pardo and Patterson, "Philosophical Foundations of Law and Neuroscience," 1249.

61. Pardo and Patterson, "Philosophical Foundations of Law and Neuroscience," 1249–50.

62. Pardo and Patterson, "Philosophical Foundations of Law and Neuroscience," 1250.

63. Pardo and Patterson, "Philosophical Foundations of Law and Neuroscience,"

Pardo and Patterson have done a great service in debunking some of the grander claims of neurolaw and in introducing Aristotle back into the mix. But Pardo and Patterson are careful to steer away from Aristotelian notions of causation. They invoke Aristotle as a sort of paradigmatic example of holism in the mind-body relation, but without offering the context for Aristotle's hylomorphism, which finally only makes sense within a thicker metaphysical matrix than that to which Pardo and Patterson are prepared to commit.

4. Pragmatism and the Camp

This is where, I suggest, pragmatism breaks down, certainly for a project in *theology* and science. We cannot really avoid the big metaphysical questions, notwithstanding the affinity in some circles today for "theology without metaphysics."[64] Why should anyone care what biologists are studying, and how they are studying it, if they are not studying *something* with its own kind of ontological integrity? Why should a theologian care about how the biologist's work relates to her own work as a "theologian" if there is no ontological distinction between "God" and "creation"?

The argument that neurobiological reductionism is self-defeating is probably the most powerful commonsense response to reductionism. For example, in his *Mind & Cosmos: Why the Materialist Neo-Darwinian Conception of Nature is Almost Certainly False*, Thomas Nagel argues that reductive materialism eliminates the epistemic basis for the phenomena of consciousness, cognition and value.[65] If human beings are nothing but complex gene replicators, there is no reason to think that we possess any capacity to get outside of ourselves and understand the world, beyond what is immediately required for survival. This would mean, among other things, that the practice of a science that could establish the objective truth of reductive materialism itself would be impossible.[66] Belief in reductive materialism requires a kind of epistemic realism that, for reductive materialism, must represent merely an epiphenomenal delusion. And this uncomfortable fact further implies that "[f]rom a Darwinian perspective, our impressions of value, if construed realistically, are completely

---

1250.

64. Cf. Hector, *Theology without Metaphysics*.

65. Nagel, *Mind & Cosmos*.

66. Nagel, *Mind & Cosmos*, chapters 3 and 4.

groundless."[67] The "entire elaborate structure of value and morality that is built up . . . by practical reflection and cultural development" would represent mere adaptations and not necessary truths about the world.[68]

Similarly, E. J. Lowe argued that the issue turns on whether we are realists about mental states—that is, whether one "considers that states of thinking and feeling really do exist."[69] The reality of mental states, for Lowe as well as for other dualists and even nonreductive physicalists, seems to be the principal driver of all contemporary nonreductive accounts of the mind. If mental states are not real, then there seems to be no possibility of reflecting on propositions such as the reality of mental states.[70]

Even *reductive* physicalists, Lowe notes, retain some notion of the reality of mental states. Lowe distinguished reductive physicalists from eliminative materialists in that "[r]eductive physicalists do not, in general, want to deny the very existence of many of the types of mental state talked about by functionalists, such as beliefs, desires and intentions."[71] Instead, reductive physicalists simply believe that "mental states of these types just *are*—that is, are identical with—certain types of brain states: just as science has revealed, say, that the temperature of a heated body of gas is in fact identical with the mean kinetic energy of its constituent molecules . . . ."[72] But this, as Lowe noted previously, is a fundamentally metaphysical claim that cannot be resolved by empirical science alone.

In the extreme anti-realist view of eliminative materialism, in contrast, "states of belief, desire and intention *simply do not exist*, and hence *a fortiori* . . . such states are not identical with physical states of any sort."[73] But this would mean, as Lowe argues, "to abandon also the very notions of truth and falsehood and therewith, it seems, the very notion of rational argument which lies at the heart of the scientific understanding of the

---

67. Nagel, *Mind & Cosmos*, 109.

68. Nagel, *Mind & Cosmos*, 109.

69. Lowe, *An Introduction to the Philosophy of Mind*, 39.

70. As the *Stanford Encyclopedia of Philosophy* puts it, "it is hard to convince oneself that, as one, for example, reflectively discusses philosophy and struggles to follow what is being said, that it is not the semantic content that is driving one's responses." See http://plato.stanford.edu/entries/dualism/.

71. Lowe, *An Introduction to the Philosophy of Mind* 63.

72. Lowe, *An Introduction to the Philosophy of Mind*, 63.

73. Lowe, *An Introduction to the Philosophy of Mind*, 63.

world."[74] "It would be ironic indeed," Lowe notes, "if the eliminative materialist, in his pursuit of a scientific theory of human behavior, could be convicted of undermining the very enterprise of science itself."[75]

The fact that even the practice of meaningful empirical science seems to require some sort of realist account of mental states, Lowe argued, provides a powerful argument for the reality of mental states. The concepts of belief, desire, and intention that eliminative materialists dismiss as "folk psychology," Lowe concluded, should not "be viewed as a proto-scientific theory of human behavior but, rather, as part of what it is to be a human being capable of engaging meaningfully with other human beings. They are not dispensable intellectual artifacts, but partially constitutive of our very humanity."[76] Or, as Keith Ward puts it, "[t]he extreme materialist view that consciousness is an illusion can only be consistently held by philosophers who are not conscious."[77]

This argument is powerful, even in evolutionary terms, because natural selection cares only about survival, not truth. As Horst notes, "once one thinks about the question of whether God or evolution is likely to design our minds so that they are capable of grasping the ultimate natures of everything in the world and the connections between them, one is likely to adopt a stance of epistemic humility on the question."[78] The retort that an organism with an inaccurate perception of its environment is unlikely to survive is demonstrably false, at least if we understand "accurate" to involve a capacity to see beyond immediate circumstances and to take in the bigger picture. The fly on my window has no idea that it is sitting on a "window" in a "building" filled with

---

74. Lowe, *An Introduction to the Philosophy of Mind*, 65.

75. Lowe, *An Introduction to the Philosophy of Mind*, 65.

76. Lowe, *An Introduction to the Philosophy of Mind*, 66. A similar argument was made against psychological behaviorism, prior to the advent of contemporary neurobiology, by Charles Taylor in *The Explanation of Behaviour* (noting that the "premise, that a purpose or set of purposes which are intrinsically human can be identified, underlies all philosophical and other reflexion concerning the 'meaning' of human existence, and this, too, would collapse if the mechanistic thesis were shown to hold"). Conor Cunningham makes a similar point: "Rather than the humanities being a proto-science, and therefore guilty of folk psychology (in a pejorative sense), science is a proto-art; for all science is thought by people, we happen to call them scientists, and therein lies science's beauty, its truth, and even its goodness." Cunningham, "Is There Life before Death," 139. See also Clark, *Can We Believe in People?*

77. Ward, *More Than Matter*, 34.

78. Horst, *Beyond Reductionism*.

"people" writing "books" and other things on "computers." Nor does the fly possess any capacities that would enable it to conduct investigations into these phenomena. The fly can, of course, sense the surface under its feet, and it can feel the oncoming pressure wave in time to zip off before my copy of Nagel's book smashes it into mush—that much, and *only* that much, is required for its survival. More than that would be inefficient and wasteful, and evolution drives organisms towards efficiency.[79]

It is at this juncture of metaphysics, ontology, and ethics that theology must *challenge* reductive neurolaw. David Eagleman will say things like: "[t]he ethical problem . . . pivots on how much a state should be able to change its citizens" or "as we come to understand the brain, how can we keep governments from meddling with it?" or that cherished civil-rights-based "social policies work to cement into place the most enlightened ideas of humanity and to surmount the basest facets of human nature." However, he never explains what terms like "should" or "meddling" or "enlightened" or "surmount" or "basest facets" could possibly mean if humans are nothing but our brains.[80] Nor does he venture any suggestion about why some behaviors should qualify for a prefrontal workout while others ought to be left unchecked, or encouraged. In a world without transcendence, why *should* one organism's immanent frame be preferred over another's? Eagleman recites notorious examples of pedophiles and mass murderers whose conduct clearly was influenced by significant brain traumas or invasive tumors. What makes their brain states or their conduct *abnormal* and therefore subject to correction? Why ought "governments" not possess the power to meddle with citizens' brain states? In an evolving sociobiological matrix, there are no "neuro-rights" (a term Eagleman inexplicably introduces and then drops); there are only game-theoretic solutions for passing along genes.

To move from extreme examples such as pedophiles and mass murderers, consider a society in which people who hold undesirable ideas and engage in other anti-social practices—say, rallies and demonstrations for political or religious causes opposed by the majority of the

---

79. Nagel's otherwise capable argument here is marred by his sympathy for "intelligent design" theories that posit gaps in natural processes represented by "irreducible complexity" in certain chemical pathways or physical systems. Nagel, *Mind and Cosmos*, 10. The epistemic argument against reductionist materialism does not require any such design-in-the-gaps claims, since "consciousness" might transcend the physical without *gaps* in the physical.

80. Eagleman, *Incognito*, 186.

populace—are sent to re-education camps for prefrontal workouts. To refine the example, let us admit that people are not in fact created equal, and that the task of determining which rallies and demonstrations are anti-social is taken on by an elite class specially bred for this task. To risk the *reductio ad Hitlerum*, visions of Aryan supremacy, Communist China during the Cultural Revolution, contemporary North Korea, and Orwell's "1984" are not far off.[81] These are not new ideas, dressed up though they may be in the trendy lingo of neuroscience.

Eagleman, to be fair, is not advocating a neuroscientific totalitarian state, but there appears to be no reason why not. There simply is no basis in neuroscience for his expressed preference for liberal democratic values or for any other notion of human dignity inscribed in the law. Having given up on a meaningful notion of persons and agency, he destroys the basis for understanding "human equality" as something that transcends differences in mental capacity.[82]

In an evolving universe, taken solely on its own terms, there is no normative force to the term "normal." There are populations, which always exhibit some degree of genetic diversity, and there is change over time. There is no sense in which organisms should conform to any "norm" external to survival in the context of the selective pressures on the organism. Perhaps a rough analogy to a "norm" would be a species' fitness landscape—that is, the parameters of the environment the species inhabits.[83] The notion is that natural selection will direct a population toward the mean fitness level as determined by the organisms' environment.[84]

---

81. See Wikipedia, "Reductio ad Hitlerum," available at https://en.wikipedia.org/wiki/Reductio_ad_Hitlerum.

82. Cf. Clark, *Biology & Christian Ethics*, 264 (noting that "[i]f our bodies and minds have been constructed from chance innovations by evolutionary selection, without any regard to Beauty or the Good, it may be true that most minor deviations will be less 'fit'. . . . But their fitness is of no serious concern to any disillusioned eye. Why should we not rearrange things to secure whatever it is we still find we want? . . . If we retain a residual, 'superstitious' belief that *pain* (not just my pain) is 'bad' we might even reckon it better to extinguish living creatures and their pain altogether."); Clark, *Can We Believe in People?* 52 (noting that "the atheistical cases against God and against 'religion' must chiefly be founded on moral indignation of a kind that only makes sense if there indisputably are Absolute Moral Norms which we can at once discern, which are more than maxims drawing their strength from the likely consequences of obeying or disobeying them, and if things could, somehow or other, be otherwise").

83. For a discussion of this concept, *see* Ridley, *Evolution*, 216–29.

84. Ridley, *Evolution*, 216–19.

Let us return to Ian Tattersall's reference to the normal distribution. We could imagine a statistical normal distribution in which the mean fitness level represents what Eagleman means by "normal" behavior. This is a great leap of imagination given the complexity of human behavioral interactions (can "*a behavior*" even be isolated from other behaviors?), but nevertheless we shall simplify for the sake of discussion. In a normal distribution, more than 25% of the set falls between one and two standard deviations from the mean.

Would Eagleman propose that 25% of the population be assigned to reeducation camps for prefrontal workouts? In the United States, this would encompass about 78 million people. According to the U.S. Census Bureau, over 1.6 million people were incarcerated in State and Federal prisons in the U.S. as of 2009.[85] Extending Eagleman's cognitive workout program to people beyond one standard deviation of the mean therefore would represent a massive expansion of the criminal justice system, without precedent in world history. Or, perhaps, Eagleman would require cognitive workouts for only the roughly 2% who fall on the tails outside two standard deviations of the mean? This would cover about 6.8 million people in the U.S.—about four times the number now incarcerated. Who would decide where to draw this line? Do the 68% within one standard deviation of the mean get to decide, or the 95% within two standard deviations?

A significant problem here—which is also a problem with Tattersall's reference to the normal distribution—is that, in strictly evolutionary terms, particularly in terms of the concept of fitness landscapes, it is doubtful whether there *is* any such thing as a homogenous normal distribution.[86] Biologists who favor the idea of fitness landscapes distinguish between "global" and "local" landscapes, and argue that segments of a broader population can move toward a fitness mean dictated by local niche conditions, which might represent a different mean to that of the aggregate population. The resulting picture is more like a set of hills and valleys rather than a single normal distribution.[87]

85. U.S. Census Compendia, Table 347, "Prisoners under Jurisdiction of State or Federal Correctional Authorities—Summary by State 1990–2009, available at http://www.census.gov/compendia/statab/2012/tables/12s0347.pdf.

86. For a brief discussion of the debate within evolutionary biology about the idea of local fitness landscapes, see Ridley, *Evolution*, 217–18.

87. See image at Wikimedia Commons, available at http://en.wikipedia.org/wiki/File:Fitness-landscape-cartoon.png. Points A and C in that diagram are local optimal

So what might the fitness landscape look like for human social behaviors? Would there be local populations in which optimal behaviors include things like forced marriage of young girls, slavery, and spousal abuse? It seems there would be, or else such behaviors would not recur so often throughout human history. Within such populations, presumably there would be no need for cognitive workouts to correct such behavior. If anything, people who fall a standard deviation or two outside this local mean (such as, perhaps, some brave young woman who desired independence and an education) would be candidates for reeducation. Curiously, this might indeed describe the socialization process for young girls in some contemporary societies that blend tribalism with radical Islamism.[88]

Biologist and new atheist popularizer Sam Harris tackled precisely the problem of the treatment of women in radical Islamist societies in an audacious TED talk, entitled "Science Can Answer Moral Questions?"[89] Early in his talk, consistent with Eagleman, Harris claims that "a suicide bomber's personality . . . is a product of his brain."[90] Yet, later, he flashes a picture of a woman wearing a Burqa, and claims that everyone in his audience knows it is unhealthy and bad for this woman to be forced to wear a Burqa "involuntarily."[91] But isn't the woman's choice to wear the Burqa, or her compliance with the social norm that impels her to wear the Burqa, a product of *her* brain? And doesn't the tradition of Burqa-wearing reflect something about social strategies in the fitness landscape of Islamic societies, with deep historical roots in the cultural dress

---

fitness peaks.

88. See Abruzzi, "Ecological Theory and the Evolution of Complex Human Communities" (noting that "Considerable controversy surrounds the application of ecological concepts in anthropological human ecology"); Pankhyo and McGrath, "Ecological Anthropology," in *Anthropological Theories*, available at http://anthropology.ua.edu/cultures/cultures.php?culture=Ecological%20Anthropology. In fact, the applicability of fitness landscapes and other ecological concepts to human cultural change is a contested question in the discipline of anthropology. See Pankhyo and McGrath, "Leading Figures." Not surprisingly, early pioneers of what has become the school of ecological anthropology include Thomas Malthus and Charles Darwin.

89. Harris, "Science Can Answer Moral Questions?" available at http://www.ted.com/talks/lang/en/sam_harris_science_can_show_what_s_right.html. TED stands for "Technology, Entertainment, Design." See http://www.ted.com/pages/about. Videos of "TED Talks" feature are freely available on the internet and have become a cultural phenomenon. See http://www.ted.com/talks.

90. Harris, "Science Can Answer Moral Questions?"

91. Harris, "Science Can Answer Moral Questions?"

practices of the ancient Middle East? Why should Harris' historically recent Western liberal democratic values trump the survival strategies of the Middle Eastern societies in which the Burqa is valued?

Even if neuroscientists could reprogram the brains of people in societies that value the Burqa, neuroscience cannot supply the normative value judgments that could tell us whether it would be good and right to do so. Various forms of pragmatism applied to ethics and law might help fill the gap, and indeed important contemporary theorists such as Richard Rorty, Jürgen Habermas, John Rawls, and others show the potential muscularity of this kind of approach.[92] These theorists, however, variously employ normative and deontological concepts that would be consumed by the universal acid of neurolaw no less than any other ethical theory. Moreover, the choice between pragmatism and a transcendental ethical theory has significant implications for political society and for positive law.

It seems, then, that the argument about whether neurobiological reductionism is self-defeating likely could never be resolved without resort to prior assumptions about what is and is not possible—that is, without first assuming the truth or implausibility of materialism—if it could be resolved at all. A typical counter-move here involves two points, which really entail several discrete arguments: (1) the fact that we are here discussing and analyzing these facts shows evolution has, indeed, supplied us with the capacity to make these truth claims; and (2) Ockham's Razor compels us to eliminate unnecessary explanations beyond natural selection as an explanation for why we're here and able to do this. In the words of the classic campfire song: "we're here because we're here because we're here because we're here."

On its own, this response seems easy to rebut. The first point could be stated as follows:

(1) Natural selection can account for every capacity we possess;

(2) We possess the capacity to examine the truth of (1);

(3) Therefore, natural selection can account for our capacity to assess the truth of the claim that natural selection can account for every capacity we possess.

---

92. See generally Ramberg, "Richard Rorty"; Bohman and Regh, "Jürgen Habermas"; Wenar, "John Rawls."

It is easy to see that this argument is invalid because premise (1) assumes the consequent. The first claim therefore is merely an assertion, not an argument.

When paired with the second claim, however, the first claim appears to possess greater force. *What else* but natural selection, after all, could explain our capacity to examine the truth of materialism and natural selection? The only other alternatives, the argument goes, involve direct divine revelation or non-material Cartesian "minds." Ockham's Razor tells us we should eliminate unnecessary explanations. If we eliminate these spooky explanations, we're left with natural selection acting on matter, which has already explained a great many things previously thought mystical. As Daniel Dennett suggests in his book *From Bacteria to Bach and Back: The Evolution of Minds*, "[i]f we can explain *self-repair in bacteria* and *respiration in tadpoles* and *digestion in elephants*, why shouldn't *consciously thinking in H. sapiens* eventually divulge its secret workings to the same ever-improving, self-enhancing scientific juggernaut?"[93]

The question here is a familiar and uncomfortable one about explanatory gaps. As the methodological discussion in chapter 4 notes, "gap" problems are particularly difficult for theology and science conversations because a "God of the gaps" is a common and inevitably failing strategy. Intelligent design advocates often rely on this strategy but they are thwarted when plausible evolutionary mechanisms are posited for supposedly irreducibly complex processes. More importantly, God of the gaps explanations create theological distortions that undermine the causal integrity of creation. Nevertheless, Horst notes that, in the mainstream philosophical literature, "[r]ecent discussions of the explanatory gaps between mind and body have generally involved three assumptions:

1. We presently find such gaps,

2. At least some such gaps are principled and abiding,

3. The psychological gaps are unique; one does not find similar gaps in the natural sciences.[94]

Horst notes that dualists in the modern philosophical literature, from Descartes to David Chalmers, rely heavily on these assumptions.[95]

---

93. Dennet, *From Bacteria to Bach and Back*.

94. Horst, *Beyond Reductionism*.

95. Horst, *Beyond Reductionism* (citing Chalmers, *The Conscious Mind*).

This kind of gap arguably differs from the "God of the gaps" because, as Horst notes, the gaps are not like "cracks in the pavement" of an otherwise developing picture of physical causes.[96] Rather, the physical sciences simply might prove incapable of explaining the mind precisely because it is not ontologically the same kind of "thing" as material things. Horst does not intend to argue for dualism here, but this, obviously, drives the debate inexorably back to basic metaphysical questions.[97]

In the end, it seems hard to escape the conclusion that materialism leads to nihilism—what C. S. Lewis called "the abolition of man."[98] If consciousness is an illusion, then nothing at all is right or wrong, and anything goes. Most contemporary materialists do not wish to become nihilists, so they try to construct ethical and legal systems consistent with materialism, including the forms of "neurolaw" examined in this book. But first they often claim that the vehemence with which some people object to their claims demonstrate that they are right.

For example, Daniel Dennett acknowledges that some of his ideas about the mind—in particular, that consciousness is an illusion—are disturbing. He seeks to disarm what he calls a "bristling" response to these threatening ideas. A bristling response, he suggests, is a conditioned response rooted in evolution that produces cognitive distortions. He implies that we should recognize and defuse the bristling response so that we can calmly and rationally evaluate his ideas.

There is no doubt that immediate emotional reactions such as "bristling" in response to threats are rooted in our evolutionary history. There is also no doubt that Dennett's strategy of pointing out this response among readers who feel threatened by the notion that human consciousness is an illusion reflects a powerful rhetorical strategy. But Dennett's suggestion that a person interested in the truth ought to recognize this response and set it aside makes no sense within the framework of his overarching claims.

"Bristling" is pervasive in nature because it *works*. Creatures in nature face *real threats* every day. A response that puts an organism on high alert and that deters the threat helps the organism survive. Far from

---

96. Horst, *Beyond Reductionism*.

97. Horst ultimately views the world in cognitivist rather than realist ontological terms. I argue in this book that Christian theology suggests a realist ontology of difference.

98. Lewis, *The Abolition of Man*; Hunter and Nedlisky, *Science and the Good*.

always representing a cognitive distortion, in nature, bristling often is a truthful, adaptive response to real threats.

The notion that consciousness is an illusion—including, for Dennett, all of our sense of will, intentionality, and moral reasoning—seems like a real threat to human existence. If everyone truly believed and acted on the belief that there is no truth content to consciousness, nothing would prevent power and violence from having the final say. Basic structures of law and society might fall away. Bristling here seems like an appropriate response.

But Dennett seems to imply that "bristling" presents cognitive distortions because the response is overdetermined to real threats. That is certainly correct. This overdetermination itself likely is adaptive. Let's say, for example, that for every twenty "knee-jerk" reactions you have, only one of them responds to a danger of serious injury to your knee. It seems like you've expended wasted energy on nineteen useless knee-jerks. But the injury to your knee on that one occasion would have been serious, meaning that the injury would have cost you as much or more, perhaps far more, than the energy you spent on the nineteen "false positive" knee-jerks. On balance, the overdetermination of knee-jerks was relatively efficient because the abundance of caution avoided a serious injury.

No doubt, then, that "bristling" behavior is overdetermined to threats. The next step in Dennett's rhetorical move is a suggestion that we sometimes need to exercise a higher level of control over our immediate threat reaction in order to assess the situation rationally. This kind of rational control allows us to calibrate our knee-jerks and move to a higher level of efficiency. If we can recognize and avoid the bristling response, we can use our calm, scientific rationality to acknowledge that, in fact, consciousness is an illusion. Further, if we use that same calm, scientific reasoning, we can show why basic structures of law and society that limit power and violence need not fall away and might even be improved.

The obvious problem here is that Dennett's metaphysical project *precludes* any such higher level of rational control. Rationality is *part of consciousness*, so in Dennett's universe "rationality" cannot exist. You might *think* you're exercising rational control over your bristling response, but that, too, is an illusion. Indeed, your "rational" response to your bristling reaction is merely another adaptive response. And Dennett's own rhetorical move of seeking to appease the bristling response through a "friendly" gesture of appealing to reason likewise is yet another merely adaptive response. It's either "nothing buttery" all the way down, or something else is going on.

Christian theology, of course, says there *is* something else going on. The relationship between theology and science is complementary here because, without denying the facts of our evolutionary history or of the embodied, neurochemical nature of our emotions and consciousness, theology supplies a metaphysical scaffolding and a narrative structure for the reality and goodness of moral concepts and of related human cultural phenomena such as positive law. Chapter 7 begins to explore how contemporary Christian theology tries to address this intersection—but often, I shall argue, without great success.

7

Mind, Law, Theology

CHAPTER 6 DISCUSSED DEBATES among analytic philosophers about neurobiological reductionism in the philosophy of mind and suggested that theology can complement philosophical perspectives that reject the inevitable nihilism of materialist reductionism. This chapter extends that discussion by examining what is probably the majority view among contemporary Christian theologians working at the intersection of theology and science: emergentism and nonreductive physicalism. I argue that this approach includes some helpful elements but ultimately is theologically inadequate. I then begin to argue for a dualist approach that draws on the "new Aristotelianism" in the modern analytic philosophy of science. This approach, I argue, helps reinvigorate classical Christian notions of natural law and the human soul.

1. Theology, Emergence, and the Soul

Many theologians—probably the mainstream of the faith and science scholarship—like many naturalistic philosophers, accept the causal closure of the physical. Instead of the soul, these contemporary theologians attempt to locate human will, intentionality, and moral responsibility in emergent properties of physical systems. The "soul" or "mind," in this sort of system, is the capacity for downward causality made possible by emergent properties of the brain, body, and environment.[1] Some con-

---

1. See, e.g., Murphy, *Bodies and Souls, or Spirited Bodies*; Barbour, *Nature, Human Nature, and God*; Green, *Body, Soul and Human Life*.

temporary theologians extend this concept of emergence to God himself, either in a thoroughgoing way through process theology, or as a partial explanation for God's interaction with the physical world.[2]

Some aspects of emergentism are helpful for explaining the problem of the mind-body relation, as discussed in more detail below. At the outset, however, it is important to note the metaphysical commitments emergentist theologians and philosophers make before embarking on their projects.

Nancey Murphy, for example, is one of the leading Christian theologians working from an emergentist/nonreductive physicalist paradigm. Murphy describes a variety of forms of physicalist reductionism against which she contrasts her nonreductive physicalism.[3] Notably, Murphy does *not* object to what she calls "ontological reductionism," which she defines as "the thesis that higher-level entities are nothing but the sum of their parts."[4] One aspect of this ontological reductionism is

> the view that as one goes up the hierarchy of levels, no new kinds of metaphysical "ingredients" need to be added to produce higher-level entities from lower. No "vital force" or "entelechy" must be added to get living beings from non-living materials; no immaterial mind or soul needed to get consciousness; no *Zeitgeist* to form individuals into a society.[5]

Murphy states that she "take[s] ontological reductionism to be entirely unobjectionable, so long as it is applied to the cosmos itself and no illegitimate inferences are drawn from it regarding the source of the cosmos."[6] Her objection is only to "causal" reductionism, which she defines as the view that "the behavior of the parts of a system (ultimately, the parts studied by subatomic physics) is determinative of the behavior of all higher-level entities; all causation is 'bottom-up'"—or, more prosaically, the view that "physics is doing all the work."[7] Murphy argues that physics cannot do "all the work" because lower-level causes are always embedded in higher-level *systems* generated by unique sets of *relations* among

---

2. For a survey of these views, see Clayton, "Toward a Constructive Christian Theology of Emergence."

3. Murphy, "Reductionism: How Did We Fall into It?" 23.

4. Murphy, "Reductionism: How Did We Fall into It," 23.

5. Murphy, "Reductionism: How Did We Fall into It," 23.

6. Murphy, "Reductionism: How Did We Fall into It," 25.

7. Murphy, "Reductionism: How Did We Fall into It," 23, 25.

higher-level elements of the systems.[8] The systems level of relationships influence outcomes, and in fact influences the re-arrangement of elements at lower levels of causality. Therefore, Murphy argues, causation cannot be reduced all the way down to the deterministic level of physics.

Robert Van Gulick follows a similar systems-oriented model in his essay on the mind/body problem in Murphy's edited volume on *Evolution and Emergence*.[9] Van Gulick also acknowledges the *a priori* metaphysical commitment of emergentist models. Nonreductive physicalism, he says, "has emerged as more or less the majority view among current philosophers of mind."[10] This view "combines a pluralist view about the diversity of what needs to be explained by science with an underlying metaphysical commitment to the physical as the ultimate basis of all that is real."[11]

Similar to Murphy, Van Gulick argues that outcomes are not determined only by the "laws of physics," but rather "by the laws of physics together with *initial boundary conditions*."[12] Natural systems supply higher-order "patterns of organization" that are irreducible to their physical constituents.[13] Van Gulick argues that these higher-order patterns of organization are real entities, no less than their physical constituents.[14] Indeed, Van Gulick argues for hypothetical worlds "that are like our world in having some lawful or causal order but which do not contain any physical matter."[15] In such worlds, "patterns exist that are very much like the patterns associated in our world with acquiring, possessing, and exploiting information."[16] This suggests that the "order of higher-level patterns" in our world reflects "a much more pervasive order that simply manifests itself in our world in physical realizations."[17] There is a very subtle move behind this claim: Van Gulick takes a non-realist

8. Murphy, "Reductionism: How Did We Fall into It," 29–33.

9. Van Gulick, "Reduction, Emergence, and the Mind/Body Problem."

10. Van Gulick, "Reduction, Emergence, and the Mind/Body Problem," 40.

11. Van Gulick, "Reduction, Emergence, and the Mind/Body Problem," 40.

12. Van Gulick, "Reduction, Emergence, and the Mind/Body Problem," 82 (emphasis added).

13. Van Gulick, "Reduction, Emergence, and the Mind/Body Problem," 82–83.

14. Van Gulick, "Reduction, Emergence, and the Mind/Body Problem," 82–82.

15. Van Gulick, "Reduction, Emergence, and the Mind/Body Problem," 85.

16. Van Gulick, "Reduction, Emergence, and the Mind/Body Problem," 85.

17. Van Gulick, "Reduction, Emergence, and the Mind/Body Problem," 85.

stance concerning physical "laws."[18] He asserts that "laws are statements or sentences in our theories of the world, not independent items among the furniture of the world itself."[19] The most basic reality, for Van Gulick, are systems of "stable self-sustaining recurrent states of the quantum flux of an irreducibly probabilistic and statistical reality."[20]

Both Murphy and Van Gulick, as leading representatives of non-reductive physicalism, pledge their *bona fides* to a non-dualistic metaphysic. But both end up substituting "systems," or, in Van Gulick's case, "information systems," for the "spiritual" or "non-physical" components of the "Cartesian" and "Aristotelian" metaphysics they eschew. Why this effort to render in physicalist terms realities that in Christian theology traditionally have been thought of as belonging to a non-physical aspect of creation?

Murphy cites the triumph of atomism over the Aristotelian ontology of matter and form.[21] Murphy credits this shift to Galileo and then to Lavoisier and Dalton.[22] From atomism in biology to reductionism in chemistry, Murphy suggests, the atomist/reductionist program continued down to the level of physics.[23] Thus, Murphy argues, "much of modern science can be understood as the development of a variety of research programs that in one way or another embody and spell out the consequences of what was originally a metaphysical theory. It has been the era in which Democritus has triumphed over Aristotle."[24]

But if Murphy wants to argue that atomistic reductionism is wrong, why not look again at Aristotle? The problem seems to relate to divine action. In a lawful or law-like universe, what "place" is there for divine action?[25] And in a lawful or law-like universe in which creatures, including humans, exercise some degree of agency, what explanatory power lies in the concept of "divine" agency?[26] Finally, if God acts in the universe,

---

18. Van Gulick, "Reduction, Emergence, and the Mind/Body Problem," 77, 86–87.

19. Van Gulick, "Reduction, Emergence, and the Mind/Body Problem," 77.

20. Van Gulick, "Reduction, Emergence, and the Mind/Body Problem," 86.

21. Murphy, "Reductionism: How Did We Fall into It," 20–21.

22. Murphy, "Reductionism: How Did We Fall into It," 20–21.

23. Murphy, "Reductionism: How Did We Fall into It," 20–21.

24. Murphy, "Reductionism: How Did We Fall into It," 21.

25. See Russell, "Introduction," 3–5.

26. Russell, "Introduction," 3–5.

why does the universe exhibit so much pain and suffering (the "theodicy" problem)?[27]

As Robert John Russell notes, the question of divine action became particularly acute because of many of the key intellectual developments of the Enlightenment:

> Newtonian mechanics seemed to depict a causally closed universe with little, if any, room for God's *special* action in specific events. With the ascendancy of deism in the eighteenth century, the scope of divine agency was limited to an initial act of creation. Moreover, David Hume and Immanuel Kant raised fundamental questions concerning the project of natural theology, challenged belief in miracles, undercut metaphysical speculation about causality and design, and restricted religion to the sphere of morality.[28]

These crises led to the split between liberal Schleiermachian Protestantism and fundamentalism, as well as to the Barthian neo-orthodox project, none of which, Russell suggests, provided adequate responses to the problem of divine action.[29]

Russell provides a helpful topology of contemporary approaches to divine action in light of this historical background.[30] These include neo-Thomism (distinguishing primary and secondary causation—the "Aristotelian" approach); process theology (God acts "persuasively" but not "exclusively" in all events); uniform action (God acts uniformly in all events and the meaning and significance of those events are subjects of human interpretation); and several "personal agent" models, in which God either acts literally and directly in the world: (1) God is immanent in and perhaps "embodied" by an organistic world; (2) God is a non-embodied agent in the world; or (3) God interacts with the world in the interstices of quantum probabilities and chaos theory.[31] These different views map onto perspectives on the possibility of divine "intervention" in the universe, including through miracles, and on the nature of such

27. Russell, "Introduction," 3–5.
28. Russell, "Introduction," 5.
29. Russell, "Introduction," 5–6.
30. Russell, "Introduction," 7–13.
31. Russell, "Introduction," 7–13.

"miracles"—for example, as suspensions of the laws of nature, or instead as acts within the laws of nature arranged in highly unusual ways.[32]

Most of the contemporary theology-and-science literature on divine action, Russell notes, explores "whether there are *objectively* special divine acts that are *neither* interventions nor suspensions of the laws of nature."[33] These include "top-down" or "whole-part" causality, in which God acts either in a higher level in nature or at the level of a physical boundary or system, and "bottom-up" approaches in which God acts directly at the quantum level in ways that indirectly affect the macroscopic world.[34] In the small sample of nonreductive physicalist accounts of "mind" above, Van Gulick's view reflects a whole-part systems view of divine action, and Murphy's reflects a "bottom-up" approach that relies on God's action in quantum improbabilities.[35]

Murphy knows that the problem of divine action "is, at base, a metaphysical problem—one that cannot be solved by anything less radical than a revision of our understanding of natural causation."[36] Since she accepts the narrative that modern science's reliance on the "laws of nature" has elided the higher levels of the medieval hierarchy of being, she must attempt to create a new metaphysic of causation.[37] According to Murphy,

> In the Medieval period, especially after the integration of the lost works of Aristotle into Western thought, God's action in the world could be explained in a way perfectly consistent with the scientific knowledge of the time. Heaven was a part of the "physical" cosmos. God's agents, the angels, controlled the movements of the "seven planets," which, in turn, gave nature its rhythms. But modern science changed all that, primarily by its dependence on the notion of *laws of nature.*[38]

And so, Murphy substitutes God's influence over quantum probabilities at the bottom of the causal layers of matter for any relation between matter and non-material transcendentals at higher orders of

32. Russell, "Introduction," 7–13.

33. Russell, "Introduction," 12.

34. Russell, "Introduction," 12.

35. See Murphy, "Divine Action in the Natural Order."

36. Murphy, "Divine Action in the Natural Order," 326.

37. Murphy, "Divine Action in the Natural Order," 325.

38. Murphy, "Divine Action in the Natural Order," 325.

creation.[39] Murphy also allows that God acts on the conscious actions of human agents, through varieties of religious experiences, consistent with her emergentist theory of mind.[40] Even here, however, God influences human consciousness "by stimulation of neurons" through bottom-up causation beginning at the quantum level.[41]

Murphy is particularly keen to avoid accounts of divine action that interfere with the law-like behavior of the universe. "Science," she says, "both presupposes for its very existence the strictly law-like behavior of all entities and processes, and constantly progresses in its quest to account for observable phenomena in terms of elegant sets of interrelated laws."[42] Consequently, an account of divine action that undermines the law-like behavior of the universe would unacceptably undermine the practice of science and destroy the program of interdisciplinarity between faith and science. Murphy argues that, since the quantum level is probabilistic rather than law-like, making space for divine action at the quantum level does not interfere with the ordinary work of the sciences.[43]

The strength of Murphy's approach and others like it is that it takes seriously how the contemporary natural and physical sciences understand physical causation. We are not exactly in Newton's universe anymore, but it is not that classical physics have been elided. Classical mechanics still accurately describe the motions of particles at the macro level and at sub-relativistic speeds—the motions of things we interact with at a phenomenological level, such as navigating a car through traffic. But classical mechanics no longer serve as the final level of explanation for such phenomena, because we are able to describe the probabilistic functions of quantum mechanics at a more basic level, including in the electrons and sub-atomic particles that make up the matter configured into a "car." And this means that the universe is no longer accurately describable as a rigid, deterministic system, but instead takes on the characteristics of a stochastic field of probabilities.[44]

39. Murphy, "Divine Action in the Natural Order," 339–57.

40. Murphy, "Divine Action in the Natural Order," 339–57.

41. Murphy, "Divine Action in the Natural Order," 349.

42. Murphy, "Divine Action in the Natural Order," 344.

43. Murphy, "Divine Action in the Natural Order," 344–45.

44. For an accessible discussion of the relation between classical and quantum mechanics, see, e.g., Barr, *Modern Physics and Ancient Faith*; Greene, *The Fabric of the Cosmos*. For a stinging critique of the failure of modern physics to deliver an integrated theory that unites classical and quantum mechanics, see Smolin, *The Trouble with Physics*.

The problems with Murphy's approach as it stands, however, are manifold, both scientifically and theologically. The first essential problem is that Murphy's approach, and others like it (such as John Polkinghorne's), depends on a causal gap. It is the old "god of the gaps" problem writ small (small as in sub-atomic). Scientifically, it is not at all clear that it will remain forever impossible to describe quantum realities in ways that close this apparent gap. Indeed, the Holy Grail of theoretical physics remains the search for a "unified theory" that would unite general relativity and quantum mechanics—a "theory of everything" ("TOE").[45] A successful TOE might or might not result in a deterministic set of unifying physical laws, but even a TOE that left the quantum realm as a stochastic space likely would elide the space for bottom-up divine intervention that Murphy hopes to preserve.

The leading candidate for producing a TOE, for example, is string theory.[46] Many versions of string theory are tied to multiverse theories, and some multiverse theories posit an infinite set of multiverses in which there is at least one universe in which every quantum possibility is realized. In such a scenario, Murphy's quantum God would vanish. There would be no need for the hypothesis that God moves our minds subatomically. Our choices in this universe would simply reflect the realization in this one universe of one set within the probability bounds determined by unifying laws, and "we" will have made different choices in other universes. All the probabilities will inevitably have been realized in all possible universes. If all possible choices are always realized, there is no room for God, or even for "choice." On the scale of the multiverse, everything simply is.

Of course, string theory and multiverses may not provide a true description of physical reality, so perhaps there is a genuine singularity, an undefinable and truly stochastic realm, at the quantum level. But banking on such gaps does not usually prove a satisfactory strategy over the long run. Moreover, contrary to Murphy's desire to develop a theory that will not impinge in any way on the practice of science, any gap theory of divine action finally depends on the failure of the modern scientific method. The modern scientific method depends precisely on the assumption that human beings are capable of closing every gap and of obtaining a TOE.

45. See Greene, *The Fabric of the Cosmos*, 29–37.

46. Greene, *The Fabric of the Cosmos*, 29–37. For a sustained critique of string theory as a scientific enterprise, see Smolin, *The Trouble with Physics*.

To claim that this is epistemically impossible is to speak a word against some of the presumptions of the modern scientific method.

Theologically, Murphy's approach is deeply problematic for at least two reasons, one relating to human freedom, and the second relating to Christology and soteriology. First, although it attempts to preserve human freedom, Murphy's approach ends up sounding much like the Baroque scholastic idea of divine "premotion" of the human will. This idea, attributed to Dominican theologian Domingo Bañez, involves God's providential first motion in the human will to move the subject towards his or her choices for or against God.[47] Bañez was the foil of the Jesuit Louis de Molina in the sixteenth-century debates over providence, predestination, and free will.[48]

As David Bentley Hart has argued, the Bañezian idea of premotion not only destroys human free will, but threatens to destroy creation itself. "It can plausibly be argued," Hart says, "that, in a very real sense, the Bañezian God does not create a world at all, and that his species of 'classical' Thomism amounts only to what the greatest Catholic philosopher of the twentieth century, Erich Przywara, called 'theophanism.'"[49] If there is "physical premotion," Hart argues persuasively, "all created actions would be merely diverse modalities of God's will."[50] And if this is so, then God is not really distinct from the created world: if God is merely "the supereminent source of all being, then—apart from some kind of *effective* divine indetermination of the creature's freedom in regard to specific goods—there is no ontological distinction between God and the world worth noting."[51] Indeed, the erasure of the ontological distinction between God and creation is precisely the move taken by emergentists who are radical panentheists or process theologians and who go a step further than Murphy and locate God (or "God-consciousness") as a product of or as embodied within or by the evolving universe.[52] In contrast to Murphy's implied Bañezian bent, combined with string theory and multiverses, such process theologians and radical panentheists can out-do Molinists: every possible universe known to "Godself" is not only known but

47. For a discussion and critique of Bañez, see Hart, "Providence and Causality," 34–56.

48. Hart, "Providence and Causality," 43.

49. Hart, "Providence and Causality," 43.

50. Hart, "Providence and Causality," 43.

51. Hart, "Providence and Causality," 43.

52. Russell, "Introduction," 8.

realized, including a universe with a purpose that is located in God.[53] Either way, little room for authentic human freedom remains.

A second problem with Murphy's approach is that its metaphysical commitments undermine important commitments in Christology and thereby compromise theological anthropology and soteriology.[54] A physicalist emergentism cannot adequately account for the dual nature of Christ. The language of Chalcedon depends on a metaphysics of transcendentals and substances. This is evident, first, in the attribute to Christ of a "reasonable soul" (ψυχῆς λογικῆς):

> he is perfect in Godhead and perfect in manhood, very God and very man, of a reasonable soul (ψυχῆς λογικῆς) and [human] body consisting, consubstantial with the Father as touching his Godhead, and consubstantial with us as touching his manhood.[55] . . .
>
> In two natures, unconfusedly, immutably, indivisibly, inseparably [united], and that without the distinction of natures being taken away by such union, but rather the peculiar property of each nature being preserved and being united in one Person and subsistence, not separated or divided into two persons, but one and the same Son and only-begotten, God the Word, our Lord Jesus Christ.[56]

The term ψυχῆς λογικῆς was adopted in opposition to the views of Apollinaris, who held that the incarnation involved the inhabiting or possession of a human body containing an animal soul with the divine Logos—that in Christ, the divine Word took the place of the human soul.[57] As John Behr notes, "[t]he most serious problem concerning

53. See Hart, "Providence and Causality," 44 (noting that the Banezian and Molinist positions are "essentially the same"). Such a move seems to inform, for example, Peters and Welker, *Anticipating Omega*. For a discussion of this notion from a panentheist perspective, see Davies, "How Many Universes?"

54. Clark, *Biology & Christian Ethics*, 92 (noting that "[t]he deconstruction of a uniquely human nature needs further commentary from Christian thinkers: after all, it is *our* nature that the Word took up, and that has been assumed to be a human one. If it was not *our nature* that he assumed, since—qua human beings—we have no nature, what happened in the Incarnation that we need to recall and ponder?"); Clark, *Can We Believe in People?*

55. The Chalcedonian Definition, translated at Early Church Texts, available at http://www.earlychurchtexts.com/public/chalcedonian_definition.htm.

56. The Chalcedonian Definition, translated at Early Church Texts, available at http://www.earlychurchtexts.com/public/chalcedonian_definition.htm.

57. See Schaff, *The Creeds of Christendom*, comment on The Chalcedonian Definition; Behr, *The Nicene Faith: Formation of Christian Theology*, Vol. 2, 392–401.

Apollinaris' account of Christ is not simply his claim that Christ did not assume a human soul or mind, but whether there remains any point of contact between Christ and us: 'He is not a man, but like a man, for he is not consubstantial with man in the highest dimension.'"[58] This leads to a "'failure to see in Christ the source and type of God's project of reshaping all of humanity together, and every person individually, in God's image, through the inner communication of divine life to a complete and normal human being.'"[59]

It is difficult to see how a physicalist emergentist anthropology such as Murphy's would avoid the same fate as applied to Christology. If there is no "soul," and the "mind" is merely the result of lower level physical processes, in what sense could Christ have had a nature "consubstantial (ὁμοούσιον) with us as touching his manhood?" It is important to note that the sense in which Christ is "consubstantial (ὁμοούσιον) with us" differs from the sense in which Christ is "consubstantial (ὁμοούσιον) with the Father as touching his Godhead" in that his consubstantiality with the Father implies a unity of essence, whereas his consubstantiality with humanity implies a unity of nature and not essence.[60] The Nicene Creed made plain that the Father, Son, and Spirit are three persons in one essence, and preserved the biblical witness to the fact that God is one.[61]

58. Behr, *Formation of Christian Theology, Vol. 2,* 399 (quoting Apollinaris, Frag. 45 [from the *Apodeixis,* GNO 3.1, 165.7–9]).

59. Behr, *Formation of Christian Theology, Vol. 2,* 399, note 160 (quoting Daley, "'Heavenly Man' and 'Eternal Christ,'" 478).

60. See Schaff, *The Creeds of Christendom,* The Chalcedonian Definition, 67 note 66.

61. As John Behr notes, the trinitarian theology of the Nicene Creed was not a new invention over against the biblical witness. See Behr, *Formation of Christian Theology, Vol. 2,* Introduction, 7. As Behr argues,

> it is not enough simply to assert the identity of the "economic" Trinity and the "immanent" Trinity, or to emphasis that the "economic" basis of our knowledge of the Trinity—that it is only the revelation of the Son in and through the Spirit that we can speak of God as Father—must correspond to how the Trinity actually is in "immanent" terms. These two dimensions of Trinitarian theology, economic and immanent, should never have been separated, even if they are subsequently reunited. That Trinitarian theology results from reflecting on how the crucified and exalted Lord Jesus Christ reveals the one and only God as Father, in and through the Holy Spirit, who also enables adopted sons crucified with Christ to call upon the same God as Father, means that Trinitarian theology has less to do with the heavenly existence of the three divine persons than with this new manner of confessing the one God—as Father, in the Son, by the Holy Spirit.

Behr, *Formation of Christian Theology, Vol. 2,* 8.

But human beings are not God, so the way in which Christ is ὁμοούσιον with us differs and relates to the transcendentals of human nature. If there *are* no transcendentals of human nature—if each person just is, as a particular person—then there does not seem to be any way in which Christ can be savingly related to *humanity*. The term ψυχῆς λογικῆς therefore continues to do crucial work in the Chalcedonian definition. It is by taking on the transcendental property of human nature shared by all persons—the ψυχῆς λογικῆς—that Christ shares in the common humanity of us all.

A response may be that the emergent mind, capable of exercising downward causality and therefore capable of moral agency, is shared by Christ with all humanity. There is simply an updating here of the Greek notion of ψυχῆς with a more scientifically accurate conception of an emergent capacity. But once this emergent capacity is conceived in this fashion, it has been remade as a transcendental, and it ceases to represent a "physicalist" account of the person.[62] In an authentically physicalist account, the fact that particular individual *homo sapiens sapiens* each possess an emergent capacity for agency is nothing but a historical accident. Within the possibilities of evolution, it may arise that some group of biologically *homo sapiens sapiens* develop a different sort of emergent capacity, or lose the existing emergent capacity. In fact, the logic of evolution says that such flux is *inevitable*—flux is simply how evolution works. There is no *physicalist* reason to identify the emergent capacity nonreductive physicalists such as Murphy equate with "mind" as a common and stable feature of human nature in which Christ could share and act savingly towards us. To make that identification is to posit a transcendental and thereby to leave the world of mere physicalism behind.

Perhaps some nonreductive physicalists would partially grant this argument with a back-handed nominalist move: go ahead and call it a "transcendental" if you like, but realize that this is merely a convenient term for something that in the long evolutionary scheme of things is really in evolutionary flux. This is a dubious move on its own merits because it cannot avoid words like "some*thing*" when referring to this property or

---

62. *Cf.* Neo-Aristotelian approaches to "substance" in Hoffman, "Neo-Aristotelianism and Substance." As will be discussed further below, I believe theological approaches like Murphy's suffer from a lack of engagement with the resurgence of Aristotelian thinking in metaphysics and the philosophy of science. See generally, Tahko, "In Defence of Aristotelian Metaphysics."

capacity we are trying to define. But it also interferes with the concept of "freedom," in which the transcendental of ψυχῆς must play a prominent role. And this, in turn, raises the question of the "laws" of nature.

2. The Laws of Nature and the New Aristotelianism

In Jewish and Christian theology, the divine command inheres not only in the *Torah* given to humans but also in God's commands that establish and govern all of creation. The creation poem of Genesis 1 is a series of spoken commands through which God brings order to primordial chaos: "Let there be Light," "Let there be a vault between the waters to separate water from water," and so-on. There is no question about whether the chaos will or will not obey. God speaks, and what God speaks *is*. The *midrash* on Genesis 1 in the Gospel of John identifies this divine command with God's Wisdom, identifies God's Wisdom with Christ, distinguishes the persons of Christ and "God," and yet identifies Christ with God: "In the beginning was the Word, and the Word was with God, and the Word was God" (Ἐν ἀρχῇ ἦν ὁ Λόγος, καὶ ὁ Λόγος ἦν πρὸς τὸν Θεόν, καὶ Θεός ἦν ὁ Λόγος) (John 1:1). In Paul's epistles the divine command and Wisdom are personified in Christ such that the *being* of the universe inheres in the *being* of Christ: "The Son is the image of the invisible God, the firstborn over all creation. For in him (ἐν αὐτῷ) all things were created: things in heaven and on earth, visible and invisible, whether thrones or powers or rulers or authorities; all things have been created through him (δι' αὐτοῦ) and for him (εἰς αὐτὸν). He is before all things (αὐτὸς ἔστιν πρὸ πάντων), and in him all things hold together (πάντα ἐν αὐτῷ συνέστηκεν)" (Col 1:15–17). Creation is *in* him (ἐν αὐτῷ), *through* him (δι' αὐτοῦ), and *for* him (εἰς αὐτὸν); he is before all things (αὐτὸς ἔστιν πρὸ); and in him (ἐν αὐτῷ) everything is συνέστηκεν—put together, synthesized, connected into an inter-locking whole, "understood."[63]

Modern scientific accounts of causality drew on a deracinated version of divine command theory in that, after Newton, the natural "laws" were divorced from being: *this* action produces *that* reaction, in causal chains that can, in theory, be described with mathematical precision through equations that do not in themselves require any *person* to

---

63. See *Strong's Greek Concordance*, 4919, available at http://biblesuite.com/greek/4920.htm.

operate. To account for the entire causal chain would be to demonstrate that each action along the chain is determined by its antecedents.

In terms of the analytic philosophy of science, this sort of flat Newtonian notion of causality has been out of favor since at least David Hume's treatment of the subject. Hume, in fact, denied that we can know causality at all, because of the problem of instance confirmability. The observation that B follows A in an observed instance does not guarantee that B will always follow A. We can only claim that B has always followed A in the past, and that B will always follow A in the future, if we assume that whatever properties affect the relations between B and A are stable, uniform, and unchanging. But since we cannot observe every instance of the relation between A and B in the past, and since we cannot presently observe the future of relations between A and B, there is no way empirically to know that A "causes" B. Hume therefore concluded that the idea of natural "laws" is semantic or a matter of custom and not necessarily real.[64]

Within the philosophy of science today, Humean approaches to natural "laws" remain important.[65] Neo-Humeans focus on instance confirmability and counterfactual support as markers of things that could be called natural "laws." The greater number of instances that can be observed of B following A, the stronger the inference that A causes B; and the greater ability of the relation between A and B to obtain across other possible worlds, the stronger the modal force of the relation between A and B. But this approach assumes that natural "laws" are

---

64. Hume, *An Enquiry concerning Human Understanding*, Part II. Hume states that "[a]ll events seem entirely loose and separate. One event follows another; but we never can observe any tie between them. They seem conjoined but never connected. And as we can have no idea of anything, which never appears to our outward sense or inward sentiment, the necessary conclusion seems to be, that we have no idea of connexion or power at all, and that these words are absolutely without any meaning, when employed either in philosophical reasoning, or in private life." Hume did not want to deny the explanatory power of causation, so he located the sense of causation in experience rather than in logical induction: "In all single instances of the operation of bodies or minds, there is nothing that produces any impression, nor consequently can suggest any idea of power or necessary connexion. But when many uniform instances appear, and the same object is always followed by the same event; we then begin to entertain the notion of cause and connexion. We then feel a new sentiment or impression, to wit, a customary connexion in the thought or imagination between one object and its usual attendant; and this sentiment is the original of that idea which we seek for."

65. See, e.g., Zilsel, "The Genesis of the Concept of Physical Law"; Ayer, "What Is a Law of Nature?"

entirely contingent. In other possible worlds, the "laws" could be different. Natural laws therefore are not embedded in a realist metaphysic, but are accidental features of the universe we happen to inhabit.

The neo-Humean approach to natural laws does not in itself avoid determinism in a weak sense. We can still speak of laws, and of causal relations, and the systems of our universe are all that obtain for us—there is no transcendence. In principle, a present observation that B followed A could be described in terms of all the relations that ever obtained in the history of the universe and that led to A and then to B given the things we would call "laws" in this universe. But this non-realist approach to natural laws does avoid determinism in a hard sense—the universe *could have been* different, and nothing *outside* the universe determines the fate of the universe or of the things (including *homo sapiens*) within it.

This sort of metaphysic underpins the contemporary debate in analytic philosophy over the problem of human free will. Camps divide over whether the concept of "freedom" requires "libertarian" or "compatibilist" free will.[66] Libertarians argue that "freedom" means, in any given situation, the ability to choose otherwise. Compatibilists argue that "freedom" does not necessarily imply a counterfactual choice, but rather implies only that an agent's capacities are functioning properly when a choice is made.

Modern philosophical theologians in the analytic mode have largely accepted these categories.[67] One attempt at a theological response to the Humean notion of natural law and causality (which also was a response to Newtonian determinism) is to invoke the need for a *first* cause. Unless the universe is eternal, something must have set the chain of causation going, and that something must itself be eternal—i.e., God. To this sort of argument, critics such as Richard Dawkins rightly reply, "But what caused God?" Philosophically, this sort of argument reflects an incapacity to move beyond Humean accounts of freedom and causality. However, an important group of contemporary philosophers are returning to Aristotle for richer accounts of freedom and causality.

In his treatise "On the Soul," Aristotle stated that the "soul" and the "body" are inseparable. For example, comparing the soul to the potential power of a cutting tool and relating it to the power of sight, Aristotle said:

66. *See* McKenna and Coates, "Compatibilism."
67. See, e.g., Baggett and Walls, *Good God.*

the soul is actuality in the sense corresponding to the power of sight and the power in the tool; the body corresponds to what exists in potentiality; as the pupil plus the power of sight constitutes the eye, so the soul plus the body constitutes the animal.[68]

Yet Aristotle never simply *equated* the soul with bodily functions. For example, he noted that "all those who define the soul by its power of knowing make it either an element or constructed out of the elements," and he is keen to refute this sort of reductionism.[69] Instead, for Aristotle, the soul is the form or source of the body:

> The soul is the *cause* or *source* of the living body. The terms cause and source have many senses. But the soul is the cause of its body alike in all three senses which we explicitly recognize. It is (a) the source or origin of movement, it is (b) the end, it is (c) the essence of the whole living body.[70]

This reference to origin, source, and movement invokes Aristotle's concept of causation. Aristotle recognized four kinds or aspects of causation: material, formal, efficient, and final.[71] The material cause is that out of which something comes, such as the bronze of a statue. The formal cause is the form or account of what it is to be something, such as the shape of a statue. The efficient cause is the primary source of change or rest, such as the sculptor who chips away at the marble. The final cause is the end for which something is done, such as the production of a sculpture.

Modern science recognizes only efficient and material causes.[72] While this may be an important methodological limitation, it is unwarranted, without further explanation, as an overarching metaphysic. Moreover, an Aristotelian or neo-Aristotelian notion of "mind" (or "soul") requires all these various senses of causation, and in particular *final* causation.[73] If some sort of Aristotelian anthropology is a response to reductive neurolaw, as Pardo and Patterson suggest (see Chapter 6.3), then we must speak of where "law" comes from, what it means for "law"

68. Aristotle, *De Anima*, II.1.

69. Aristotle, *De Anima*, II.2.

70. Aristotle, *De Anima*, II.4. (emphasis added).

71. See, e.g., Falcon, "Aristotle on Causality."

72. For a discussion of causation in modern science, see Murphy, "Divine Action, Emergence, and Scientific Explanation."

73. See Shields, "Aristotle's Psychology."

to be "law," and of the ends or purposes of "law." That is, we must speak of "law" as having some transcendent *telos*, some *source* that also implies its *ends*.

In fact, even in the academic philosophy of science literature, there has been a resurgence in Aristotelian thinking about the *powers* and *dispositions* of things.[74] This move has been spurred in large part by Roy Bhaskar and other philosophers of science who espouse an approach they call "critical realism."[75] As noted in chapter 4, a related move is made by many "science and religion" scholars, although their version of "critical realism" differs in some important respects from the Bhaskar school.[76] Nevertheless, there are important areas of overlap, particularly in relation to anthropology and the problem of "mind."[77]

74. See Groff and Greco, *Powers and Capacities in Philosophy*.

75. For a definition of critical realism, see Hartwig, *Dictionary of Critical Realism*, 96: "A movement in philosophy, social theory and cognate practices that seeks to under labour for science and other ways of knowing in order to promote the cause of TRUTH and FREEDOM, hence the transformation of social structures and other constraints that impeded that cause and their replacement with wanted and needed ones, or emancipation."

76. Hartwig, *Dictionary of Critical Realism*, 98. The *Dictionary of Critical Realism* suggests that

> In another neck of the realist philosophical woods, the "critical realism" of the Canadian Jesuit philosopher-theologian Bernard Lonergan (1904–84) appears to commit the epistemic fallacy in viewing the real as that which is known, . . . as does that of the French Thomist philosopher, Jacques Maritain. . . . The current movement in theology known as "critical realism" . . . was significantly influenced by the tradition of representative realism, but is currently being taken in a strongly Bhaskarian direction by Alister McGrath (2002). By and large, while there are obvious commonalities between all these various kinds of realisms, one can say that Bhaskarian CR is sharply distinguished from the others by its robustly transcendental and immanently critical method, its outright rejection of empiricism and positivism, its thoroughgoing emergentism, its understanding of social science as necessarily explanatory critical (entailing rejection of the fact-value and theory-practice dichotomies) and its explicitly emancipatory stance.

77. The *Dictionary of Critical Realism* states that "CR's major contribution on this subject is *synchronic emergent powers materialism* . . . which shares with Searle's biological naturalism . . . a refusal of the basic terms of debate set out by dualism and reductionism, on the basis that both are rooted in an ontological idealist-materialist dichotomy. Dualism leaves consciousness as a mysterious non-corrigible intangible, whilst reductionism, in the name of materialism, puts aside the totality of a conscious being which is the very property that gives rise to questioning the nature of mind in the first place. SEPM argues that consciousness is an emergent non-reducible property of the material brain." Hartwig, *Dictionary of Critical Realism*, 314–15.

Bhaskar's metaphysic is phenomenological, realist, and essentialist.[78] Bhaskar argues that

> [t]he world consists of things, not events. Most things are complex objects, in virtue of which they possess an ensemble of tendencies, liabilities, and powers. It is by reference to the exercise of their tendencies, liabilities, and powers that the phenomena of the world are explained. Such continuing activity is in turn referred back for explanation to the essential nature of things.[79]

Similarly, Nancy Cartwright and John Pemberton state that "Aristotelian powers . . . are part of the basic ontology of nature—at least as nature is pictured through the lens of modern science."[80] Cartwright and Pemberton argue that, although "[t]he scientific revolutionaries made fun of this kind of Aristotelianism," the notion that there are "powers" in nature that can combine to produce various sorts of "canonical effects" is essential to a nonreductive understanding of nature and to the practice of science itself.[81] They wish to elide Hume's skepticism about causation by showing how "nomological machines" produce predictable effects that support meaningful claims of causation.[82] For Cartwright and Pemberton, such effects result from a nomological machine's "emergent powers which are not to be found in its components."[83] Nomological machines, then, are not reducible to underlying "laws," but rather employ powers that *are* the canonical effects they contribute to the machine.[84] Moreover, powers are not arbitrary in relation to nomological machines. For Cartwright and Pemberton, "arrangement matters."[85] This ontological move—rendering "powers" as emergent features of nature—thus eliminates the problems of reduction and instance confirmability that so

---

78. See Bhaskar, *A Realist Theory of Science.*

79. Bhaskar, *A Realist Theory of Science,* 51.

80. Cartwright and Pemberton, "Aristotelian Powers: Without Them, What Would Modern Science Do?" See also Groff, "Whose Powers? Which Agency?" 209 (noting that "[i]t is fair to date to the mid-1970s the contemporary retrieval of causal power for which Hume couldn't locate an original impression"); Guenin, "Developmental Potential."

81. Cartwright and Pemberton, "Aristotelian Powers," 93–94.

82. Cartwright and Pemberton, "Aristotelian Powers," 94.

83. Cartwright and Pemberton, "Aristotelian Powers," 94.

84. Cartwright and Pemberton, "Aristotelian Powers," 95.

85. Cartwright and Pemberton, "Aristotelian Powers," 109.

troubled Hume.[86] As Cartwright and Pemberton conclude, their account of powers "has major implications for debates about levels and about reduction. The arrangement of parts is immanent in the whole but not in each of the parts. Machine arrangements can have emergent powers not possessed by the parts."[87]

Further, as Ruth Groff observes, realism about powers as stable emergent properties of machine arrangements "carries with it implications for the theorizing of human agency."[88] Groff argues that among the emergent powers of human beings is the power to act as genuine causative agents.[89] In a chapter that explores the link between powers and agency, Groff invokes Brian Ellis' canonical discussion of how realism about essential powers differs from Humeanism.[90] Ellis identified his view with Leibniz: "Like Leibniz," Ellis says, "I suppose that laws of nature are grounded in intrinsically powerful properties."[91] For Ellis, Groff, and other neo-Aristotelian philosophers of science, human beings possess dispositional properties relating to natural powers. For example, a person who comes in from the cold and sits by a fire becomes warm due to the fire's power to warm, and now that person also has the power "to warm some other thing, such as the body of anyone who wants to come and cuddle."[92] This, she argues, implies a space for ethical action: the person who obtains the fire's power to warm may share or not share that power with others.[93]

3. From "Is" to "Ought"

The new Aristotelianism in the philosophy of science therefore provides one important response to neurolaw's reductionist claims. If the "laws of nature" are not so much deterministic rules as powers and potentialities,

86. Cartwright and Pemberton, "Aristotelian Powers," 105 (noting that, in contrast to Hume, "[o]ur account is a powers account precisely because we take exercisings seriously as a central part of scientific ontology").

87. Cartwright and Pemberton, "Aristotelian Powers," 111.

88. Groff, "Whose Powers? Which Agency?" 207.

89. Groff, "Whose Powers? Which Agency?" 208.

90. Groff, "Whose Powers? Which Agency?" 211.

91. Groff, "Whose Powers? Which Agency?" 211.

92. Groff, "Whose Powers? Which Agency?" 218.

93. Groff, "Whose Powers? Which Agency?" 218. For a discussion of how this claim implies the naturalistic fallacy, see section 3 below.

then the neurochemistry of the brain empowers and enables, but does not *determine* the capacity of "mind." This perspective connects contemporary philosophy of science with the pre-modern perspectives on ethics and natural law discussed in chapter 1.

But generally these neo-Aristotelian philosophers are attempting to speak of powers as something emergent from lower orders of nature, without any prior referent or antecedent end. As Charlotte Witt notes, Aristotle's ontology of causal powers requires "the central presence of teleology."[94] Witt argues that "[w]ithout the teleological thread it is unclear on what basis it makes sense to extend a realist theory of causal powers from natural causation to human activity."[95] A notion of Aristotelian teleology, Witt suggests, is missing "from many contemporary versions of realist theories of causal powers."[96] This lack of teleology raises the specter of the "is/ought" fallacy and the related naturalistic fallacy.

This problem of the is/ought fallacy is central to James Davidson Hunter's and Paul Nedelisky's excellent book *Science and the Good: The Tragic Quest for the Foundations of Morality*.[97] As discussed in chapter 3, neurolaw is one manifestation of the "new moral science" critiqued by Hunter and Nedelisky. The practitioners of this "new moral science" are mostly positivists of one sort or another. According to Hunter and Nedelisky, the facts of human evolution and neurochemistry do not entail ethical imperatives because they are merely facts about what is. The neo-Aristotelians and other neo-Hegelian idealists (including, it seems, Nedelisky) attempt to avoid the is/ought fallacy through emergence.

There are several reasons, however, why this is the wrong line of critique, and why a neo-Aristotelian or Hegelian approach without a transcendent God fails. First, Hunter and Nedelisky do not really grapple with how neuroscientific reductionists handle the "is-ought" problem. Second, Hunter and Nedelisky overlook the "naturalistic fallacy," which is related to but in this case more powerful than the "is-ought" distinction. Third, and most importantly, Hunter and Nedelisky do not address the central question of metaphysics.

A good conversation partner here is Patricia Churchland. In her book *Braintrust: What Neuroscience Tells Us about Morality*, Churchland

---

94. Witt, "Aristotelian Powers."

95. Witt, *"Aristotelian Powers,"* 137.

96. Witt, *"Aristotelian Powers,"* 130.

97. Hunter and Nedelisky, *Science and the Good.*

notes that Hume's "is-ought" rule is a narrow claim that refers to deductive logic.[98] Churchland grants that an "ought" statement cannot be derived from an "is" statement as a matter of formal logic. She argues, however, that "ought" statements can be *inferred* from "is" statements, "drawing on knowledge, perception, emotions, and understanding, and balancing considerations against each other."[99] As Churchland notes, "I ought to go to the dentist" is a valid inference from the fact that "I have a horrendous toothache."[100] Similarly, Churchland suggests, more complex social practices, including moral behavior, usually develop through inferences from various facts rather than from cold deductive logic.[101] Given Churchland's understanding of what an "ought" can comprise, she escapes the "is-ought" rule.

The understanding of what an "ought" can comprise, however, is the rub. Churchland's description of how most people navigate moral issues certainly is correct, and in fact is consistent with millennia of reflection on virtue ethics: ethical frameworks and moral choices are lived out in the complexity of the real world, not only in the sterile chamber of deductive logic.

Because of her commitment to naturalism, however Churchland cannot refer the "ought" to the higher purposes and ends—the *telos*—of classical virtue ethics. Instead, she refers generally to human wellbeing and suggests that some kind of consequentialism is the best basis for legal rules that support human wellbeing.[102] This seems to catch Churchland in a problem related to the "is-ought" rule—the naturalistic fallacy. As G. E. Moore first argued, human wellbeing, defined as health, pleasure, or any other property natural to humans, cannot define the "good."[103] As Moore noted, when people say "Pleasure is good, we cannot believe that they merely mean Pleasure is pleasure and nothing more than that."[104]

Churchland thinks Moore constructed a "mystical moat around moral behavior."[105] Her response to the naturalistic fallacy is that a

---

98. Churchland, *Braintrust*, 6–7.

99. Churchland, *Braintrust*, 6.

100. Churchland, *Braintrust*, 7.

101. Churchland, *Braintrust*, 8.

102. Churchland, *Braintrust*, 175–81.

103. Moore, *Principia Ethica*, § 10 ¶ 3.

104. Moore, *Principia Ethica*, § 11(2).

105. Churchland, *Braintrust*, 188.

scientific term can include more than one aspect of meaning. She suggests, "consider these scientifically demonstrated identifications: light (A) is electromagnetic radiation (B), or temperature (A) is mean molecular kinetic energy (B). Here, the A and B terms are not synonymous, but the property measured one way was found to be the same as the property measured another way."[106] As another more prosaic example, she suggest, "Suppose I discover that my neighbor Bill Smith (A) is the head of the CIA (B): are the expressions 'my neighbor Bill Smith' and 'the head of the CIA synonymous?' Of course not."[107]

Churchland is of course correct that a term can include more than one aspect of meaning, but that is not what her examples demonstrate, and in any event, she completely misses Moore's point. Churchland's second example is irrelevant. "Bill Smith" and "Head of the CIA" are not categories that overlap at all except for the contingent historical fact that at some point in time Bill Smith serves in that role. Obviously, Bill Smith cannot be reduced to his role as Head of the CIA, nor can the role of Head of the CIA be reduced to the individual who currently occupies it, Bill Smith. If Bill Smith ceases to serve as Head of the CIA, he will still be Bill Smith and there will still be a Head of the CIA. If anything, this example reinforces Moore's arguments against reductionism. Not only are the terms not "synonymous," they are not even close to coextensive.

Churchland's example of light and electromagnetic radiation is no more availing. First, "radiation" is, in fact, a synonym for "light."[108] In at least one range of meaning—particularly the range of meaning employed by the natural sciences—"electromagnetic radiation" does mean "light" and "light" does mean "electromagnetic radiation," without remainder. So, in the scientific domain that is Churchland's immediate concern, this example belies her point.

"Light," of course, carries a much broader semantic range of meaning than this narrow scientific one. To say "you light up my life," for example, has nothing to do with electromagnetic radiation. Churchland might respond that the experience of having one's life lit up by a lover can be described in the entirely material terms of hormones and neurochemistry. But this response only begs the question whether a person's subjective conscious experience can be reduced to such material terms.

106. Churchland, *Braintrust*, 188.

107. Churchland, *Braintrust*, 188.

108. See Thesaurus.com, "light," available at https://www.thesaurus.com/browse/light?s=t.

And, in any event, "light" now signifies something very different from "electromagnetic radiation."

The example of "temperature" and "mean molecular kinetic energy," which invokes the Boltzmann constant, is more interesting. While it is true that the average kinetic energy of molecules in a gas is proportional to temperature, mean molecular kinetic energy is *not* a precise measure of some absolute quantity of temperature. A measurement of mean kinetic energy assumes that every molecule in the gas acts like an independent point mass. This is important for measuring heat transfer and entropy. It is not, however, a real measure of the specific heat of a gas, because each molecule has some degree of freedom in its rotation and vibration and does not act like an independent point mass. Moreover, kinetic theory only applies to gases, and even for gases, is only one way of thinking about temperature. And things become even more interesting when "quantum thermodynamics" enters the picture, which raises major unresolved questions about the relationship between the classical laws of thermodynamics and the thermodynamics of systems at the quantum level.[109]

Even if Churchland wants to suggest something like "mean molecular energy : temperature :: (individual brain chemistry + social evolution) : altruism," the analogy breaks down on several levels. First, as discussed above, the left side of the analogy only applies to one specific set of conditions. Moving to the right side of the analogy, this would mean that "altruism" can be related to "individual brain chemistry + social evolution" only if "altruism" is used here in a unique way in relation to a specific kind of system. But this would once again beg the question whether this relation describes anything about a real world or is only a specific, limited kind of model. And even if it were otherwise a fair model within its own limited sphere, it would leave open the question whether, as with quantum thermodynamics, there are other levels of possible description, perhaps even with different rules.

This, however, is a quite generous account of the analogy. Mean molecular energy and temperature are related to each other proportionately, which is why one can be used to measure the other. Brain chemistry and evolution, in contrast, are not in the same kind of proportionate relation to altruism or any other kind of ethically significant conduct. We cannot take the mean level of serotonin in the brains of humans in a society

109. See Castelvecchi, "Battle between Quantum and Thermodynamic Laws Heats Up"; Wolchover, "The Quantum Thermodynamics Revolution."

and come up with any predictable measure of altruism. Brains and social structures are too complex for correlations here, outside very broad normal distributions, much less for inferring causation between any discrete element of brain chemistry or social evolution and something like levels of altruism. The notion that there might be a Boltzmann constant for moral behavior is statistically absurd.

Finally, and most importantly, "mean molecular energy : temperature :: (individual brain chemistry + social evolution) : altruism," is not really the right analogy. The right analogy is "mean molecular energy . temperature .. (individual brain chemistry + social evolution) : the *goodness* of altruism." Again, the analogy breaks down here on its own terms. Behavior described as altruistic might be morally good, or morally bad, or morally indifferent, or any of these things under different circumstances. Measuring the sheer instances of a behavior is not a moral judgment. A moral judgment entails a measure of value the leads to some kind of imperative, prohibition, or exhortation: altruism is *good* so people *ought* to be altruistic if they have extra and others are in need. No one says "that container of oxygen *ought* to obey Boltzmann's constant or we will judge it to be bad oxygen." The oxygen has no agency and Boltzmann's constant invariably will apply in the domain of classical physics. This means Churchland cannot avoid the naturalistic fallacy after all.

This analysis also hints at the deeper metaphysical questions Churchland refuses to address. She describes the individual components of each set—light (A) and electromagnetic radiation (B); and temperature (A) and mean molecular kinetic energy (B)—as "properties." As the *Stanford Encyclopedia of Philosophy* notes, however, "[q]uestions about the nature and existence of properties are nearly as old as philosophy itself."[110] Any discussion of "properties" invokes the distinction between universals and particulars and other basic problems in metaphysics and ontology.[111] Churchland cannot dismiss these enormous metaphysical problems with a hand-wave and then discourse about supposedly interchangeable "properties" of light and radiation. Yet this is exactly what she does, when she confidently asserts that "[w]hat does not exist is a Platonic Heaven wherein the Moral Truths reside—no more than there is a Platonic Heaven wherein the Physical Truths reside."[112] No contemporary

110. Orilia and Swoyer, "Properties."

111. See Orilia and Swoyer, "Properties."

112. Churchland, *Braintrust*, 181.

philosopher would frame an answer exactly as Plato did, but the question whether "properties" are real, and whether any such realist claim can be justified absent immaterial entities, is the same kind of question Plato asked.

This focus on metaphysics returns us to Hunter and Nedilisky's critique of scientism in ethics. The problem is not merely that an "ought" of ethics cannot be derived from an "is" of evolutionary psychology or neurobiology. The problem is that the "is" of scientism is merely a natural phenomenon. A chemical state in the brain is a chemical state in the brain, not a moral value. A subjective feeling produced by hormones released because of a chemical state in the brain is a subjective feeling—and, for reductive neuroscience, an illusion—not a moral value. There is no ought, period.

The classical accounts of law surveyed in chapter 1 avoid the naturalistic fallacy because the source of moral value *transcends* nature. The new Aristotelianism, along with other Hegelian idealist approaches, attempts to circumvent the naturalistic fallacy but makes it only part way around. One reason for this shortfall is a failure to understand the classical Christian doctrine of creation, which leads the neo-Aristotelians into the naturalistic fallacy when they try to connect their theory with ethics. For example, Ellis argues that powers "are not imposed by God on things that are intrinsically powerless, nor are they just regular patterns of behavior that happen to be displayed by such things, just as if they were imposed by God."[113] Ellis' conception of how natural powers might relate to divine causation here betrays a failure to understand the traditional Christian doctrine of creation *ex nihilo*. God neither stamps pre-existing matter with powers, nor randomly imbues things with powers by fiat. In the traditional Christian conception, created things have dispositions, powers, and capacities because they participate in the being of the living Triune God, and moreover the dispositions, powers, and capacities of all things are finally oriented towards a *telos* in God, who is not part of creation.

In fact, as Eleonore Stump has noted, "what is distinctive about this contemporary resurgence of Aristotelianism in metaphysics is its subtle difference from standard versions of Aristotelianism, such as that which can be found in the high Middle Ages, in the work of Aquinas, for

---

113. Churchland, *Braintrust*, 212 (quoting Ellis, *Scientific Essentialism*, 265).

example."[114] Stump notes that contemporary neo-Aristotelianism meshes with Aquinas' thought in that both understand a material thing to comprise a dynamically organized system that cannot be elided through reduction.[115] For Aquinas, this system-level dynamic configuration was the "form" that gave the thing its "function."[116] But contemporary neo-Aristotelians are generally committed to the principle of the causal closure of the physical.[117]

Aquinas, Stump suggests, would agree with the causal closure of the physical with respect to the integrity of secondary causation.[118] Using the paradigmatic example of water as a composition of matter with emergent properties, Stump notes that Aquinas would not posit any "mental stuff or panentheistic stuff or anything else non-physical which is responsible for the causal power of a water molecule to form a hydrogen bond."[119] But Aquinas would *not* accept causal closure at the level of what Stump calls the "micro-physical," because the fundamental particles that make up hydrogen and oxygen atoms taken in isolation do not each possess the powers of a water molecule.[120] The "form" of the water molecule, for Aquinas, inheres only in its configuration as a system.

This is particularly important, Stump notes, for Aquinas' treatment of the human person. A neo-Aristotelian account of the human person may be "nonreductive" based on the emergent property of "mind," but it remains "physicalist" in that it recognizes no source beyond the physical.[121] The neo-Aristotelian person therefore remains subject to a dissolution into matter. For Aquinas, in contrast, a human person is a whole system with an integral form that is not subject to dissolution into

---

114. Stump, "Emergence, Causal Powers, and Aristotelianism in Metaphysics."

115. Stump, "Emergence, Causal Powers, and Aristotelianism in Metaphysics," 51–52.

116. Stump, "Emergence, Causal Powers, and Aristotelianism in Metaphysics," 51–52.

117. Stump, "Emergence, Causal Powers, and Aristotelianism in Metaphysics," 51–52.

118. Stump, "Emergence, Causal Powers, and Aristotelianism in Metaphysics," 51–52.

119. Stump, "Emergence, Causal Powers, and Aristotelianism in Metaphysics," 51–52.

120. Stump, "Emergence, Causal Powers, and Aristotelianism in Metaphysics," 51–52.

121. Stump, "Emergence, Causal Powers, and Aristotelianism in Metaphysics," 51–52.

matter—that survives death.[122] And, although Stump does not explicitly make this connection in her discussion of neo-Aristotelian metaphysics, for Aquinas the human form—the soul—finds its true *telos* in the final resurrection, when united again with matter and participating fully in the beatific vision of God.

"Natural" law in the classical accounts surveyed in chapter 1 concerns the moral principles within nature that refer to causes outside nature. The new Aristotelianism in the philosophy of science refers to powers and capacities in things as emergent properties *of* matter that supervene on matter. The earlier Aristotelian perspective on causality recognizes that formal causes *impose* upon matter and that final causes draw matter towards something *beyond* itself. The new Aristotelianism would leave the powers and capacities of the laws of nature as emergent brute facts, which means a theory of ethics relating to those powers and capacities would still fall prey to the naturalistic fallacy. The earlier Aristotelian perspective on causality, along with the earlier Platonic perspective on the ideal (or, relatedly, the earlier Hebrew perspective on God's power in creation), as taken up within Christian theology, escape the naturalistic fallacy—concerning divine commands, the laws of nature, the truths of reason, the capacities of the human brain and mind, and natural law.

122. Stump, "Emergence, Causal Powers, and Aristotelianism in Metaphysics," 51–52.

8

The Soul of the Law

CHAPTER 7 IDENTIFIED AN important stream within the contemporary philosophy of science literature concerning the laws of nature that advocates for a new Aristotelianism focused on the powers of entities rather than on laws. This new Aristotelianism echoes pre-modern philosophical and theological arguments about essence and existence and makes space for a reinvigorated concept of the soul as the powers and capacities of human beings to act or not act in certain ways. But the new Aristotelianism seems to fall prey to the naturalistic fallacy, no less than materialist ethics, without formal and final causes that transcend nature.

At the conclusion of chapter 7, we suggested that the new Aristotelianism needs theology. This chapter moves the discussion into how a coherent theory of natural law could be articulated and defended in light of this neo-Aristotelian perspective. First, we briefly examine and critique the "new" natural law movement. Next, we examine four contemporary thinkers who provide insights for our perspective on natural law: Jean Porter, Stanley Hauerwas, Christos Yannaras, and Robert Spaemann. We then synthesize the different perspectives of these thinkers into an account of human uniqueness in relationship with the transcendent source of the law of love.

1. The New Natural Law

In recent decades, there has been a resurgence in natural law theory among some analytic philosophers. Philosophers such as Germain Grisez, John Finnis, and Robert George have spearheaded a movement in "new" natural law theory that is designed to appeal, at least in its first principles, to all rational persons regardless of religious or theological commitments.[1] The "new" natural law theory, however, turns out to represent another effort to define "law" without theological context.[2]

Finnis identifies seven goods that he claims are self-evident to all rational persons: (1) life; (2) knowledge; (3) play; (4) aesthetic experience; (5) sociability or friendship; (6) practical reasonableness; and (7) religion.[3] These goods are not ordered hierarchically, but Finnis explains that the principles of practical reason enable human beings to make rational decisions about how all these goods could be instantiated in an ordered society. The first principle of practical reason, for Finnis, is the Thomistic aphorism that "good is to be pursued and done and evil is to be avoided."[4]

The new natural law theory is controversial and problematic. Indeed, the subtle critique implied by the adjective "new" demonstrates that many ethicists attracted to theories of inherent moral goods find the Grisez-Finnis approach troubling.[5] In his critique of the Grisez-Finnis approach, for example, Russell Hittinger argues that the fundamental problem with that approach "lies in a failure to interrelate systematically

---

1. See George, *In Defense of Natural Law*; May, "Germain Grisez on Moral Principles and Moral Norms." May argues that Grisez's version of natural law theory, though it posits general principles of practical reason to which all persons have access, is also specifically Christian in that Grisez also recognizes some additional moral principles that can be known only through revelation.

2. Some Catholic moral theologians have described debates between the new natural law theorists and proportionalists as a "schism." See Salzman, *What Are They Saying about Catholic Ethical Method*, 17. As Salzman notes, the new natural law theorists criticize Aquinas for coming close to committing the naturalistic fallacy (deriving an "is" from an "ought") and further criticize the subsequent manualist tradition for actually committing the naturalistic fallacy.

3. Finnis, *Natural Law and Natural Rights*, 81.

4. Finnis, *Natural Law and Natural Rights*; Grisez, *The First Principle of Practical Reason*. Finnis relies heavily upon Grisez for this point.

5. The adjective "new" was first applied by Russell Hittinger in *A Critique of the New Natural Law Theory*.

practical reason with a philosophy of nature."[6] Hittinger notes that Grisez believes "speculative reason, including its metaphysical mode, is able to affirm little, if anything, concerning God as an end of human striving."[7] This leads Grisez and Finnis away from associating their method too closely with Augustine, Aquinas, or other pre-modern Christian natural law theorists. Indeed, notwithstanding their reference to Aquinas' first principle concerning pursuing good and avoiding evil, Grisez and Finnis eschew the label of "Thomist," in part to avoid interpretive disputes surrounding Aquinas' own work.[8]

The new natural law theorists are keen to distinguish themselves from both materialistic monism and Cartesian dualism.[9] Patrick Lee and Robert George, for example, argue that human beings are animals with a capacity for agency. The capacity for intentional agency, they suggest, is the principle of action that defines human beings as body-soul composites.[10] Without the sense organs and the brain, the human person cannot understand and cannot will, yet understanding and willing cannot merely be identified with sense organs or the brain.[11]

Although other animals can also perform acts of understanding and willing, Lee and George argue, "human beings fundamentally differ from other animals because they [human beings] perform actions which manifest a transcendence of matter not possessed by other animals."[12] Human beings are capable of conceptual thought, which "radically distinguishes them from other animals."[13] For Lee and George, conceptual thought differs from sense perception in that "[w]hat one senses, perceives, or imagines—what one grasps in *bodily* cognitive acts—is always a *this*, with a particular, albeit sometimes vague, contour," whereas conceptual

---

6. Hittinger, *A Critique of the New Natural Law Theory*, 8.

7. Hittinger, *A Critique of the New Natural Law Theory* 20.

8. Hittinger, *A Critique of the New Natural Law Theory*, 8–9. Grisez responded to Hittinger in "A Critique of Russell Hittinger's Book, A Critique of the New Natural Law Theory." Hittinger responded with a terse paragraph in which Hittinger said "[a]t least in this piece, he [Grisez] reduces the philosophical issues to an argument from authority, which in this case is his own." Hittinger, "Response to Professor Grisez's Critique."

9. Lee and George, *Body-Self Dualism*.

10. Lee and George, *Body-Self Dualism*, 17.

11. Lee and George, *Body-Self Dualism*, 17.

12. Lee and George, *Body-Self Dualism*, 52.

13. Lee and George, *Body-Self Dualism*, 56.

thought is capable of obtaining insight about "a nature, property or form that can be (and usually is) instantiated in many, innumerable cases and which grounds explanations for why things (or relations, as in logic) are as they are."[14] Moreover, the human capacity for conceptual thought allows humans to "reflect back upon themselves and their place in reality."[15] Animals other than humans, Lee and George claim, "give no evidence at all" of being capable of conceptual thought or self-reflection.[16] It is therefore the capacity for rationality that defines what human beings *are* and that render humans capable, in ways other animals are not, of free choice and moral agency.[17]

For Lee and George, the *kind* of freedom humans possess is libertarian freedom: "that is, . . . not determined by the events that preceded it, but . . . determined by the person making the choice in the very act of choosing."[18] In at least some choices, Lee and George insist, "the events and realities" antecedent to the choice, including the person's "character," are not sufficient to bring about the choice, such that the person "could have chosen the other option, or not chosen at all, under the very same conditions."[19] The "principal objection" to this libertarian position, Lee and George assert, is the "principle of rational explanation"—the notion that a *rational* choice is *determined* by rationality or else the "choice" is irrational and random and not a "choice."[20] They rebut this argument by distinguishing a "rational" choice from a "moral" or "best" choice.[21] A "rational" choice, they assert, is simply one in which "one sees a distinctive benefit" in the choice.[22]

Lee and George argue that their anthropology is "not incompatible with theologically based key propositions" concerning the *imago Dei*, the immortality of the soul, and the resurrection of the body.[23] The same sort of argument is common to all new natural law theorists: rational arguments, understood on their own terms, establish a foundation for

14. Lee and George, *Body-Self Dualism*, 56.

15. Lee and George, *Body-Self Dualism*, 56.

16. Lee and George, *Body-Self Dualism*, 56.

17. Lee and George, *Body-Self Dualism*, 59–60.

18. Lee and George, *Body-Self Dualism*, 60.

19. Lee and George, *Body-Self Dualism*, 60.

20. Lee and George, *Body-Self Dualism*, 64.

21. Lee and George, *Body-Self Dualism*, 64.

22. Lee and George, *Body-Self Dualism*, 64.

23. Lee and George, *Body-Self Dualism*, 50–51.

further theological reflection. The project thus represents a "natural theology" of ethics and law.

This brief discussion of Lee and George's notion of "rationality," agency, embodiment, and the soul, however, demonstrate precisely why their project ultimately fails. A very particular metaphysic of "nature" is already smuggled into Lee and George's presumptively neutral discussion of agency. They betray their presumptions when they argue that the deterministic assumptions of the scientific method do not define the limits of "every entity which exists."[24] "In fact," they note, "renowned scientists such as Werner Heisenberg held this very position."[25] "Free choices and thoughts," they suggest, "are entities of this sort" (the sort that are not explicable by the scientific method). This passing reference to the Heisenberg Uncertainty Principle and to "free choices and thoughts" as "entities" obviously encodes a metaphysic of "nature," being reason and causality—and one derived straight from Kant and Paley.

In this sense, the new natural law theorists engage in the same sort of "natural theology" as proponents of "intelligent design" ("ID") theory. These kinds of natural theologies represent an apologetic program dictated by modernity. They accept the premise that human rationality is a neutral arbiter among competing truth claims and argue that facts "consistent with" Christianity can be ascertained by all rational persons from self-evident first principles. ID theorists do not claim their proofs establish there is a God, nor do new natural law theorists claim their principles require a divine source. Both, however, claim that their efforts clear a common ground on which theists and non-theists can parlay.

There are many empirical, philosophical, and theological problems with these claims. Empirically, neither ID theory nor the new natural lawyers take evolutionary biology seriously on its own terms. ID theorists consistently misunderstand or misrepresent what evolutionary biology means by "randomness" in natural selection. ID theorists claim that against the random background noise of natural history there are discernible patterns of "design" from which it can be inferred that a "Designer" exists. Such patterns may take the form of specified informational content in DNA or of "irreducibly complex" biomechanical systems such as the bacterial flagellum.[26] The empirical problem is that "randomness" in evolutionary

---

24. Lee and George, *Body-Self Dualism*, 63.

25. Lee and George, *Body-Self Dualism*, 63

26. See Behe, *Darwin's Black Box*; Behe, *The Edge of Evolution*.

theory, properly understood, is a statement about *ex ante* predictability and not about *ex post* observations. No evolutionary biologist would deny that there is "order" evident in the observable universe—that DNA molecules provide "instructions" for the expression of particular proteins and that there are complex biological structures with specific functions in particular organisms. The evolutionary biologist's claim, however, is that the higher level order inherent in something like a particular complex biological structure is not predictable from *a priori* observations of the genetic material and biosphere existing at any earlier time.[27] The order that *presently* exists is a *contingent* order, and that contingency is bound up in billions of years of evolutionary history that could have unfolded in paths too vast to quantify.[28] Life as we know it is orderly, but not necessary.

In a similar fashion, the new natural lawyers suggest that some moral principles are the necessary result of basic principles of rationality, such as the law against non-contradiction. This inherently is a claim that these principles of rationality are a fundamental and necessary property of the universe and that the moral principles derived from them are likewise necessary.[29] Such a claim, however, fails to comprehend the contingency of biological evolution. The moral principles the new natural lawyers are concerned with purport to govern *human* activity. Human beings are a product of biological evolution, like all other life on earth. Our beliefs about rationality may be no more than epiphenomena of contingent processes. The principles of logic and reason may *appear to us* inviolable, but this appearance may simply reflect our rather puny status as large-brained primates adapted to one of the billions upon billions of planets orbiting one of the billions upon billions of stars in one of the billions upon billions of galaxies in what we perceive to be the universe—which may only be one of billions upon billions of universes in the multiverse, or one of infinite universes or multiverses.

27. See, e.g., Ridley, *Evolution,* 5 (noting that "[e]volution does not proceed along some grand, predictable course. Instead, the details of evolution depend on the environment that a population happens to live in and the genetic variants that happen to arise (by almost random processes) in that population").

28. Ridley, *Evolution,* 5. There are, however, some evolutionary biologists who do not identify with ID theory but who argue that the "convergence" of common biological forms within separate evolutionary pathways suggests that the contingency of evolutionary history is highly constrained by universal boundary conditions. See Morris, *Life's Solution.*

29. See chapter 4.8 for a discussion of contingency in theology and science.

Philosophically, then, both ID theorists and the new natural lawyers adopt a naïve form of foundationalism. They assume that a scientific, ethical, and/or legal system can be established from the bottom up based on rational foundations that cannot be challenged and that are sufficient to support the resulting edifice. This sort of naïve foundationalism, however, consistently fails, because the supposed foundations turn out to require more basic unverifiable assumptions for their own support.

Theologically, both ID theorists and the new natural lawyers claim they are not making theological claims—that is, they proceed from an a-theistic starting point. Instead, they suggest that their arguments are neutrally accessible to religious and non-religious people and stand on their own, even though they are *consistent* with various theological and religious claims. The unintended result of this position is a further *separation* of "faith" and "reason." It looks like a Kantian move because it is a response to the modern Kantian turn that is resigned, at least for the sake of argument, to separation of reason and sentiment. The "God" resulting from this modern form of apologetic ends up looking flatly immanent, defined, constrained, and revealed entirely by human reason. Indeed, the "God" of this apologia seems to *be* human reason. In this way, the theological problems with ID theory and the new natural law are related to the philosophical problems, which in turn are related to fundamental failures to take either evolutionary biology or theology seriously. The lonely primate mind stretching out from within the incomprehensibly vast sea of the multiverse (whether "real" or only imaginatively counterfactual) remains incapable of establishing its own existence, much less the existence of universal "laws" or of its God.

Hittinger is therefore correct when he argues that "[w]e should admit the truth: it is not advisable to suppress the issues in a philosophy of nature and then, as it were, to take the ethics and run."[30] As Christian theology has always recognized, if "nature" is in fact "creation," a gift of the transcendent and yet personal creator-God, then what it *means* to "reason", to "be," and to "act"—what it means to be *free*—differs radically from any concepts in which such a God is absent. The very intelligibility of the universe *depends* on the first fact, that the universe is "creation." In "creation" there are no "acts" apart from "being"; causes are not univocal; and there is neither determinism nor "libertarian" freedom. In "creation," what is "good" and "true" is not designated as such in virtue of its

---

30. Hittinger, *A Critique of the New Natural Law Theory*, 194.

correspondence with a neutral rationality, but rather what is "rational" is designated as such in virtue of its participation in and orientation towards its final cause in God. As Hittinger notes, "[a]ny effort to extract a part of the ethic [of common morality based in a shared notion of creation] in the absence of its proper foundations, or to assign that part to some other foundation, is tantamount to constructing a materially different ethic."[31]

2. Jean Porter and "Nature as Reason"

In contrast to the new natural lawyers, Jean Porter develops a theory of natural law in conversation with a traditioned account of nature and reason. Porter notes that the scholastic concept of natural law, like Grisez and Finnis' approach, understood natural law as a "product of reason."[32] But, Porter argues, the scholastics "interpreted reason itself in theological terms."[33] Like Hittinger, Porter argues that modern attempts to articulate a universally compelling and rationally defensible natural law ethic have failed because there simply is no possibility of rational inquiry outside culturally specific traditions.[34]

Although Porter adopts Alasdair MacIntyre's critique of pure reason abstracted from tradition, she returns to Aquinas in an effort to retain some notion of "nature" that is neither opposed to "grace" nor collapsed into "grace." For Porter, the necessary bridge is teleology.[35] Aquinas' account of natural law, Porter argues, "is essentially teleological—that is to say, it is developed and structured through reflection on the purpose, or end, of human life, and the way this end incorporates and brings order to the diverse inclinations of our complex specific nature."[36]

Porter also accepts the "critical realist" stance in theology and science, which commits her to "construing nature in a way that is responsive to our best speculative understanding of the world around us, which

31. Hittinger, *A Critique of the New Natural Law Theory*, 195.

32. Porter, *Nature as Reason*, 27.

33. Porter, *Nature as Reason*, 27.

34. Porter, *Nature as Reason*, 29. Porter acknowledges the influence of Alasdair MacIntyre when she asserts that "[w]e need not adopt the deep skepticism of some postmodernists in order to defend the possibility that rational inquiry can *only* take place within some context of culturally specific practices, mores, and traditions." Porter, *Nature as Reason*, 7

35. Porter, *Nature as Reason*, 49–50.

36. Porter, *Nature as Reason*, 50.

today comes to us largely, though not exclusively, through the natural sciences."[37] Indeed, Porter specifically relies on Alister McGrath's approach to critical realism.[38] However, Porter criticizes what she perceives as naïve realism in McGrath's understanding of "science" and the scientific portrait of "nature." Porter wishes to navigate between outright postmodern social constructivism and modern foundationalism. She finds her way via a kind of "speculative realism" through which MacIntyrean tradition-specific inquiry "can in some instances attain to a highly developed theoretical account of a given subject matter, of such a kind as to reveal proper divisions and causal connections within a field of inquiry."[39]

Porter's approach to the nature-grace question reflects this critical realist orientation. She suggests that Aquinas' connection between the virtues and the natural law requires "a kind of happiness that is connatural to the human person."[40] Porter argues that Aquinas maintained a clear distinction between nature and grace that was central to his theology, but that Aquinas never assumed the existence of a state of "pure nature."[41] The first humans, for Porter's Aquinas, were created in a state of grace. Human nature has been distorted, but not entirely erased, by original and actual sin. There are virtues and principles of action that are proper to human nature as it now is, yet there are also pervasive human tendencies (such as narrow self-love) that are not proper to human nature as such. Moreover, there are virtues and principles of action that are in excess of human nature as it now is—that are infused—but that move human persons back toward the state of grace (beatitude).[42] For Porter, this distinction allows us to reflect on human nature as it now is and to develop principles of "natural law" that are appropriate to human nature but that do not imply the *ad extra* of grace.[43] Nature, for Porter's Aquinas, "broadly considered is intelligible on its own terms, and as such it has independent theological significance as a reflection of the wisdom

37. Porter, *Nature as Reason*, 58.

38. Porter, *Nature as Reason*, 58–59.

39. Porter, *Nature as Reason*, 64.

40. Porter, *Nature as Reason*, 379.

41. Porter, *Nature as Reason*, 384.

42. Porter, *Nature as Reason*, 384–85.

43. Porter, *Nature as Reason*, 385. Porter states that "just as we can distinguish, albeit imperfectly, between what is natural to the human person as such and what reflects particular social/cultural expressions, so we can distinguish between what is natural to us and what stems from grace."

of God."[44] Porter contrasts this with what she describes as the contemporary Catholic view, in which the nature-grace distinction is maintained only as a formal doctrinal principle, because "everything is permeated by grace, and at any rate all creation is a gratuitous gift of God."[45]

Porter argues that the nature-grace distinction is vital to the Thomistic dictum that grace does not pervert nature but perfects nature. The infused virtues do not wash out or cancel the acquired virtues. "'Nature as reason,'" Porter says, "informs the infused as well as the acquired virtues, even though the two kinds of virtues are specifically different, insofar as they are directed toward distinct ends."[46] In particular, for Porter, the acquired virtue of justice, which is reflected in ordinary relationships of obligation, is complemented and completed by the infused virtue of charity.[47] Justice and love do not compete: love fulfills justice. This move allows Porter to offer a positive concept of human rights. Reflection on human nature as such, on Porter's reading of the scholastics, "implies that all persons are naturally equal in some respects."[48] This notion of natural equality "leads to an expansive construal of the scope of justice, and it also implies limits on the scope of authority and obedience."[49]

3. Stanley Hauerwas' Critique of Natural Law

Porter's line of argument at times seems to run in the direction of some Protestant critiques of natural law, as she acknowledges.[50] She notes that "[r]ecently, Protestant reappraisals [of natural law theory] have retrieved aspects of the earlier tradition that many Catholic theologians have rejected, particularly its emphasis on prerational nature as a source for moral discernment."[51] One of these Protestant thinkers is Stanley Hauerwas.[52]

---

44. Porter, *Nature as Reason*, 386–87.

45. Porter, *Nature as Reason*, 386.

46. Porter, *Nature as Reason*, 389.

47. Porter, *Nature as Reason*, 390–91.

48. Porter, *Nature as Reason*, 394.

49. Porter, *Nature as Reason*, 394

50. Porter, *Nature as Reason*, 40.

51. Porter, *Nature as Reason*, 40.

52. Porter, *Nature as Reason*, 40.

Hauerwas has been critical of natural law because, he argues, "the power of natural law as a systematic idea was developed in and for the Roman imperium and then for 'Christendom.' Thus, ironically, 'natural law' became the means of codifying a particular moral tradition."[53] Hauerwas is particularly concerned about what he understands as a conflation of nature and grace in Catholic natural law ethics.[54] This approach, Hauerwas suggests, "is bound to use Christ to underwrite the integrity of the 'natural,' since he [Christ] is seen as epitomizing the fulfillment of the human vocation."[55] But for Hauerwas these categories of the "natural" and the "graced," as well as the categories ordinarily emphasized in Protestant ethics—covenant and redemption—are abstractions that should not take priority over the narrative of the community shaped by God's love for the world in Christ.[56] Otherwise, the rightness or wrongness of particular actions is derived from "nature" and specifically Christian convictions only offer, at best, some supplemental motivation for an abstract "morality."[57] This means that learning how to be "moral" becomes an exercise in the analysis of logical propositions rather than a specific sort of communal formation in particular virtues, habits, and practices.[58] The church then loses its ability to function as a counter-cultural community, particularly in Western democracies with historic links to modern natural law theories.[59]

One of the most disturbing results of the tendency to identify what is "natural" with the prevailing culture, Hauerwas suggests, is that "violence and coercion become conceptually intelligible from a natural law standpoint."[60] The language of natural "rights," he says, "in spite of its potential for good, contains within its logic a powerful justification for violence."[61] This is in part a result of grounding ethical reflection in

53. Hauerwas, *The Peaceable Kingdom*, 51. Hauerwas bemoans the fact that "[m]oral theologians came to look more like lawyers than theologians. They were people skilled in adjudication of cases for the troubled conscience (no mean or small skill)."

54. Hauerwas, *The Peaceable Kingdom*, 56.

55. Hauerwas, *The Peaceable Kingdom*, 56.

56. Hauerwas, *The Peaceable Kingdom*, 57.

57. Hauerwas, *The Peaceable Kingdom*, 57.

58. Hauerwas, *The Peaceable Kingdom*, 58.

59. Hauerwas, *The Peaceable Kingdom*, 59.

60. Hauerwas, *The Peaceable Kingdom*, 61.

61. Hauerwas, *The Peaceable Kingdom*, 61.

anthropology, even an anthropology connected to Christology: "[i]t is certainly right that life in Christ makes us more nearly what we should be, but that is not to say we must start with the human to determine what it means to be a disciple of Christ. While the way of life taught by Christ is meant to be an ethic for all people, it does not follow that we can know what such an ethic involves 'objectively' by looking at the human."[62] Instead, also echoing Alasdair MacIntyre, Hauerwas notes that all action is historically situated.[63] The emphasis on narrative reminds us "that we do not know what it means to call God creator or redeemer apart from the story of his activity with Israel and Jesus. The language of creation and redemption, nature and grace, is a secondary theological language, that is sometimes mistaken for the story itself."[64]

Given this emphasis on the particularity of the Christian narrative, how does Hauerwas avoid the specter of voluntarism? Would Hauerwas agree with other Protestant versions of divine command ethics that God could counterfactually have issued any command at all—say, a command to torture babies—and thereby established that command as "moral"?[65] In response to these concerns, Hauerwas refers to God's inherent character, which we learn "most clearly . . . in the life and death of Jesus Christ."[66] The "foundation" of Christian ethics is not in any form of rational foundationalism, but rather "[i]f we have a 'foundation' it is the story of Christ."[67] This foundation is not given in excess of reason, but is itself a claim about reality—a *metaphysical* claim, although Hauerwas does not use the term "metaphysics" in this text.[68] God's commands "make sense within his purpose of creating a people capable of witnessing in the world to the kingdom."[69]

62. Hauerwas, *The Peaceable Kingdom*, 58.

63. Hauerwas, *The Peaceable Kingdom*, 61.

64. Hauerwas, *The Peaceable Kingdom*, 62–63.

65. Hauerwas, *The Peaceable Kingdom*, 65–66.

66. Hauerwas, *The Peaceable Kingdom*, 67. Hauerwas does not reference the Euthyphro Dilemma here, but he is responding in classical fashion to the concerns raised by the Dilemma. Cf. Baggett and Walls, *Good God* (discussing the Euthyphro Dilemma and potential responses).

67. Porter, *Nature as Reason*, 65–66.

68. Porter, *Nature as Reason*, 67–68.

69. Porter, *Nature as Reason*, 69.

4. Christos Yannaras: Law and Freedom

Christos Yannaras is an often-overlooked Greek Orthodox theologian who has written extensively on theological anthropology and ethics.[70] In *The Freedom of Morality*, Yannaras addresses the seeming aporia between "freedom" and the strictures of "morality." Yannaras grounds his account in the personal and relational being of the Triune God. God's personal existence as Trinity constitutes his being, and therefore God's being is free, not contingent on some prior essence.[71] "When the Christian revelation declares that 'God is love, (1 Jn 4.16)'" Yannaras argues, "it is not referring to one among many properties of God's 'behavior,' but to what God *is* as the fullness of trinitarian and personal communion." Human existence "derives its ontological significance from the fact of divine love, the only love which gives substance to being."[72] Human persons, who are created to partake in the divine love, therefore must be "free" creatures.[73]

Human freedom does not imply a capacity for absolutely libertarian choice. It is, rather, "the freedom of love and of personal communion," a capacity to relate existentially to God.[74] As such, human beings are not subject to any kind of "natural predetermination."[75] A human being can reject this relationship, but to do so is to reject "the ontological precondition for his existence . . . ."[76]

The ostensibly libertarian choice to pursue one's own purposes apart from God is in fact a rejection of the self and the foreclosure of the freedom of love. The fall occurs when the human person "freely renounces his possibility of participating in true life, in personal relationship and loving communion—the only possibility for man to *be* as a hypostasis of personal distinctiveness."[77] The fall fragments the communality of human beings with God, each other, and the rest of creation. The fall "has irrevocably split nature, and condemned the will of all other human persons to be merely an individual will expressing and enforcing

---

70. For a brief biography of Yannaras, see Yannaras, *The Freedom of Morality*.

71. Yannaras, *The Freedom of Morality*, 18.

72. Yannaras, *The Freedom of Morality*, 19.

73. Yannaras, *The Freedom of Morality*, 19.

74. Yannaras, *The Freedom of Morality*, 20.

75. Yannaras, *The Freedom of Morality*, 25.

76. Yannaras, *The Freedom of Morality*, 25.

77. Yannaras, *The Freedom of Morality*, 29.

the necessities of the fragmented nature."[78] This is a kind of non-being or non-existence, not a juridical category.[79] For Yannaras, "[t]he God of the Church as known and proclaimed by Orthodox experience and tradition has never had anything to do with the God of the Roman juridical tradition, the God of Anselm and Abelard . . . ."[80] Judgment and hell are states of self-imposed exclusion from communion with God and therefore from genuine human existence.[81]

Yannaras' relational ontology leads him to view the biblical law not as a deontological code of obligation imposed from above, but rather as a gracious description of the principles of communion already present, as it were, from below. For Yannaras, *Torah* is analogous to principles of aesthetics in art and music.[82] The law was given to Israel to identify and demarcate what it meant to participate in the life of the covenant community. Christ's fulfillment of the law is the full realization of love, through which the law is disclosed as thoroughly personal, indeed as a *person*, "the very person of Christ, the perfect image of God."[83]

The *telos* of the law therefore is love.[84] This *telos* of the law means that Christian faith and practice are not matters of positivistic legal observance. Instead, Christian faith and practice center on the communal life of the church and in particular on the Eucharistic meal, by which we participate in Christ's fulfillment of the law through self-giving love.[85] This embodied practice demonstrates that Christian anthropology is non-dualistic. "The distinction between soul and body," Yannaras notes, "is not an ontological distinction, like that between nature and person or between nature and energies; it does not relate to man's *being*, to his *mode of existence*."[86] The soul and the body are "distinct natural energies" of "the one human nature."[87]

Yannaras does not apply these observations to secular positive law, but he does address the role and nature of the church canons. Here he

78. Yannaras, *The Freedom of Morality*, 31.
79. Yannaras, *The Freedom of Morality*, 35.
80. Yannaras, *The Freedom of Morality*, 35.
81. Yannaras, *The Freedom of Morality*, 35–36.
82. Yannaras, *The Freedom of Morality*, 54.
83. Yannaras, *The Freedom of Morality*, 56.
84. Yannaras, *The Freedom of Morality*, 56.
85. Yannaras, *The Freedom of Morality*, 92–111.
86. Yannaras, *The Freedom of Morality*, 111.
87. Yannaras, *The Freedom of Morality*, 112.

interprets St. Paul's treatment of the law in terms of transcendence. He argues that, for Paul, the law is a form of separation leading to death, but that "[t]he cross of Christ, that ultimate consequence of the Law, the fulfillment of the curse and of death, is the end of the Law and transcendence of the Law."[88] The church canons, then, cannot be understood legalistically, in ways that suggest separation and death. Instead, the canons are ascetical principles that reflect "the ontology of the Church, the mode of existence within the church body."[89] They demonstrate, within the context of their times and places, the corporate ascetical disciplines required to transcend the passions that separate us from full participation in God's life. It is finally not through deontological rules but through "physical acts of asceticism, practical rejection of individuality, fasting, continence, freedom from the cares of the consumer, participation of the body in prayer and the labor of serving others"—the practices of the life of faith—that human persons become free from "subservience to natural necessity" and "confinement in existential individuality."[90]

5. Robert Spaemann: Law and Persons

Robert Spaemann is another philosophical theologian who has addressed freedom, virtue, and causality in a richly theological key. In his book *Persons*, Spaemann seeks to integrate a teleological and relational account of theological anthropology. Like Yannaras, Spaemann ties the nature of human "persons" to God's personal nature as Trinity. But while Yannaras, in the vein of the Cappadocian fathers, focuses on *relationality*, Spaemann, in the vein of Augustine and the Western doctors, focuses on knowledge, and particularly on self-knowledge.

"Persons," Spaemann notes, "are not something else the world contains, over and above inanimate objects, plants, animals, and human beings. But human beings are connected to everything else the world contains at a deeper level than other things to each other. That is what it means to say that they are persons."[91] Where Yannaras tends to see individuation as a product of the fall, however, Spaemann argues that individuation is part of any living organism's, and any person's, ontology: "The

---

88. Yannaras, *The Freedom of Morality*, 176.

89. Yannaras, *The Freedom of Morality*, 188.

90. Yannaras, *The Freedom of Morality*, 267.

91. Spaemann, *Persons*, 4.

coming-to-be of a new something, individuation, cannot be described as an emergent property. If drive, or pursuit, individuate experience, life cannot be comprehended as the *property* of an existent but only as it's *being*. 'Life is the being of living things'. Persons are living things, and their being is life, their individuation that of a living organism."[92] Indeed, for Spaemann, individual self-reflexivity demonstrates that materialist reductionism fails.

Nevertheless, for Spaemann, the ability to *transcend* individuality is a uniquely *human* quality among the creatures of the earth. "No beast reflects upon the fact that the world surrounding it is no more than its world, relative to it specific organization," he notes, and "[n]o beast thinks beyond the scope of its own surrounding world to conceive itself as simply a feature of some other animals world, a barrack meetings that are meaningless to itself."[93] Like Yannaras, Spaemann wishes to preserve God's freedom concerning creation, and to connect human persons to God's creative freedom. But Spaemann follows Aquinas in recognizing each individual human person as a "divine idea." The divine idea of a person is not in itself a person—"a human being is not called a person unless he or she exists outside God's mind, extra causum." This means, for Spaemann, that "[e]xistence carries with it the moment of sheer facticity, which cannot be got round, and which implies God's sheer creative freedom."[94] Yet this sheer facticity, this contingency of personal existence on God's creative gift, shows that self-knowledge requires a personal encounter with transcendence: "The reality of a human person and all its depth and complexity is accessible only to someone who invests something of himself or herself in the encounter. It is not the most impersonal, but the most personal observation that reveals most of what reality is in itself. It is one of those persistent prejudices of modern thought to think that the less subjective something is, the more objective."[95]

---

92. Spaemann, *Persons*, 43.

93. Spaemann, *Persons*, 64.

94. Spaemann, *Persons*, 71.

95. Spaemann, *Persons*, 89.

6. Synthesis: Reason, Virtue, Freedom, and the Relational Self

From this brief discussion of four contemporary philosophical theologians—Jean Porter, Stanley Hauerwas, Christos Yannaras, and Robert Spaemann—we can discern four themes that have always been important to the Christian tradition concerning human nature and law. Porter reflects streams of the tradition drawn from Aquinas and Aristotle. Hauerwas draws from some of those same streams but also adds the more critical perspective of the anabaptist witness. Yannaras develops ideas in some of the Greek fathers and Plato about human freedom and community. Spaemann represents the Augustinian perspective of self-reflection leading to self-transcendence. In these contemporary examples, then, we can see a microcosm of historical Christian thought about creation, natural law, and human nature: Greek-patristic, Augustinian, Thomistic, and pietist.[96]

First, Porter reminds us that creation is imbued with reason precisely because it is God's very good creation, and the reason of creation implies a concept of natural law and of attendant virtues. Some human dispositions and actions are good, right, and just, and some are ugly, destructive, and wrong, because the creation and its human creatures participate in the God who is creator. This concept of natural law, however, requires specifically theological and metaphysical claims about God, creation, and the relation between God and creation. In contrast to the "new" natural law theory, it cannot stand alone as a supposed deliverance of reason apart from a particular theological tradition.

Second, the life, death, and resurrection of Jesus Christ, as narrated in the Gospels, is central to any properly Christian concept of the virtues. Hauerwas cautions us that we learn the virtues by learning from Christ, not by making general observations about creation. To some degree, Hauerwas' anabaptist-influenced ethic stands in tension with Porter's version of Catholic natural law theory. But if Christ is the logic of creation—if, as chapter 4 of this book on method suggests, we only really see the human creature when we see Christ—then there is less distance between Porter

---

96. I do not mention the Magisterial Reformers here, who in their own way each also reflect these four streams of Christian thought about humanity, culture, and law. And, of course, the examples profiled here are only examples, to which many other important contemporary figures could be added. Further, all these theologians in their own ways draw from the foundational biblical narratives, which are rich sources of reflection about human nature and law. For more, see my *Law and Theology*.

and Hauerwas than might otherwise seem to be the case. To see Christ *is* to see creation as it is meant to be.[97]

Third, Yannaras examines the central question of human freedom. Human beings are free creatures. But because creation is rooted in God's being, a radically libertarian concept of human freedom fails. Freedom is living in accord with the goodness of the life we are given as creatures. Sin—the "fall" of humanity—is a refusal of our humanity. Law is not an arbitrary restriction imposed from above, but rather is a dynamic aspect of establishing a community that is able to live authentically human lives in a community of love.

Finally, Spaemann points us to the human subject as knower, in particular as a knower of him- or herself as an individual. To deny that this is a true kind of knowledge, as must be the case for any kind of materialistic reductionism, is to deny the self that is supposed to be making the denial—an absurdity. Yet, Spaemann does not offer a form of Cartesian solipsism because, like Yannaras, he understands the human self as a creature of the Triune God, made for communion. Self-knowledge requires self-transcendence. The self is only truly known in its encounter with other humans and with God. Spaemann's Augustinian focus on self-transcendence and encounter with the other allows us to connect his anthropology with Yannaras' communitarian account of freedom.

Porter and Hauerwas address the notion of natural law, and Yannaras begins to touch on positive law through his discussion of canon law.[98] In *Persons*, Spaemann does not address law, but we can add law to Spaemann's account as follows: law is a structure that supports the turn of the human subject out from itself towards the other. One self relates to another self, without denying the self and without damaging the other, via mediating structures that facilitate cooperation, communication, and mutual regard. Among these mediating structures is positive law. When these mediating structures work, it is because they partake in the structure of the divine being itself, the Trinitarian structure of perfect regard and love.

Consistent with the methodological perspective in chapter 4, this traditioned account of human persons and law offers a different, and superior, narrative to reductive neurolaw. It accounts for human subjectivity

97. See also Williams, *Christ the Heart of Creation.*

98. For a discussion of the difference between natural law and positive law and the development of these concepts in the Christian theological tradition, see my *Law and Theology.*

and relationality, and locates human relationships and cultural products, including positive law, within a framework of meaning—all achievements that reductive neurolaw cannot claim if it really is true to its reductionist method. Further, this traditioned account is not *contrary* to any claim of the natural sciences, provided the natural sciences are understood as a domain of knowledge in relation to a broader whole (as suggested by critical realism, other metaphysically realist but nonreductive episte-mologies, and by various forms of idealism). Nor does it require a kind of "intelligent design"/"God of the gaps" argument as is the case for the "new" natural law.

In fact, our traditioned narrative is *more consistent* with the natural sciences than reductive neurolaw in light of the "new Aristotelianism" in the contemporary analytic philosophy of science. If "laws of nature" are better thought of as "powers and capacities" than as deterministic rules, our neurobiology *enables*, but does not *determine* human actions. To reduce something to a deterministic rule is to elide the thing reduced. To relate something to a basic power or capacity is to enable it as something itself. While some of the new Aristotelian philosophers of science still bracket or reject final causes, and others opt for a kind of pantheistic Hegelian idealism, Christian theologians can suggest that our tradition has noted God as the source and end of nature's powers and capacities for thousands of years, and that we see no reason to opt for something less explanatory or more convoluted. This, at least, is a conversation about *human* goods, which is a conversation reductive neurolaw simply cannot entertain.

9

Law, Violence, and Original Sin

CHAPTERS 7 AND 8 articulate a vision of natural law proceeding from the transcendent source of God's being, which is love. This vision, we argue, is truer to the phenomena of human existence than rival theories.

One important hurdle for our theological account, however, remains. Our account so far has been vague about the distinction between natural law (or eternal law), divine commands, and positive law (or temporal law). This distinction surfaces the problem of the violence of the law. A command, whether a direct divine command or a command of human positive law, implies coercion. Even natural law, which reflects the divine commands that spoke creation into existence ("Let there be light!" Gen 1:3) can be viewed as coercive, in that no created thing (including any created person) has a say in whether it wants to be spoken into existence.

To break a legal command invokes a penalty. When Adam ate from the Tree of the Knowledge of Good and Evil, he broke the divine command and was expelled from the Garden. A person convicted of murder by the state is imprisoned, and in some parts of the world, could be executed. A person who is negligent or breaches a contract must pay damages in a civil judgment, with the threat of criminal contempt of court looming at least on the distant horizon if the judgment is not satisfied. Behind the benefits of the rule of law lie threats of force. Law, then, seems inescapably violent.

In fact, the violence of the law, particularly the retributive violence of the criminal law, is what motivates many neurolaw scholars to seek an alternative in neuroscience. It sounds more humane to suggest a therapeutic intervention than a prison sentence—and no doubt it *is* more humane for many kinds of crimes. A discussion of sentencing reform and restorative justice, however, could proceed without the far more radical step of dismissing moral accountability altogether before the bar of neuroscience. Yet the nagging question remains whether the seemingly elegant narrative of God, creation, and natural law is only a smokescreen for violence. In this respect, reductive neurolaw forces us to confront questions about power and violence raised for decades by critical legal theory from the historical margins of race, gender, and non-traditional sexual orientation.

This final chapter suggests that these concerns are addressed (not solved, but at least addressed) by the Christian doctrines of sin and redemption, and indeed that a focus on law in relation to human nature sheds important light on the contested and difficult doctrine of "original" sin. Christian teaching about sin and redemption shows why authentic law is a gift of love, not an imposition of violence, and thereby highlights why the new Aristotelianism in the philosophy of science needs notions of formal and final causes.

1. Law and Violence

In "nature red in tooth and claw," it seems that "law" is a function of power and violence. An argument for any form of "natural law" therefore must grapple with the problem of originary violence. Is the *origin* of law found in power and violence or cooperation and peace? In the earthly city, it seems, positive law *always* finally implies violence. Chairman Mao once quipped that "political power grows out of the barrel of a gun."[1] On the first day of law school, my constitutional law professor, distinguished federal appellate Judge John J. Gibbons, introduced me to the study of law

---

1. "Problems of War and Strategy" (November 6, 1938), Selected Works, Vol. II, 224, available at http://www.marxists.org/reference/archive/mao/selected-works/volume-2/mswv2_12.htm. In this text, Mao argued that a proletariat revolution could not occur in China without an armed struggle against Japanese imperialism. He further noted that "[o]ur principle is that the Party commands the gun, and the gun must never be allowed to command the party." Thus, even Mao recognized that violence cannot comprise the fundamental principle of society.

with this quote, and I do the same with my constitutional law students. Judge Gibbons' purpose was to contrast the arbitrary rule of power from the rule of law. It was a masterful lesson: a *polis* grounded in commonly held constitutional legal principles functions by reason and not by power.

This is not only true of extreme cases. One thing practicing lawyers learn quickly that is not taught in law school is that a victory in court in a civil case does not automatically translate into money in the bank. The court issues a judgment, which in itself is just a piece of paper with some text requiring one party to pay the other the amount awarded. That paper in itself has no inherent value. There is money in the bank only if the judgment is executed upon and the responsible party transfers funds or assets in full or partial satisfaction of the judgment. The case is not really over when the final judgment is issued: the money still must be paid or collected.[2]

The reason why parties comply with judgments finally is coercive power. Failure to comply with a court order can lead to sanctions for contempt of court, which may include fines, seizure of assets by armed U.S. Marshalls, or jail time. Of course, many, perhaps most, civil litigants routinely comply with judgments without direct threat of contempt sanctions. We might attribute this to the social contract through which parties bring their disputes before a constitutionally appointed judge for a decision under the rule of law. But a judgment's final inherent value—and the reason why judgments can often be used as security for third-party transactions—lies in what stands behind the paper: the power of the U.S. federal government.

Sometimes judgments remain unsatisfied because the losing party lacks sufficient assets from which the judgment could be paid. And, of course, some parties game the system by using corporate law and other means to render themselves judgment proof. But even here, the coercive power of the law is evident: the *winning* party cannot lawfully extract the judgment's value from an insolvent or defaulting party through revenge killings, beat-downs, cement loafers, or other forms of self-help commonly employed by organized crime gangs. To do so is to risk arrest and incarceration by armed government police forces. Of course, the law's

---

2. A judgment also may have value if it can be used as security for a loan or other transaction involving a third party. Even in such cases, the value of the judgment as an asset inheres only in the probability that the amounts finally will be collected.

coercive power is even more immediately evident in criminal cases. No one does jail time only because of a social contract.[3]

Experiences such as these make us wonder whether Judge Gibbons' real purpose in offering the quote from Mao was more subtle than an easy contrast between totalitarianism and constitutional democracy. *Even in a constitutional democracy*, political authority is finally secured by the barrel of a gun. The constitutional social contract in itself is a thin veil that is easily torn. Many citizens refuse the terms of the social contract and live outside the bounds of the law.

Some Christian theologians criticize the liberal notion of constitutional democracy and the social contract itself, on theological grounds, and argue for forms of Christian socialism or other types of governmental structures.[4] But even under such structures—indeed, perhaps even more so—the peace that is the goal of the governmental form must be secured by the force of law. There is no form of earthly *polis* in which the law is entirely consensual. Human experience tells us that some will *not* desire the peace of the city. Scripture and tradition tell us the same. There is no earthly city without a police power.

2. Law, Force, and Absence

Jacques Derrida has noted that the language of the law is inherently violent. In his essay *Force of the Law: The "Mystical Foundation of Authority,"* Derrida notes that the phrase "to enforce the law" reminds us that "law is always an authorized force, a force that justifies itself or is justified in applying itself, even if this justification may be judged from elsewhere to be unjust or unjustifiable."[5] Indeed, Derrida argues, "there is no such thing

---

3. This is not to suggest that the prison system in the United States functions effectively. Strict mandatory sentencing guidelines for non-violent offenses, the disproportionate number incarcerated of young African-American men, and the perverse incentives of the prison-industrial complex raise numerous issues about the function of prisons in contemporary culture. See, e.g., The Sentencing Project, "Facts about Prisons and People in Prison" (Jan. 2014), available athttp://sentencingproject.org/doc/publications/inc_Facts%20About%20Prisons.pdf. Nevertheless, very few informed commentators argue that incarceration should be eliminated for *every* class of offender (say, violent sex offenders or mass murderers). In any event, whatever sort of rehabilitative program might be suggested in place of prison, such programs must at some point be mandatory and thus backed by coercion and force.

4. See, e.g., Milbank, *Theology and Social Theory*.

5. Derrida, "Force of the Law."

as law (*droit*) that doesn't imply *in itself, a priori, in the analytic structure of its concept,* the possibility of being 'enforced,' applied by force."[6] Derrida asks in this essay a perennial question for the rule of law: how is the force or violence of the law distinguished from violence that is unjust?

Derrida's essay was written in French but delivered at an American law school in an English translation.[7] He playfully notes the irony that his contractual agreement to deliver the essay as a keynote address in a symposium on law and deconstruction required—forced—him to use a language that was not his native tongue. This very act of translation, with its inevitable changes in nuance and idiom, fails to do justice to the original text. In the same way, legal concepts often lose the force of their meaning in translation.

A basic example, for Derrida, is the German term *Gewalt*.[8] In English and French, the term is often translated "violence," but in the German idiom it also signifies "legitimate power, authority, public force," including *Gesetzegebende Gewalt* (legislative power), *Geistliche Gewalt* (the spiritual power of the church), and *Staatsgewalt* (the authority of the state).[9] But what is the difference between bare *Gewalt* and legitimate *Gewalt*? The modifiers "legislative," "church," and "state" represent institutions that at some time came into being and claimed legitimate power through some act of "originary violence."[10] What transmutes unjust originary violence into justified authority?

Derrida refers here to one of Pascal's *Pensées*: "Justice, force.—It is just that what is just should be obeyed; it is necessary that what is strongest should be followed."[11] There is no justice, Derrida concludes, without force; and the compulsion to follow arises from the strength of the force applied rather than anything inherent in the law.[12] "Justice," then is merely a word applied to the strong. Derrida again quotes Pascal: "And so, since it was not possible to make the just strong, the strong have been made just."[13]

---

6. Derrida, "Force of the Law," 925.

7. Derrida, "Force of the Law," 920.

8. Derrida, "Force of the Law," 927.

9. Derrida, "Force of the Law," 927.

10. Derrida, "Force of the Law," 927.

11. Derrida, "Force of the Law," 935 (quoting Pascal, *Pensées*, ¶298).

12. Derrida, "Force of the Law," 935, 937.

13. Derrida, "Force of the Law," (quoting Pascal, *Pensées*, ¶298).

But if justice is only power, why do people ever obey the law, rather than living in perpetual revolt? Derrida refers to another of Pascal's Penseés, which refers in turn to Montaigne's concepts of custom and equity. Pascal seems at first to suggest that there is indeed a transcendent source of justice: "Justice without might is helpless; might without justice is tyrannical. Justice without might is gainsaid, because there are always offenders; might without justice is condemned."[14] But Pascal immediately notes that "justice" seems impossible to define and quickly devolves to power:

> Justice is subject to dispute; might is easily recognised and is not disputed. So we cannot give might to justice, because might has gainsaid justice and has declared that it is she herself who is just. And thus, being unable to make what is just strong, we have made what is strong just.[15]

For Pascal, the notion of "natural law" offers no succor:

> Men admit that justice does not consist in these customs, but that it resides in natural laws, common to every country. They would certainly maintain it obstinately, if reckless chance which has distributed human laws had encountered even one which was universal; but the farce is that the caprice of men has so many vagaries that there is no such law. Theft, incest, infanticide, parricide, have all had a place among virtuous actions. Can anything be more ridiculous than that a man should have the right to kill me because he lives on the other side of the water, and because his ruler has a quarrel with mine, though I have none with him?[16]

Finally, Pascal says, the foundation of authority is "mystical" and cannot be reduced to first principles:

> The result of this confusion is that one affirms the essence of justice to be the authority of the legislator; another, the interest of the sovereign; another, present custom, and this is the most sure. Nothing, according to reason alone, is just itself; all changes with time. Custom creates the whole of equity, for the simple reason that it is accepted. It is the mystical foundation of

---

14. Pascal, *Penseés*, ¶294.
15. Pascal, *Penseés*, ¶298.
16. Pascal, *Penseés*, ¶298.

its authority; whoever carries it back to first principles destroys it.[17]

Derrida notes that in this paragraph on the mystical foundation of authority, Pascal is referencing Montaigne.[18] Montaigne, Derrida points out, referred to the "legitimate fictions" of the law "on which it founds the truth of its justice."[19] Derrida finds a distinction between Pascal and Montaigne. The heart of the problem, for Pascal, is sin: "There are, no doubt, natural laws; but this fine thing called reason has corrupted everything," Pascal says, and further "Our justice comes to nothing before divine justice."[20] But it is possible, says Derrida, to "set aside the functional mechanism of the Pascalian critique, if we dissociate it from Christian pessimism," and to find in Montaigne "the basis for a modern critical philosophy" of law and justice.[21] For Derrida, the mystical authority of justice derives from performativity.[22] The discourse of "law" itself possesses a mystical performative power from which it derives its force.

Because law is founded in a mystical performative power, for Derrida, law is always subject to deconstruction.[23] This may be a "stroke of luck for politics, and for all historical progress," Derrida suggests, for law then is infinitely malleable.[24] But the paradox, he argues, is that justice in itself, "outside or beyond law," is not deconstructible because justice is itself a performative act of deconstruction.[25] That is, "Deconstruction is justice."[26] As a mystical event, justice simply presents itself to us as "an experience of the impossible." "It is just that there be

17. Pascal, Penseés, ¶298.

18. Derrida, "Force of Law," 939 (citing Pascal, Penseés ¶94 and Montaigne, Essais III, XIII, De l'expérience).

19. Derrida, "Force of Law," 939.

20. Derrida, "Force of Law," 939 (quoting Pascal, Penseés ¶294 and 233 ("The finite is annihilated in the presence of the infinite, and becomes a pure nothing. So our spirit before God, so our justice before divine justice").

21. Derrida, "Force of Law," 941.

22. Derrida, "Force of Law," 943.

23. Derrida, "Force of Law," 943. Derrida states that "[t]he structure I am describing here is a structure in which law (droit) is essentially deconstructible, whether because it is founded, constructed on interpretable and transformable textual strata (and that is the history of law (droit), its possible and necessary transformation, and sometimes its amelioration), or because its ultimate foundation is by definition unfounded."

24. Derrida, "Force of Law," 943, 945.

25. Derrida, "Force of Law," 945.

26. Derrida, "Force of Law," 945.

law," Derrida says, "but justice is incalculable, it requires us to calculate with the incalculable; and aporetic experiences are the experiences, as improbable as they are necessary, of justice; that is to say of moments in which the decision between just and unjust is never insured by a rule."[27] The experience of law and justice, for Derrida as well as Pascal, is an experience of absence.

3. Biopolitics in the State of Exception

In the Auschwitz death camp there is a room in Cell Block 11 containing a long table and several chairs. When the camp was in operation, a Gestapo judge sat at the table hearing cases against prisoners charged with "serious" crimes, such as attempted escape or political subversion. At one end of the courtyard outside Cell Block 11 stands a brick wall, still pockmarked with bullet holes, against which those condemned by the judge were executed.[28]

None of those "tried" in the Auschwitz court had the benefit of representation by counsel. There are no published law codes or judicial precedents specifying any rules of due process or substantive limitations on judicial power. There is no record of any acquittals.

Not all the inmates of Auschwitz-Birkenau, of course, appeared before the Getsapo court—indeed, the vast majority never received any judicial process. Many, particularly the very young or old, the sick and infirm, were sorted for the gas chambers immediately upon debarking the train inside the gates of Birkenau. Others were gassed after some time working in the camp factories. Many died of exhaustion and disease, and still others were summarily executed by their guards. At Auschwitz-Birkenau alone, about a million people died in this fashion, without even a false veneer of law.[29]

So why is there a court room in Cell Block 11? Why were some prisoners put through show trials before they were executed?

Theologian Miroslav Volf tells the story of his involuntary service in the Yugoslavian military and his interrogation by his commander,

27. Derrida, "Force of Law," 947.

28. A photograph of the execution wall is available at the U.S. Holocaust Museum, http://www.ushmm.org/wlc/en/media_ph.php?ModuleId=10005189&MediaId=752.

29. See *Auschwitz: Inside the Nazi State*, available at http://www.pbs.org/auschwitz/40–45/killing/; U.S. Holocaust Museum, Holocaust Encyclopedia, "Auschwitz," available at http://www.ushmm.org/wlc/en/article.php?ModuleId=10005189.

"Captain G."[30] Volf was accused of serving as a CIA spy and of subverting the communist regime because he had married an American and studied theology. He was threatened with eight years in prison at the hands of a military tribunal. As a soldier, he was not entitled to legal counsel. "To be accused was to be condemned," he recalls, "and to be condemned was to be ruined . . . unless I confessed."[31] After many weeks of this practice, Volf's interrogations abruptly ended. Why was Volf never tried?

History offers countless other examples of such summary justice, and untold multitudes have suffered similar abuse without any historical memory. It seems that powerful human beings need to cloak their violence against the powerless with a simulacrum of judicial process.

In his book *Homo Sacer*, Italian political philosopher Giorgio Agamben observes that in the state of exception the law is "suspended."[32] When faced with a perceived threat or emergency, the sovereign declares a "state of exception" under which the ordinary rules of procedure, evidence, and judgment no longer apply. In the state of exception there is no law but the will of the sovereign, and thus there is no "law" at all.

Agamben highlights the problem of the relation between constituting and constituted power. Constituted power is that which is exercised with an existing state/juridical framework. Constituting power is that which legitimates the state/juridical framework in the first instance.[33] Agamben suggests that the problem of constitutive power "is increasingly dismissed as a prejudice or a merely factual matter," creating a circularity by which the problem of legitimate power simply is referred to a constitutional document, which hangs in mid-air.[34] The fundamental problem, he argues, is metaphysical: what is the relation between potentiality (the possibility of constituting law) and actuality (law as constituted). "Until a new and coherent ontology of potentiality . . . has replaced the ontology founded on the primacy of actuality and its relation to potentiality," he argues, "a political theory freed form the aporias of sovereignty remains unthinkable."[35]

30. Volf, *The End of Memory*.

31. Volf, *The End of Memory*, 3.

32. Agamben, *Homo Sacer*.

33. Agamben, *Homo Sacer* § 3.1, 39–40.

34. Agamben, *Homo Sacer* § 3.1, 40.

35. Agamben, *Homo Sacer* § 3.2, 44.

Agamben demonstrates that this problem of constituting and constituted power is a manifestation of the Aristotelian relationship between potentiality and act, *dynamis* and *energia*.[36] How, if at all, is potentiality different from act? Potentiality in the Aristotelian sense, Agamben argues, is the ability not to do or be: "'Every potentiality is impotentiality of the same and with respect to the same'" or "'What is potential can both be and not be.'"[37] This means that when potentiality passes into act, that which is potential "sets aside its own potential not to be (its *adynamia*)."[38] Therefore, it is through potentiality that "Being founds itself *sovereignly*," for the passage to actuality implies the sovereign freedom not to be or act.[39] This means that constituting power is never exhausted by constituted power. Sovereign power can remain in reserve, as un-given potentiality.[40] As Conor Cunningham notes, Agamben plays on the voluntarist notion of *potentia dei absoluta*.[41]

Agamben then explores the figure of *homo sacer*, the person in Roman law placed under the sacred ban. The *homo sacer* was not subject to execution by the state, but neither was it a crime of homicide for anyone to kill him. This placed the *homo sacer* paradoxically both under and outside the law. The same dynamic, Agamben notes, obtained in the Germanic *wargus*, the "werewolf," who is banned from the city and its law.[42] Agamben defines this as the origin of politics: "[n]ot simple natural life, but life exposed to death (bare life or sacred life) is the originary political element."[43]

---

36. Agamben, *Homo Sacer* § 3.3, 44–48. For a critique of Agamben on this point, see Cunningham, "Nihilism and Theology." Cunningham argues that Agamben seeks "to develop his constructive, demonic, nihilism (after all, the Devil wants a kingdom, so there is no point in going all napalm on us), by way of reinterpreting Aristotle's division of actuality and potentiality. He does this in a bid to 'decreate' us."

37. Agamben, *Homo Sacer* § 3.3, 44–48 (quoting Aristotle, *Metaphysics* 1046a, 32; 1050b, 10).

38. Agamben, *Homo Sacer* § 3.3, 46. This is how Agamben construes Aristotle's statement that "[a] thing is said to be potential if, when the act of which it is said to be potential is realized, there will be nothing im-potential (that is, there will be nothing able not to be)." Agamben, *Homo Sacer* § 3.3, 45 (quoting Aristotle, *Metaphysics*, 1047a, 24–26).

39. Agamben, *Homo Sacer* § 3.3., 45.

40. Agamben, *Homo Sacer* § 3.3, 46.

41. Cunningham, "Nihilism and Theology," 325–44.

42. Agamben, *Homo Sacer* § 6.1, 104–5.

43. Agamben, *Homo Sacer* § 4.1, 88.

Agamben thereby deconstructs the Hobbseian response to the state of nature: the city and its laws do not limit the violence of the state of nature, but rather the state of nature exists within the city, in the human condition of bare life, through which the citizen may become *homo sacer/ wolf-man* in the state of exception.[44] The potential of the state of exception, moreover, bears within it the potential for the dissolution of the city itself: "[t]he transformation into a werewolf corresponds perfectly to the state of exception, during which (necessarily limited) time the city is dissolved and men enter into a zone in which they are no longer distinct from beasts."[45] Thus, "[t]he state of nature is, in truth, a state of exception, in which the city appears for an instant (which is at the same time a chronological interval and a nontemporal moment) *tanquam disoluta*."[46]

The paradigm of this dynamic, Agamben argues, is the concentration camp. In the camp, the governing "law" is pure biopolitics, the assertion of power over the body, as evidenced vividly in the gruesome Nazi medical experiments on inmates.[47] "The camp," Agamben says, "was also the most absolute biopolitical space ever to have been realized, in which power confronts nothing but pure life, without any mediation."[48] "Law" and "fact" become indistinguishable in the camp: the fact of bare life is law.[49] And as Western politics have come to define humanity in terms of bare life, to perpetuate the state of exception, and thereby to declare all persons not persons but rather *homo sacer* and *wargus*, the camp has superseded the city as our basic political paradigm.[50]

Agamben does not resolve this aporia, but he concludes with an appeal to reconstitute Western metaphysics.[51] As Graham Ward has noted, Agamben makes use of Pauline thinking about the person, about faith and love, "but there is no analysis of the third in the Pauline trilogue of virtues—hope."[52]

The Christian concept of hope finally is eschatological. For eschatological hope, "the end is like the beginning." This means the original

44. Agamben, *Homo Sacer* § 4.1, 88.

45. Agamben, *Homo Sacer* § 6.2, 107.

46. Agamben, *Homo Sacer* § 6.3, 109.

47. Agamben, *Homo Sacer* § 6.5, 154–59.

48. Agamben, *Homo Sacer* § 7.3, 171.

49. Agamben, *Homo Sacer* § 7.3, 170.

50. Agamben, *Homo Sacer*, 181.

51. Agamben, *Homo Sacer*, 188.

52. Ward, *The Politics of Discipleship*, 179.

beginning has somehow been lost. Prior to modern evolutionary science, Christian theology referred to the doctrine of the fall to account for this loss.

In chapter 5, we noted that the story of human beginnings is a story of deep time. It is now clear—unless we wish to adopt the epistemology of the young-earth creationists—that selfishness, death, and violence characterized "nature" for many billions of years prior to the emergence of "humans" and for the four million years or so of "human" evolutionary history prior to the emergence of *homo sapiens sapiens*. Indeed, a leading introduction to the modern philosophy of biology bears the title "Sex and Death," an apt summary of the brute facts of evolution.[53]

In our theological narrative, however, law is not merely something that epiphenomenally emerges from the evolutionary soup of brain chemistry. Law is in some sense a given property of the universe, and is in some sense a constituent element of the human soul, present in our created goodness, prevenient in our fallenness, perfected in our resurrection with Christ. Law is part of the origin of each person's form—of each person's soul. In chapter 5, we did not try to connect the "cultural explosion" in recent human evolutionary history with any details of the Genesis creation accounts, but we did suggest that the connections between language, writing, and positive law may provide a way of understanding what it means to be human persons. We now refer to a patristic source who is particularly helpful in our effort to develop this account: Athanasius.

4. Law, the Origin of the Soul, and Original Sin: Athanasius

In Athanasius we see a connection between the divine ideas, human ontology, and law. The human fall away from the divine pattern was a fall away from the law of love. Christ restores human nature by restoring the law of love.

The pattern of Genesis 2 suggests that God created the soul of Adam ("the breath of life") and imprints on Adam's soul the law of the Garden ("you shall not eat of it"). This pattern is discussed in St. Athanasius' *On the Incarnation*.[54] Athanasius notes that all of creation is God's good gift.

---

53. Sterelny and Griffiths, *Sex and Death*.

54. Athanasius, *On the Incarnation of the Word*.

Human beings, however, we given additional gifts: God made them in his image and "[gave] them a share of the power of his own Word, so that having as it were shadows of the Word and being made rational, they might be able to abide in blessedness, living the true life which is really that of the holy ones in paradise." But because of their rational nature, human beings were given a power to choose whether to live in accordance with this gift of life. The Garden and the law were therefore given to provide the means for human beings to choose to live in accordance with the grace of reason:

> And knowing again that free choice of human beings could turn either way, he secured beforehand, by a law and a set place, the grace given. For bringing them into his own paradise, he gave them a law, so that if they guarded the grace and remained good, they might have the life of paradise—without sorrow, pain or care—besides having the promise of their incorruptibility in heaven . . . .[55]

But when human beings turned against God and transgressed the law, they lost the gift of incorruptibility and were returned to their "natural state," which in fact dissolved them as "human":

> For the transgression of the commandment returned them to the natural state, so that, just as they, not being, came to be, so also they might rightly endure in time the corruption unto non-being. For if, having a nature that did not once exist, they were called into existence by the Word's advent [*parousia*] and love for human beings, it followed that when human beings were bereft of the knowledge of God and had turned to things which exist not—evil is non-being, the good is being, since it has come into being from the existing God—then they were bereft also of eternal being.[56]

The fall as a turn from the law, then, for Athanasius, produced an ontological change in the human person precisely in the loss of direct and full participation in God's eternal being secured by the law in the Garden. The loss of the law in the Garden reduces the human being towards non-being:

> But this, being decomposed, is to remain in death and corruption. For the human being is by nature mortal, having come

---

55. Athanasius, *On the Incarnation of the Word* § 1.3.

56. Athanasius, *On the Incarnation of the Word* § 1.4.

into being from nothing. But because of his likeness to the One who Is, which, if he had guarded through his comprehension of him, would have blunted his natural corruption, he would have remained incorruptible, just as Wisdom says: "Attention to the laws is the confirmation of incorruptibility" (Wis 6:18).[57]

As Athanasius suggests, the Garden is symbolic of the potentially harmonious relations between humans and God, humans and non-human creation, and among all humans with each other. But Adam's sin resulted in his expulsion from the Garden, and the Cherubim with flaming swords bar the way back. Judicially, then, Adam has been placed outside the law. This is his curse, his sentence for lawbreaking.

Outside the Garden, of course, Adam and his heirs remain accountable to the law and can still hear God's commands. This is evident in Cain's murder of Abel. Cain is banished in punishment for his crime, but God pronounces a law of protection over Cain: "anyone who kills Cain will suffer vengeance seven times over."[58] Yet Cain was capable of murder because the law was no longer constitutive of his soul in the way possible only in the Garden. The law had become something at least partially external, at least partially inaccessible. He became alienated from the law, in a state of exception. His knowledge of the law remained—he knew murder was evil—but his power to keep the law failed.

This separation is symbolized by the cherubim and flaming swords that bar access to the Tree of Life (Gen 3:24). The Tree of Life is the pure law of love. To eat from the Tree of Life is to take the law of love into the soul, to nourish the soul. As the fruit of the Tree of Life metabolized into the body (we are speaking metaphorically here, of course), the law pervades a person's being, body and soul. Without the Tree of Life, a person may know the difference between good and evil, but doing the good is a struggle, and indeed the tendency is away from the good. When eating of the Tree of Life, the soul is so joined to the pure law of love that the law is ecstatic delight.[59]

---

57. Athanasius, *On the Incarnation of the Word* § 1.4.

58. Gen 4:15.

59. The Tree of Life, Wisdom, and Torah are linked in Jewish tradition. See Proverbs 3:13–18; "Torah: The Tree of Life," available at https://reformjudaism.org/torah-tree-life; "Etz Chayim: The Tree of Life in the Bible and Beyond," available at https://www.chabad.org/parshah/article_cdo/aid/2277982/jewish/Etz-Chayim-The-Tree-of-Life-in-the-Bible-and-Beyond.htm.

We, as Adam's heirs, are born outside the law. But as gift, law continually presents itself to us without coercion or violence. The Tree of the Knowledge of Good and Evil was not locked behind a wall that had to be breached, nor was it surrounded by armed Cherubim. It was, rather, at the center of the Garden, open and accessible. The most severe penalty, of course, was attached to God's command not to eat: death. Yet here God's perlocutionary act of uttering the command and delineating its penalty—of establishing "law"—was inseparable from the gift of justice which flowed from God's being. There was no distinction between "justice" and "law," for the gift of "life" is participation in the life of God. To refuse participation in God's life by equating the self with God is to engage in the absurd performance of death. The act, therefore, is its own penalty, and not something externally imposed by force of will. It is self-chosen, self-imposed, an exile of the self from the self as created from God's ecstatic generosity.

It is sometimes suggested by Eastern Orthodox scholars that the East retained a higher view of post-lapsarian human capacities and individual human responsibility than the parts of the Western tradition that have been deeply influenced by Augustine.[60] That may be true, but as noted above, even for Athanasius the fall produced an ontological change in that the human person is no longer constituted by the Garden and the law. It is not the sort of change that appears in the paleontological or genetic record of human evolution, but it is rather a loss of direct participation in the life of God. As Athanasius stated: "[b]ut human beings, turning away from things eternal and by the counsel of the devil turning towards things of corruption, were themselves the cause of corruption in death, being, as we already said, corruptible by nature but escaping their natural state by the grace of participation in the Word, had they remained good."[61]

60. See, e.g., Harrison, "The Human Person as Image and Likeness of God." Bishop Kallistos Ware (*The Orthodox Way*, 62) states that:

> For the Orthodox theological tradition . . . Adam's original sin affects the human race in its entirety. . . . But does it also imply an inherited guilt? Here Orthodoxy is more guarded. Original sin is not to be interpreted in juridical or quasi-biological terms, as if it were some physical "taint" of guilt, transmitted through sexual intercourse. This picture, which normally passes for the Augustinian view, is unacceptable to Orthodoxy. The doctrine of original sin means rather that we are born into an environment where it is easy to do evil and hard to do good; easy to hurt others, and hard to heal their wounds; easy to arouse men's suspicions, and hard to win their trust.

61. Athanasius, *On the Incarnation of the Word*, § 2.1.

This sense of ontological change in Athanasius' account of the fall is richly teleological. Humans were made to grow in participation in the life of God, but by sin they have moved in the direction of dissolution. In fact, he says, "the race of human beings would have been utterly dissolved had not the Master and Savior of all, the Son of God, come for the completion of death."[62] Moreover, although human beings were expelled from the Garden, God did not leave sinful humanity entirely bereft of law: "since the negligence of humans descended gradually to lower things, God again anticipated such weakness of theirs, sending the law and the prophets, known to them, so that if they shrank from looking up to the heavens and knowing the Creator, they might have instruction from those close by."[63] The law and prophets were sent not only for the Jews, but for all of humanity: "they were for the whole inhabited world a sacred school of the knowledge of God and the soul."[64] Nevertheless, humans remained "irrational" and "did not raise their gaze to the truth" of the law.[65]

For this reason God sent Christ: "what should be done, except to renew again the 'in the image,' so that through it human beings would be able once again to know him? But how could this have occurred except by the coming of the very image of God, our Savior Jesus Christ?" But to state this in such a diachronic fashion is not entirely true to Athanasius' sense of God's continual presence in creation through Christ: "For the Word unfolded himself everywhere, above and below and in the depths and in the breadth: above, in creation; below, in the incarnation; in the depths, in hell; in breadth, in the world. Everything is filled with the knowledge of God."[66] The presence of the Word in all of creation and all of history is an aspect of providence:

> And, as being in all creation, he is in essence outside everything
> but inside everything by his own power, arranging everything,
> and unfolding his own providence in everything to all things,
> and giving life to each thing and to all things together, contain-
> ing the universe and not being contained, but being wholly, in
> every respect, in his own Father alone. So also, being in the hu-
> man body, and himself giving it life, he properly gives life to the
> universe also, and was both in everything and outside all. And

62. Athanasius, *On the Incarnation of the Word*, § 2.9.

63. Athanasius, *On the Incarnation of the Word*, § 3.12.

64. Athanasius, *On the Incarnation of the Word*, § 3.12.

65. Athanasius, *On the Incarnation of the Word*, § 3.12.

66. Athanasius, *On the Incarnation of the Word*, § 3.16.

being made known from the body through the works, he was not unseen even from the working of the universe.[67]

Athanasius' account of the fall, then, while it does involve judicial-legal categories, is also an ontological account grounded in relationality.

5. Law, Participation, and Grace

If the fall is a fall away from the law, are we saved by returning to the law and keeping it? The answer in the Pauline theology of the New Testament, and in the Christian tradition as it developed in both the East and West, is no. Because of the ontological effects of sin, we cannot keep the law. We do not have libertarian freedom. As we are, we are bound to the powers of sin and death. But the powers of sin and death are not powers or capacities of our created nature. They are not our proper *telos*. They are a corruption, a lawlessness, not a law. The powers of sin and death are a suspension, an incursion—and they have been defeated by Christ.

We are then, as humanity in Christ, free to return to the law of love. But this freedom, for Porter, Hauerwas, Yannaras, and Spaemann, as well as for Paul, Athanasius, Augustine, and Aquinas, is not just a libertarian, voluntarist freedom to choose this or that. To be human is to be able to know the source and end of the self, and thereby to know that one *is* known by God. To be "free" is to be "human," to be "know fully as I am known" (1 Cor 13:12), to find life, fellowship, and love in God.[68] The truly "natural" law—the law of love, the law of the Garden—is the receipt of the gift of life from God who creates, redeems, and fulfills human "being" in Christ.

This *telos* supplies what is missing from neo-Aristotelian accounts of natural powers and capacities and their relationship to ethics. "Love" is not an emergent property of pre-existing matter. Love is the *reason* for matter, the reason for creation. Love is a power and capacity donated by God, who *is* love, which enables human action. To act in accordance with the law of love is to act in a way that is authentically and freely human. The divine commands and the human positive law can nudge us in the direction of the law of love. But the law of love is realized, fulfilled, and made human in the true Adam, Christ, who is the hope of history, the hope of our return from the state of exception.

---

67. Athanasius, *On the Incarnation of the Word*, § 3.17.

68. See Schindler, *The Perfection of Freedom* (noting that "our current conception of freedom is deeply problematic" because it focuses on means rather than on ends).

Conclusion

IN THIS BOOK I have argued that "law" is a constituent element of human nature. Law is embedded in our material nature but also transcends it and points to something beyond ourselves. The capacity to formulate positive law is unique to humans among all the creatures of the earth. Some other creatures can construct fascinating systems of social discipline, but none can formulate codes or institutions of positive law. The human capacity for lawmaking is different in kind from any similar capacity in other animals—or at least, it is so different in degree that it is essentially different in kind.

The paleoanthropological record suggests that this kind of cultural capacity did not arise before the very recent cultural explosion among anatomically modern humans, and the historical record suggests that positive law developed at the dawn of systems of writing in the ancient Near East. The Bible's second creation narrative in Genesis 2 in this sense is consistent with the paleoanthropological and historical evidence: it was to Adam, to humans, and not to the other animals, that God gave the primal command not to eat from the Tree of the Knowledge of Good and Evil. This command marks the historical beginning of humanity and identifies the elusive "historical Adam," not as an individual genetic progenitor, but as a community standing before, under, and within the law. The human record of positive law demonstrates both our capacity for transcendence and our failure to achieve the ideal of the law of love—that is, both our original goodness and our original sin.

In contrast to this theological narrative, I have traced a theme in contemporary Western jurisprudence that seeks identify "law" with neuroscience, called "neurolaw." Some neurolaw scholars argue that "law," like everything else we think of as "mind" or "consciousness," is merely an epiphenomenon of brain processes shaped by evolution. This trend, I have argued, reflects the efforts of legal positivists who, since the nineteenth century, have sought to elide concepts of transcendence from jurisprudence and to render positive law as a kind of quantifiable science. If the neurolawyers are right, the *adam*—the humanity—I think I have found in the law is just another ghost in the machine.

But legal positivism, I have suggested, is itself part of a deeper flow of the intellectual currents of modernity, which have at their headwaters a number of assumed and usually unexamined metaphysical claims. In the chapter 4, I explored the question of method in "theology and science," and argued for a method that refuses to bracket such metaphysical questions. I claimed, in fact, that the metaphysical assumptions of Christian theology—that the Triune God revealed in the incarnate Christ is the transcendent creator of the cosmos—make better sense of the phenomena of human persons, including both our deep evolutionary history and our remarkably recent capacity for cultural institutions such as positive law, than materialist explanations.

The doctrine of the Trinity, Christology, and a proper understanding of God's relationship to creation, I have suggested, are essential to understand the idea of natural law. In our efforts to formulate what we mean by the claim that God is Triune, we see that the divine *hypostases* are delimited by love, which flows from their mutual indwelling in the one divine *ousia*. The order of God's being is an order of love, and from this order flows the order of creation, which, as given, is not a necessary order but a contingent order defined in its particulars by God' free, gracious decision to create. As God's free, contingent act of creation participates in his eternal, unchanging being, so God's contingent, historical commands to the human creatures prepared to hear them participate in God's eternal law of love. As God's act of creation was not a moment "in time" but rather encompassed and encompasses the generation *of* time, so God's creation of Adam is not a definable moment in the paleoanthropological or genetic record but rather is the generation of a new kind of being in relationship to God through the reception of the divine command embodying the law of love.

The record of human history, though it includes love, is not in its essence a record of love. We are alienated from the law of love and live in a state of exception under which the rule of the law of love seems suspended. It is here, I have argued, that robust Christology is required. The *true* Adam, the Adam we *can* identify in recorded history, is Christ. Christ fulfilled the law of love through his incarnation, life, and atoning death on the cross, and Christ inaugurated his reign under the law of love through his resurrection. Only in Christ can we know that the first Adam, the Adam lost to us in the complex history of human evolution, truly existed, because we can know the second Adam who brings humanity to its completion by fulfilling the law of love. In reductive neurolaw we see the end of the law, that is, the dissolution of "law" as any kind of thing. In Christian theology, I have argued, we see the true end of the law, that is, the culmination of the powers and potentialities of creation, including those of human persons, in the embrace of God's eternal perichoretic love.

Bibliography

Abruzzi, William S. "Ecological Theory and the Evolution of Complex Human Communities." *Advances in Human Ecology* 5 (1996) 111–56.

Adams, Marilyn McCord. "Ockham on Will, Nature, and Morality." In *The Cambridge Companion to Ockham*, edited by Paul Vincent Spade, 245–72. Cambridge: Cambridge University Press, 1999.

Adams, Nicholas, George Pattison, and Graham Ward, eds. *The Oxford Handbook of Theology and Modern European Thought*. Oxford: Oxford University Press, 2015.

Agamben, Giorgio. *Homo Sacer: Sovereign Power and Bare Life*. Translated by Daniel Heller-Roazen. Stanford, CA: Stanford University Press, 1998.

Alcalde, David. *Cosmology without God? The Problematic Theology Inherent in Modern Cosmology*. Eugene, OR: Cascade, 2019.

"Answers in Genesis." Website, available at http://www.answersingenesis.org.

Aristotle. *The Basic Works of Aristotle*. Edited by Richard McKeon. Reprint, New York: Modern Library, 2001.

———. *De Anima*. Translated by J. A. Smith. Oxford: Clarendon, 1931.

Ashworth, E. Jennifer. "Medieval Theories of Analogy." In *The Stanford Encyclopedia of Philosophy*, available at https://plato.stanford.edu/entries/analogy-medieval/. Stanford, CA: The Metaphysics Laboratory, Fall 2017 ed.

Athanasius. *On the Incarnation: Saint Athanasius*. Yonkers, NY: St Vladimir's Seminary Press, 2012.

Ayer, A. J. "What Is a Law of Nature?" *Revue Internationale de Philosophie* 10.36 (1956) 144–65.

Baggett, David, and Jerry L. Walls. *Good God: The Theistic Foundations of Morality*. New York: Oxford University Press, 2011.

Balthasar, Hans Urs von. *Theo-Logic, Vol. 2: Truth of God*. San Francisco: Ignatius, 2004.

———. *The Theology of Karl Barth*. 3rd ed. San Francisco: Ignatius, 1992.

Bar-Yosef, Ofer. "The Upper Paleolithic Revolution." *Annual Review of Anthropology* 31 (2002) 363–93.

Barr, Stephen M. *Modern Physics and Ancient Faith*. New ed. Notre Dame, IN: University of Notre Dame Press, 2003.

Behe, Michael J. *Darwin's Black Box: The Biochemical Challenge to Evolution*. 2nd ed. New York: Free, 2006.

———. *The Edge of Evolution: The Search for the Limits of Darwinism*. Reprint, New York: Free, 2008.

Behr, John. *Formation of Christian Theology, Vol. 2: The Nicene Faith*. Crestwood, NY: St St Vladimir's Seminary Press, 2004.

———. *The Mystery of Christ: Life in Death*. Crestwood, NY: St Vladimir's Seminary Press, 2006.

Behr, John, and Conor Cunningham, eds. *The Role of Death in Life: A Multidisciplinary Examination of the Relationship between Life and Death*. Veritas. Eugene, OR: Cascade, 2015.

Belanger, Jerome D. *The Complete Idiot's Guide to Raising Chickens*. Indianapolis, IN: Alpha, 2010.

Benedict, Pope XVI. *'In the Beginning':A Catholic Understanding of the Story of Creation and the Fall*. Grand Rapids: Eerdmans, 1990.

Berman, Harold J. *Law and Revolution: The Formation of the Western Legal Tradition*. Reprint, Cambridge: Harvard University Press, 1983.

———. *Law and Revolution, II: The Impact of the Protestant Reformations on the Western Legal Tradition*. Cambridge: Belknap, 2006.

Bhaskar, Roy. *The Possibility of Naturalism: A Philosophical Critique of the Contemporary Human Sciences*. 4 ed. London: Routledge, 2014.

———. *A Realist Theory of Science*. London: Verso, 2008.

Bhaskar, Roy, Margaret Archer, Andrew Collier, Tony Lawson, and Alan Norrie, eds. *Critical Realism: Essential Readings*. London: Routledge, 1998.

Block, Ned, Owen J. Flanagan, and Guven Guzeldere, eds. *The Nature of Consciousness: Philosophical Debates*. Cambridge, MA: Bradford, 1997.

Boersma, Hans. *Heavenly Participation: The Weaving of a Sacramental Tapestry*. Grand Rapids: Eerdmans, 2011.

Boesch, Christophe. *The Real Chimpanzee: Sex Strategies in the Forest*. New York: Cambridge University Press, 2009.

Bouteneff, Peter C. *Beginnings: Ancient Christian Readings of the Biblical Creation Narratives*. Grand Rapids: Baker Academic, 2008.

Brook, John Hedley. "Science and Secularization." In *The Cambridge Companion to Science and Religion*, edited Peter Harrison, 103–24. Cambridge: Cambridge University Press, 2010.

Burrell, David B., C.S.C. *Freedom and Creation in Three Traditions*. Notre Dame, IN: University of Notre Dame Press, 1993.

Cartwright, Nancy, and John Pemberton. "Aristotelian Powers: Without Them, What Would Modern Science Do?" In *Powers and Capacities in Philosophy: The New Aristotelianism*, 93–112. London: Routledge 2012.

Castelvecchi, Davide. "Battle between Quantum and Thermodynamic Laws Heats Up." *Nature*, March 30, 2017.

Church, U. S. Catholic. *Catechism of the Catholic Church*. 2nd ed. New York: Doubleday, 2003.

Churchland, Patricia S. *Braintrust: What Neuroscience Tells Us about Morality*. Reprint, Princeton: Princeton University Press, 2018.

Cicero, Marcus Tullius. *The Republic and The Laws*. Edited by Jonathan Powell. Translated by Niall Rudd. Reissue, New York: Oxford University Press, 2009.

———. *The Treatises of M.T. Cicero*. Boston: Wentworth, 2016.

Clark, Stephen R. L. *Biology and Christian Ethics*. Cambridge: Cambridge University Press, 2000.

———. *Can We Believe in People? Human Significance in an Interconnected Cosmos.* Brooklyn, NY: Angelico, 2020.

Clayton, Philip. "Toward a Constructive Christian Theology of Emergence." In *Evolution and Emergence: Systems, Organisms, Persons*, edited by Nancey Murphy and William J. Stoeger, SJ, 315–44. Oxford: Oxford University Press 2007.

Coakley, Sarah. *Sacrifice Regained: Evolution, Cooperation and God.* Gifford Lectures 2012. Available at https://www.giffordlectures.org/lectures/sacrifice-regained-evolution-cooperation-and-god.

Cobb, John B., Jr. *A Christian Natural Theology. Second Edition: Based on the Thought of Alfred North Whitehead.* 2nd ed. Louisville, KY: Westminster John Knox, 2007.

Cobb, John B., Jr. and David Ray Griffin. *Process Theology.* Philadelphia: Westminster, 1976.

Conn, Harvie M., ed. *Inerrancy and Hermeneutic: A Tradition, a Challenge, a Debate.* Grand Rapids: Baker, 1988.

Cooper, John W. *Body, Soul, and Life Everlasting: Biblical Anthropology and the Monism-Dualism Debate.* Grand Rapids: Eerdmans, 1989.

Creation Museum website, available at http://creationmuseum.org/.

Critchley, Simon. *Continental Philosophy: A Very Short Introduction.* New York: Oxford University Press, 2001.

Cunningham, Conor. *Darwin's Pious Idea: Why the Ultra-Darwinists and Creationists Both Get It Wrong.* Grand Rapids: Eerdmans, 2010.

———. *Genealogy of Nihilism.* London: Routledge 2002.

———. "Nihilism and Theology: Who Stands at the Door?" In *The Oxford Handbook of Theology and Modern European Thought*, edited by Nicholas Adams, 325–44. Oxford: Oxford University Press 2012.

Cunningham, Mary B. *The Cambridge Companion to Orthodox Christian Theology.* Cambridge: Cambridge University Press, 2009.

Davies, Paul. "How Many Universes?" In *God's Action in Nature's World: Essays in Honor of Robert John Russell*, edited by Robert J. Russell, Ted Peters, and Nathan Illanger, 217–24. London: Routledge 2006.

Dawkins, Richard. *The God Delusion.* Boston: Mariner 2008.

Dembski, William A. *The End of Christianity: Finding a Good God in an Evil World.* Nashville: B&H Academic, 2009.

———. *Intelligent Design: The Bridge between Science and Theology.* Downers Grove, IL: IVP, 1999.

Dennett, Daniel C. *Consciousness Explained.* Boston: Back Bay, 1992.

———. *From Bacteria to Bach and Back: The Evolution of Minds.* New York: Norton, 2017.

Dennett, Daniel C., and Alvin Plantinga. *Science and Religion: Are They Compatible?* New York: Oxford University Press, 2010.

Derrida, Jacques. "Force of the Law: The 'Mystical Foundation of Authority.'" *Cardozo Law Review* 11 (1989–90) 920–1045.

Dod, Bernard G. "Aristoteles Latinus." In *The Cambridge History of Later Medieval Philosophy*, edited by Norman Kretzmann et al., 45–79. Cambridge: Cambridge University Press, 1982.

Dore, Isaak. *The Epistemological Foundations of Law.* Durham, NC: Carolina Academic, 2007.

Eagleman, David. *Incognito: The Secret Lives of the Brain*. Reprint, New York: Vintage, 2012.

Ellis, Brian. *Scientific Essentialism*. New York: Cambridge University Press, 2001.

Elshtain, Jean Bethke. *Sovereignty: God, State, and Self*. New York: Basic, 2008.

Enns, Peter. *Evolution of Adam: What the Bible Does and Doesn't Say about Human Origins*. Grand Rapids: Brazos, 2012.

Epperly, Bruce G. *Process Theology: A Guide for the Perplexed*. London: T. & T. Clark, 2011.

Ernst, Zachary. "Game Theory in Evolutionary Biology." In *The Cambridge Companion to the Philosophy of Biology*, edited by David Hill and Michael Ruse, 304–23. Cambridge: Cambridge University Press, 2007.

Falcon, Andrea, "Aristotle on Causality." In *The Stanford Encyclopedia of Philosophy*. Stanford, CA: The Metaphysics Laboratory, Summer 2019 ed., available at https://plato.stanford.edu/entries/aristotle-causality/.

Feigenson, Neal. "Brain Imaging and Courtroom Evidence: On the Admissibility and Persuasiveness of fMRI." In *Law, Mind and Brain*, edited by Michael Freeman and Oliver R. Goodenough, 23–54. Farnham, UK: Ashgate, 2009.

Fergusson, David. *Creation*. Grand Rapids: Eerdmans, 2014.

Feyerabend, Paul. *Against Method*. 4th ed. New York: Verso, 2010.

Finnis, John. *Natural Law and Natural Rights*. 2ND ed. New York: Oxford University Press, 2011.

Fitzpatrick, Peter, and Alan Hunt. "Introduction to Critical Legal Studies." *Journal of Law and Society* 14.1 (1987) 1–3.

Freeman, Michael, and Oliver R. Goodenough. *Law, Mind and Brain*. London: Routledge, 2017.

George, Robert P. *In Defense of Natural Law*. Rev. ed. New York: Oxford University Press, 2001.

———. *Natural Law and Moral Inquiry: Ethics, Metaphysics, and Politics in the Thought of Germain Grisez*. Washington, DC: Georgetown University Press, 1998.

Gignilliat, Mark S. *A Brief History of Old Testament Criticism: From Benedict Spinoza to Brevard Childs*. Grand Rapids: Zondervan Academic, 2012.

Gould, Stephen J. "Nonoverlapping Magesteria." *Natural History* 106.2 (1997) 16–22.

Graziano, Michael S. A. *God Soul Mind Brain: A Neuroscientist's Reflections on the Spirit World*. Freedonia, NY: Leapfrog, 2010.

Greco, John, and Ruth Groff, eds. *Powers and Capacities in Philosophy: The New Aristotelianism*. London: Routledge, 2012.

Green, Joel B. *Body, Soul, and Human Life: The Nature of Humanity in the Bible*. Milton Keynes, UK: Paternoster, 2008.

Greene, Brian. *The Fabric of the Cosmos: Space, Time, and the Texture of Reality*. New York: Vintage, 2005.

Gregory, Brad S. *The Unintended Reformation: How a Religious Revolution Secularized Society*. Reprint, Cambridge: Belknap, 2015.

Gregory of Nazianzus. *Oration 28*. In *On God and Christ: St. Gregory of Nazianzus—The Five Theological Orations and Two Letters to Cledonius*, translated by Lionel Wickham. Crestwood, NY: St. Vladimir's Seminary Press, 2002.

Grisez, Germain. "A Critique of Russell Hittinger's Book, *A Critique of the New Natural Law Theory*." *New Scholasticism* 62 (1988) 438–65.

Groff, Ruth, ed. *Revitalizing Causality: Realism about Causality in Philosophy and Social Science*. London: Routledge, 2008.

———. "Whose Powers? Which Agency?" In *Powers and Capacities in Philosophy: The New Aristotelianism*, edited by John Greco and Ruth Groff, 207–28. London: Routledge, 2012.

Guenin, Louis M. "Developmental Potential." In *Contemporary Aristotelian Metaphysics*, edited by Tuomas E. Tahko, 156–73. Cambridge: Cambridge University Press, 2012.

Hackney, James R., Jr. *Under Cover of Science: American Legal-Economic Theory and the Quest for Objectivity*. Durham, NC: Duke University Press Books, 2007.

Hallanger, Nathan. *God's Action in Nature's World: Essays in Honour of Robert John Russell*. Edited by Ted Peters. London: Routledge, 2006.

Harris, Sam. "Science Can Answer Moral Questions." Available at http://www.ted.com/talks/lang/en/sam_harris_science_can_show_what_s_right.html.

Harrison, Peter, ed. *The Cambridge Companion to Science and Religion*. Cambridge: Cambridge University Press, 2010.

Harrison, Peter, and Jon H. Roberts, eds. *Science without God? Rethinking the History of Scientific Naturalism*. Oxford: Oxford University Press, 2019.

Hart, David Bentley. *The Beauty of the Infinite: The Aesthetics of Christian Truth*. Grand Rapids: Eerdmans, 2004.

———. *The Experience of God: Being, Consciousness, Bliss*. New Haven, CT: Yale University Press, 2014.

———. "Providence and Causality: On Divine Innocence." In *The Providence of God: Deus Habet Consilium*, edited by Francesca Aran Murphy and Philip G. Ziegler, 34–56. London: T. & T. Clark, 2009.

Hartwig, Mervyn, ed. *Dictionary of Critical Realism*. London: Routledge, 2007.

Hasker, William. *The Emergent Self*. Ithaca, NY: Cornell University Press, 1999.

Hauerwas, Stanley. *The Peaceable Kingdom: A Primer in Christian Ethics*. Notre Dame, IN: University of Notre Dame Press, 1991.

———. *With the Grain of the Universe: The Church's Witness and Natural Theology*. Grand Rapids, MI: Brazos, 2001.

Haught, John F. *Making Sense of Evolution: Darwin, God, and the Drama of Life*. Louisville, KY: Westminster John Knox, 2010.

Haywood, John, Charles Freeman, Paul Garwood, and Judith Toms. *Historical Atlas of the Ancient World 4,000,000–500 BC*. Southampton, UK: Metro, 2000.

Heller, Michael. *Creative Tension: Essays on Science & Religion*. Philadelphia: Templeton, 2003.

Henry, John. "Religion and the Scientific Revolution." In *The Cambridge Companion to Science and Religion*, edited by Peter Harrison, 39–58. Cambridge: Cambridge University Press, 2010.

Hittinger, Russell. *A Critique of the New Natural Law Theory*. Reprint, Notre Dame, IN: University of Notre Dame Press, 1988.

———. *The Teachings of Modern Roman Catholicism on Law, Politics, and Human Nature*. Edited by John Witte Jr. and Frank Alexander. New York: Columbia University Press, 2007.

———. "Response to Professor Grisez's Critique." *New Scholasticism* 62 (1988) 466.

Hobbes, Thomas. *The Elements of Law: Natural and Politic*. Edited by Ferdinand Tonnies. London: Routledge, 2019.

Hoffman, Joshua. "Neo-Aristotelianism and Substance." In *Contemporary Aristotelian Metaphysics*, edited by Tuomas E. Tahko, 140–55. Cambridge: Cambridge University Press 2011.

Holmes, Oliver Wendell, Jr. "The Path of the Law." *Harvard Law Review* 10 (1987) 457–78.

Horst, Steven. *Beyond Reduction: Philosophy of Mind and Post-Reductionist Philosophy of Science*. New York: Oxford University Press, 2007.

Hume, David. *An Enquiry concerning Human Understanding: With Hume's Abstract of A Treatise of Human Nature and A Letter from a Gentleman to His Friend in Edinburgh*. Edited by Eric Steinberg. 2nd ed. Indianapolis: Hackett, 1993.

Hummel, Charles E. *The Galileo Connection: Resolving Conflicts between Science and the Bible*. Nottingham, UK. IVP, 1986.

Hunsinger, George. *Evangelical, Catholic, and Reformed: Essays on Barth and Other Themes*. Grand Rapids: Eerdmans, 2015.

———. *Reading Barth with Charity*. Grand Rapids: Baker Academic, 2015.

Hunter, James Davison, and Paul Nedelisky. *Science and the Good: The Tragic Quest for the Foundations of Morality*. New Haven, CT: Yale University Press, 2018.

Hyers, Conrad. *The Meaning of Creation: Genesis and Modern Science*. Atlanta: John Knox, 1984.

Israel, Jonathan I. *Radical Enlightenment: Philosophy and the Making of Modernity 1650–1750*. Oxford: Oxford University Press, 2002.

James, Frank. "On Wilberforce and Huxley." *Astronomy and Geophysics* 46 (2005) 1.9.

Jefferson, John, Roger Nicole, J. Ramsey Michaels. *Inerrancy and Common Sense*. Grand Rapids: Baker, 1980.

Johnson, Vincent R., and Alan Gunn. *Studies in American Tort Law*. 4 ed. Durham, NC: Carolina Academic, 2009.

Jolls, Christine, Cass R. Sunstein, and Richard Thaler. "A Behavioral Approach to Law and Economics." *Stanford Law Review* 50 (1998) 1471–1548.

Jones, Owen D., Jeffrey D. Schall, and Frances X. Shen. *Law & Neuroscience*. New York: Wolters Kluwer Law & Business, 2014.

Jones, Steven, Robert Martin, and David Pilbeam, eds. *The Cambridge Encyclopedia of Human Evolution*. New York: Cambridge University Press, 2009.

Korobkin, Russell B. "What Comes after Victory for Behavioral Law and Economics?" *University of Illinois Law Review* (2011) 1653–74.

Korobkin, Russell B., and Thonmas S. Ulen. "Law and Behavioral Science: Removing the Rationality Assumption from Law and Economics." *California Law Review* 88 (2000) 1051–1144.

Kelsey, David H. *Eccentric Existence: A Theological Anthropology*. Louisville, KY: Westminster John Knox, 2009.

Kennedy, David, and William W. Fisher III, eds. *The Canon of American Legal Thought*. Princeton, NJ: Princeton University Press, 2006.

King, Gary, Robert O. Keohane, and Sidney Verba. *Designing Social Inquiry: Scientific Inference in Qualitative Research*. Princeton, NJ: Princeton University Press, 1994.

Kramer, Samuel Noah. *History Begins at Sumer: Thirty-Nine Firsts in Recorded History*. 3rd ed. Philadelphia: University of Pennsylvania Press, 1988.

Kretzmann, Norman, Anthony Kenny, Jan Pinborg, and Eleonore Stump, eds. *The Cambridge History of Later Medieval Philosophy: From the Rediscovery of Aristotle* to the Disintegration of Scholasticism, 1100–1600. Cambridge: Cambridge University Press, 1988.

Kuksewicz, Z. "Criticisms of Aristotelian Psychology and the Augustinian-Aristotelian Synthesis." In *The Cambridge History of Later Medieval Philosophy*, edited by Norman Kretzmann, Anthony Kenny, and Jan Pinborg, 623–28. Cambridge: Cambridge University Press, 1982.

Landesman, Charles. *Leibniz's Mill: A Challenge to Materialism*. Notre Dame, IN: University of Notre Dame Press, 2011.

Langston, Douglas C. "Scotus and Ockham on the Univocal Concept of Being." *Franciscan Studies* 39 (1979) 105–29.

Lee, Daniel. *Popular Sovereignty in Early Modern Constitutional Thought*. New York: Oxford University Press, 2016.

Lee, Patrick. *Body-Self Dualism in Contemporary Ethics and Politics*. New York: Cambridge University Press, 2009.

Letwin, Shirley Robin. *On the History of the Idea of Law*. New York: Cambridge University Press, 2005.

Lewis, C. S. *The Abolition of Man*. Reprint, San Francisco: HarperOne, 2009.

Lindbeck, George A. *The Nature of Doctrine: Religion and Theology in a Postliberal Age*. Louisville, KY: Westminster John Knox, 1984.

Lindberg, David C. "The Fate of Science in Patristic and Medieval Christendom." In *The Cambridge Companion to Science and Religion*, edited by Peter Harrison, 21–38. New York: Cambridge University Press, 2010.

Lohr, C. H. *From the Rediscovery of Aristotle to the Disintegration of Scholasticism, 1100–1600*. Cambridge: Cambridge University Press, 1988.

———. "The Medieval Interpretation of Aristotle." In *The Cambridge History of Later Medieval Philosophy*, edited by Norman Kretzmann, Anthony Kenny, and Jan Pinborg, 91–98. Cambridge: Cambridge University Press, 1982.

Long, D. Stephen. *Saving Karl Barth: Hans Urs von Balthasar's Preoccupation*. Minneapolis: Fortress, 2014.

Lowe, E. J. *An Introduction to the Philosophy of Mind*. Cambridge: Cambridge University Press, 2000.

———. *Personal Agency: The Metaphysics of Mind and Action*. Reprint, Oxford: Oxford University Press, 2010.

Lucas, J. R. "Wilberforce and Huxley: A Legendary Encounter." *The Historical Journal* 22 (1979) 313–30.

Ludlow, Peter, Yujin Nagasawa, and Daniel Stoljar, eds. *There's Something about Mary: Essays on Phenomenal Consciousness and Frank Jackson's Knowledge Argument*. Cambridge, MA: Bradford, 2004.

MacArthur Foundation Research Network on Law and Neuroscience Website, available at http://www.lawneuro.org/.

Machuga, Ric. *In Defense of the Soul: What It Means to Be Human*. Grand Rapids: Brazos, 2002.

MacIntyre, Alasdair. *Whose Justice? Which Rationality?* Notre Dame, IN: University of Notre Dame Press, 1988.

Madueme, Hans, and Michael Reeves, eds. *Adam, the Fall, and Original Sin: Theological, Biblical, and Scientific Perspectives*. Grand Rapid: Baker Academic, 2014.

Mahoney, Edward P. "Sense, Intellect, and Imagination." In *The Cambridge History of Later Medieval Philosophy*, edited by Norman Kretzmann, Anthony Kenny, and Jan Pinborg, 605–11. Cambridge: Cambridge University Press, 1982.

Marsden, George. *Understanding Fundamentalism and Evangelicalism*. Grand Rapids: Eerdmans, 1990.

May, William E. "Germain Grisez on Moral Principles and Moral Norms: Natural and Christian." In *Natural Law & Moral Inquiry: Ethics, Metaphysics, and Politics in the Work of Germain Grisez*, edited by Robert George, 3–35. Washington DC: Georgetown University Press, 1998.

McConnell, Michael W., Robert F. Cochran Jr, and Angela C. Carmella. *Christian Perspectives on Legal Thought*. New Haven, CT: Yale University Press, 2001.

McCormack, Bruce L. "Karl Barth's Version of an 'Analogy of Being': A Dialectical No and Yes to Roman Catholicism." In *The Analogy of Being: Invention of the Antichrist or the Wisdom of God?* edited by Thomas Joseph White, OP, 88–147. Grand Rapids: Eerdmans 2011.

———. *Orthodox and Modern: Studies in the Theology of Karl Barth*. Grand Rapids: Baker Academic, 2008.

McCumber, John. *Time and Philosophy: A History of Continental Thought*. Montréal: McGill-Queen's University Press, 2011.

McGrath, Alister E. *Dawkins' God: From The Selfish Gene to The God Delusion*. 2nd ed. Malden, MA: Wiley, 2015.

———. *The Foundations of Dialogue in Science and Religion*. Malden, MA: Wiley-Blackwell, 1991.

———. *The Open Secret: A New Vision for Natural Theology*. Malden, MA: Wiley-Blackwell, 2008.

———. *Science and Religion: A New Introduction*. 2nd ed. Malden, MA: Wiley-Blackwell, 2009.

———. *A Scientific Theology: Reality*. Grand Rapids: Eerdmans 2002.

McKenna, Michael, and D. Justin Coates. "Compatibilism." *The Stanford Encyclopedia of Philosophy*. Stanford, CA: Metaphysics Research Lab, Summer 2020 ed., available at https://plato.stanford.edu/entries/compatibilism/.

Merzenich, Michael. *Soft-Wired: How the New Science of Brain Plasticity Can Change Your Life*. 2nd ed. San Francisco: Parnassus, 2013.

Michener, Ronald T. *Postliberal Theology: A Guide for the Perplexed*. London: T. & T. Clark, 2013.

Migliore, Daniel L. *Faith Seeking Understanding: An Introduction to Christian Theology*. 3rd ed. Grand Rapids: Eerdmans, 2014.

Milbank, John. *Beyond Secular Order: The Representation of Being and the Representation of the People*. Oxford: Wiley-Blackwell, 2014.

———. "Foreword." In *Imaginative Apologetics: Theology, Philosophy and the Catholic Tradition*. Edited by Andrew Davison. Grand Rapids: Baker Academic, 2012.

———. *Theology and Social Theory: Beyond Secular Reason*. 2nd ed. Oxford: Wiley-Blackwell, 2006.

Milbank, John, and Simon Oliver, eds. *The Radical Orthodoxy Reader*. London: Routledge, 2009.

Milbank, John, Catherine Pickstock, and Graham Ward, eds. *Radical Orthodoxy: A New Theology*. London: Routledge, 1998.

Mithen, Steven. *The Prehistory of the Mind: A Search for the Origins of Art, Religion and Science*. London: Orion, 1998.

Moore, G. E. *Principia Ethica*. Reprint, New York: CreateSpace, 2016.

Morris, Simon Conway. *Life's Solution: Inevitable Humans in a Lonely Universe*. Cambridge: Cambridge University Press, 2005.

Muers, Rachel. *Modern Theology*. London: Routledge, 2012.

Murphy, Francesca Aran, and Philip G. Ziegler, eds. *The Providence of God: Deus Habet Consilium*. London: T. & T. Clark, 2009.

Murphy, James Bernard. *The Philosophy of Positive Law: Foundations of Jurisprudence*. New Haven, CT: Yale University Press, 2005.

Murphy, Nancy. *Bodies and Souls, or Spirited Bodies?* New York: Cambridge University Press, 2006.

———. "Divine Action, Emergence, and Scientific Explanation." In *The Cambridge Companion to Science & Religion*, edited by Peter Harrison, 244–59. Cambridge: Cambridge University Press 2010.

———. "Divine Action in the Natural Order: Buridan's Ass and Schrodinger's Cat." In *Chaos and Complexity: Scientific Perspectives on Divine Action*, edited by Robert John Russell, Nancey Murphy, and Arthur R. Peacocke, 325–57. 2nd ed. Rome: Vatican Observatory, 1997.

———. "Reductionism: How Did We Fall into It and How Can We Emerge from It." In *Evolution and Emergence: Systems, Organisms, Persons*, edited by Nancey Murphy and William J. Stoeger, SJ, 19–39. Oxford: Oxford University Press 2007.

Nagel, Thomas. *Mind & Cosmos: Why the Materialist Neo-Darwinian Conception of Nature Is Almost Certainly False*. New York: Oxford University Press, 2012.

Neff, Stephen C., ed. *Hugo Grotius on the Law of War and Peace: Student Edition*. Critical ed. New York: Cambridge University Press, 2012.

Nishimoto, Vu, et al. "Reconstructing Visual Experiences from Brain Activity Evoked by Natural Movies." *Current Biology* 21.19 (2011) 1641–46.

Nozick, Robert. *Anarchy, State, and Utopia*. Reprint, New York: Basic, 2013.

Numbers, Ronald L. *The Creationists: From Scientific Creationism to Intelligent Design*. Exp. ed. Cambridge: Harvard University Press, 2006.

———, ed. *Galileo Goes to Jail and Other Myths about Science and Religion*. Reprint, Cambridge: Harvard University Press, 2010.

Oakley, Francis, "Medieval Theories of Natural Law: William of Ockham and the Significance of the Voluntarist Tradition." *Natural Law Forum* 1 (1961) 65–83.

Oberheim, Eric. *Feyerabend's Philosophy*. Berlin: de Gruyter, 2006.

Ockham, William of, and Stephen F. Brown. *Ockham—Philosophical Writings: A Selection*. Translated by Philotheus Boehner O.F.M. Rev. ed. Indianapolis: Hackett, 1990.

O'Donovan, Oliver. *Resurrection and Moral Order: An Outline of Evangelical Ethics*. Grand Rapids: Eerdmans 1994.

O'Donovan, Oliver, and Joan Lockwood O'Donovan, eds. *From Irenaeus to Grotius: A Sourcebook in Christian Political Thought*. Grand Rapids: Eerdmans, 1999.

Oliver, Simon. "Introducing Radical Orthodoxy: From Participation to Late Modernity." In *The Radical Orthodoxy Reader*, edited by John Milbank and Simon Oliver, 3–28. London: Routledge, 2009.

Opderbeck, David W. *Law and Theology: Classic Questions and Contemporary Perspectives*. Minneapolis, MN: Fortress, 2019.

Orilia, Francesco, and Chris Swoyer. "Properties." In *The Stanford Encyclopedia of Philosophy*. Stanford, CA: The Metaphysics Laboratory, Summer 2020 ed., available at https://plato.stanford.edu/archives/sum2020/entries/properties.

Pannenberg, Wolfhart. *Toward a Theology of Nature*. Louisville, KY: Westminster John Knox, 1993.

Pardo, Michael, and Dennis Patterson. "Philosophical Foundations of Law and Neuroscience." *University of Illinois Law Review* (2010) 1211-50.

Pankhyo, Maria, and Stacy McGrath. "Ecological Anthropology." In *Anthropological Theories: A Guide Prepared for Students*, available at http://anthropology.ua.edu/cultures/cultures.php?culture=Ecological%20Anthropology

Paul II, John, Pope. Address of John Paul II to the Members of the Pontifical Academy of Sciences, The Pontifical Academy of Sciences, ACTA 17, The Four Hundredth Anniversary of the Pontifical Academy of Sciences (Vatican City 2004).

———. "Fides et Ratio." Encyclical Letter, September 14, 1998, available at http://www.vatican.va/content/john-paul-ii/en/encyclicals/documents/hf_jp-ii_enc_14091998_fides-et-ratio.html.

———. Letter of His Holiness John Paul II to Rev. George V. Coyne, SJ Director of the Vatican Observatory, June 1, 1988, available at http://www.vatican.va/holy_father/john_paul_ii/letters/1988/documents/hf_jp-ii_let_19880601_padre-coyne_en.html

Percy, Pam. *The Field Guide to Chickens*. St. Paul, MN: Voyageur, 2006.

Peters, Ted, and Michael Welker. *Anticipating Omega: Science, Faith, and Our Ultimate Future*. Göttingen: Vandenhoeck & Ruprecht, 2006.

Pascal, Blaise. *Penseés*. New York: Penguin Classics, 1995.

Placher, William C. *Unapologetic Theology: A Christian Voice in a Pluralistic Conversation*. Louisville, KY: Westminster John Knox, 1989.

Plantinga, Alvin. *God, Freedom, and Evil*. Reprint, Grand Rapids: Eerdmans, 1989.

———. *Warrant and Proper Function*. New York: Oxford University Press, 1993.

———. *Warrant: The Current Debate*. New York: Oxford University Press, 1993.

———. *Warranted Christian Belief*. New York: Oxford University Press, 2000.

———. *Where the Conflict Really Lies: Science, Religion, and Naturalism*. New York: Oxford University Press, 2011.

Pickstock, Catherine. "Duns Scotus: His Historical and Contemporary Significance." In *The Radical Orthodoxy Reader*, edited by John Milbank and Simon Oliver, 116–47. London: Routledge, 2009.

Pius, Pope XII. Encyclical Humani Generis of the Holy Father Pius XII, August 12, 1950, ¶37, available at http://www.vatican.va/holy_father/pius_xii/encyclicals/documents/hf_p-xii_enc_12081950_humani-generis_en.html.

Polanyi, Michael. *Scientific Thought and Social Reality: Essays*. New York: International Universities Press, 1974.

———. *The Tacit Dimension*. Reprint, Chicago: University of Chicago Press, 2009.

Porter, Jean. *Nature as Reason: A Thomistic Theory of the Natural Law*. Grand Rapids: Eerdmans, 2004.

Poythress, Vern S. *Redeeming Science: A God-Centered Approach*. Wheaton, IL: Crossway, 2006.

Przywara, Erich. *Analogia Entis: Metaphysics—Original Structure and Universal Rhythm*. Translated by John R. Betz and David Bentley Hart. Grand Rapids: Eerdmans, 2014.

Rawls, John. *A Theory of Justice*. 2nd ed. Cambridge: Belknap, 1999.

Ridley, Mark, ed. *Evolution*. 2nd ed. New York: Oxford University Press, 2004.

Ruse, David L., and Michael Hull. *The Cambridge Companion to the Philosophy of Biology*. Cambridge: Cambridge University Press, 2007.

Russell, Robert J. *Chaos and Complexity: Scientific Perspectives on Divine Action*. Edited by Nancey Murphy. Notre Dame, IN: University of Notre Dame Press, 1996.

Ryl, Gilbert. *The Concept of Mind*. Chicago: University of Chicago Press 1949.

Salzman, Todd A. *What Are They Saying about Catholic Ethical Method?* New York: Paulist, 2003.

Sawyer, G. J., and Viktor Deak. *The Last Human: A Guide to Twenty-Two Species of Extinct Humans*. New Haven, CT: Yale University Press, 2007.

Schaff, Philip. *The Creeds of Christendom: With a History and Critical Notes*. Sydney: Wentworth, 2019.

Schindler, D. C. *The Perfection of Freedom: Schiller, Schelling, and Hegel between the Ancients and the Moderns*. Eugene, OR: Wipf and Stock, 2012.

———. "Hans Urs von Balthasar, Metaphysics, and the Problem of Ontotheology." 1 *Analecta Hermeneutica* 1 (2009) 102–13.

Scotus, John Duns. *Duns Scotus on the Will and Morality*. Edited by William A. Frank. Translated by Alan B. Wolter. Washington, DC: Catholic University of America Press, 1997.

———. *On Being and Cognition: Ordinatio 1.3*. Translated by John van den Bercken. New York: Fordham University Press, 2016.

Shields, Christopher, "Aristotle's Psychology." In *The Stanford Encyclopedia of Philosophy* Stanford, CA: The Metaphysics Laboratory, Winter 2016 ed., available at https://plato.stanford.edu/entries/aristotle-psychology/.

Nishimoto, Shinji, et al. "Reconstructing Visual Experiences from Brain Activity Evoked by Natural Movies." *Current Biology* 21.19 (2011) 1641–46.

Silva, Moises. "Old Princeton, Westminster, and Inerrancy." In *Inerrancy and Hermeneutic: A Tradition, a Challenge, a Debate*, edited by Harvey M. Conn, 15–35. Grand Rapids: Baker, 1988.

Smith, Christian. *What Is a Person? Rethinking Humanity, Social Life, and the Moral Good from the Person Up*. Chicago: University of Chicago Press, 2010.

Smolin, Lee. *The Trouble with Physics: The Rise of String Theory, the Fall of a Science, and What Comes Next*. Reprint, Boston: Mariner, 2007.

Spade, Paul Vincent, ed. *The Cambridge Companion to Ockham*. Cambridge: Cambridge University Press, 1999.

Spaemann, Robert. *Persons: The Difference between "Someone" and "Something."* Translated by Oliver O'Donovan. Oxford: Oxford University Press, 2006.

Sterelny, Kim, and Paul E. Griffiths. *Sex and Death: An Introduction to Philosophy of Biology*. Chicago: University of Chicago Press, 1999.

Stoeger, William R., SJ. *Evolution and Emergence: Systems, Organisms, Persons*. Edited by Nancey Murphy. New York: Oxford University Press, 2007.

Stout, Jeffrey. *Ethics After Babel: The Languages of Morals and Their Discontents*. Boston: Beacon, 1988.

Stump, Eleanore. "Emergence, Causal Powers, and Aristotelianism in Metaphysics." In *Powers and Capacities in Philosophy: The New Aristotelianism*, edited by John Greco and Ruth Groff, 48–68. London: Routledge, 2012.

Tahko, Tuomas E., ed. *Contemporary Aristotelian Metaphysics*. New York: Cambridge University Press, 2012.

Tamanaha, Brian Z. *Law as a Means to an End: Threat to the Rule of Law*. Cambridge: Cambridge University Press, 2010.

Tattersall, Ian. *The Fossil Trail: How We Know What We Think We Know about Human Evolution*. 2nd ed. New York: Oxford University Press, 2008.

———. *Masters of the Planet: The Search for Our Human Origins*. Reprint, New York: St. Martin's Griffin, 2013.

Taylor, Charles. *Explanation of Behavior*. London: Routledge & Kegan Paul, 1964.

———. *A Secular Age*. Reprint, Cambridge: Belknap, 2018.

———. *Sources of the Self: The Making of the Modern Identity*. Cambridge, MA: Harvard University Press, 1992.

Thijssen, Hans. "Condemnation of 1277." In *The Stanford Encyclopedia of Philosophy*, available at https://plato.stanford.edu/entries/condemnation/. Stanford, CA: The Metaphysics Laboratory Winter 2018 ed.

Tyson, Paul, "Can Modern Science Be Theologically Salvaged? Reflections on Conor Cunningham's Theological and Metaphysical Evaluation of Modern Evolutionary Biology." *Radical Orthodoxy: Theology, Philosophy, Politics* 2.1 (2014) 118–39. available at http://journal.radicalorthodoxy.org/index.php/ROTPP/article/view/67.

Tomberlin, H., and Peter van Inwagen, eds. *Alvin Plantinga*. Boston: Springer, 1985.

Torrance, Thomas F. *Reality & Evangelical Theology: The Realism of Christian Revelation*. Reprint, Eugene, OR: Wipf and Stock, 2003.

Torrey, R. A., and A. C. Dixon. *The Fundamentals: A Testimony to the Truth*. Grand Rapids: Baker, 1994.

University of Pennsylvania Center for Neuroscience & Society website, available at http://neuroethics.upenn.edu/index.php/section-blog/28-articles/72-science-and-the-soul

Valliere, Paul. *The Teachings of Modern Orthodox Christianity on Law, Politics, and Human Nature*. Edited by John Witte Jr and Frank Alexander. New York: Columbia University Press, 2007.

VanDoodewaard, William. *The Quest for the Historical Adam: Genesis, Hermeneutics, and Human Origins*. Grand Rapids: Reformation Heritage, 2015.

Van Til, Cornelius. *The Defense of the Faith*. Edited by K. Scott Oliphint. 4th ed. Phillipsburg, NJ: P & R, 2008.

Van Gulick, Robert. "Reduction, Emergence, and the Mind/Body Problem: A Philosophic Overview and Who's in Charge Here? And Who's Doing All the Work?" In *Evolution and Emergence: Systems, Organisms, Persons*, edited by Nancey Murphy and William J. Stoeger, SJ, 74–87. Oxford: Oxford University Press, 2007.

Volf, Miroslav. *The End of Memory: Remembering Rightly in a Violent World*. Grand Rapids: Eerdmans, 2006.

Waal, Frans de. *Chimpanzee Politics: Power and Sex among Apes*. 25th anniversary ed. Baltimore, MD: Johns Hopkins University Press, 2007.

Walton, John H. *Ancient Near Eastern Thought and the Old Testament*. 2nd ed. Grand Rapids: Baker Academic, 2018.

Ward, Graham. *The Politics of Discipleship: Becoming Postmaterial Citizens*. Grand Rapids: Baker Academic, 2009.

Ward, Keith. *More Than Matter? What Humans Really Are*. Oxford: Lion, 2010.

Ward, Lee. *The Politics of Liberty in England and Revolutionary America*. Cambridge: Cambridge University Press, 2010.

Ware, Kallistos. *The Orthodox Way*. Rev ed. Crestwood, NY: St Vladimir's Seminary Press, 1995.

Warfield, Benjamin B. *Evolution, Science, and Scripture: Selected Writings*. Edited by Mark A. Noll and David N. Livingstone. Grand Rapids: Baker, 2000.

Warren, Rick. *The Purpose Driven Life: What on Earth Am I Here For?* 10th Anniversary ed. Grand Rapids: Zondervan, 2013.

Watson, Alan, ed. *The Digest of Justinian, Volume 1*. Rev. ed. Philadelphia: University of Pennsylvania Press, 2009.

Webster, John, ed. *The Cambridge Companion to Karl Barth*. Cambridge: Cambridge University Press, 2000.

Westphal, Merold. *Overcoming Onto-Theology: Toward a Postmodern Christian Faith*. New York: Fordham University Press, 2001.

White, Thomas Joseph, OP, ed. *The Analogy of Being: Invention of the Antichrist or Wisdom of God?* Grand Rapids: Eerdmans, 2010.

Williams, Rowan. *Christ the Heart of Creation*. London: Bloomsbury Continuum, 2018.

Wilson, David Sloan. *Evolution for Everyone: How Darwin's Theory Can Change the Way We Think about Our Lives*. Reprint, New York: Delta, 2007.

Wilson, Edward O. *Sociobiology: The New Synthesis. Twenty-Fifth Anniversary Edition*. 2nd ed. Cambridge: Belknap, 2000.

Wippel, John F. "Essence and Existence." In *The Cambridge History of Later Medieval Philosophy*, edited by Norman Kretzmann, Anthony Kenny, and Jan Pinborg, 385–410. Cambridge: Cambridge University Press, 1982.

Witt, Charlotte. "Aristotelian Powers." In *Revitalizing Causality: Realism about Causality in Philosophy and Social Science*, edited by Ruth Groff, 129–38. London: Routledge, 2008.

Witte, John Jr. *Christianity and Law: An Introduction*. New York: Cambridge University Press, 2008.

———. *God's Joust, God's Justice: Law and Religion in the Western Tradition*. Grand Rapids: Eerdmans, 2006.

———. *The Reformation of Rights: Law, Religion and Human Rights in Early Modern Calvinism*. New York: Cambridge University Press, 2008.

Witte, John Jr., and Frank S. Alexander, eds. *The Teachings of Modern Christianity on Law, Politics, & Human Nature: Volume One*. New York: Columbia University Press, 2006.

———, eds. *The Teachings of Modern Christianity on Law, Politics, & Human Nature: Volume Two*. New York: Columbia University Press, 2006.

Wolters, Alan. *The Transcendentals and Their Function in the Metaphysics of Duns Scotus*. St. Bonaventure, NY: The Franciscan Institute 1946.

Wright, Joshua, and Douglas H. Ginsburg. "Behavioral Law and Economics: Its Origins, Fatal Flaws, and Implications for Liberty." *Northwestern Law Review* 106 (2012) 1033–88.

Wolchover, Natalie. "The Quantum Thermodynamics Revolution." *Quanta Magazine*, May 2, 2017.

Yannaras, Christos. *The Freedom of Morality*. Translated by Elizabeth Briere. Crestwood, NY: St Vladimir's Seminary Press, 1984.

Zilsel, E. "The Genesis of the Concept of Physical Law." *Philosophical Review* 51 (1942) 245–79.

Index

A

Abelard, Peter, 197
Abraham, 15, 103
absolute power of God, 34
act, 16–17, 21, 23, 25, 29–31, 161–
    62, 184, 186–87, 190, 207,
    212, 217, 219, 222
actuality, 172, 211–12
Adam, 34, 83, 86–87, 99, 101–4,
    125, 214, 216–17, 221–23,
    225, 228, 231
Agamben, Giorgio 8, 211–13, 225
agency, 44, 115, 149, 168, 174–75,
    180, 186, 188, 229
    degree of, 44, 160
    human, 53–54, 105, 175
    intentional, 186
    moral, 41, 43, 168, 187
agent, 27, 30–31, 162
    causative, 175
    free moral, 97
    intentional, 141
    nonembodied, 161
ages, 16, 35, 58, 78, 96
    geological, 60
Alcalde, David, 81
Alexander, Frank, 229, 236, 237
altruism, 79, 81, 126, 179–80
    supernormal, 94–95
altruistic, 95, 180
analogical, 25, 28, 33, 92
analogy, 11, 24–25, 27–28, 33–34,
    37, 144, 149, 179, 225, 232,
    237

analytic philosophy, 7, 170–71
animals, 13, 24, 33, 83, 120, 143,
    172, 186–87, 198, 221
Anselm of Canterbury, 197
anthropology, 60, 92, 151, 173, 187,
    195, 201, 225
apologetics, 77, 95, 190
aporias, 196, 211, 213
Aquinas, Thomas, 5, 18–19, 22, 24–
    27, 31, 76–78, 80, 89, 94–95,
    181–83, 185–86, 191–92,
    199–200
Archer, Margaret, 226
Aristotelianism, 5, 174, 181
Aristotelian Powers, 174–76, 226,
    237
Aristotle, 11–12, 14, 18, 21–22,
    24–26, 33, 144–45, 160, 162,
    171–72, 212, 225, 230–31
Athanasius of Alexandria, 214–19,
    225
atheism, 65, 82
atomism, 160
Augustine of Hippo, 18–19, 22,
    24–25, 38, 76, 89, 99–100,
    102, 186, 217, 219
Auschwitz, 210

B

Babylon, 15–16, 54
bacteria, 126–27, 153, 227
Balthasar, Hans Urs von, 91–93,
    103, 225, 235
Bañez, Domingo, 165

Barth, Karl, 71–72, 76, 78–79, 89,
    91–92, 225, 230, 232, 237
Bayesian coherentism, 65
behavioral law and economics,
    50–51, 230, 237
behaviors, 44, 51, 121, 126–27,
    141–43, 148, 150–51, 158,
    163, 180–81, 196
Behe, Michael, 188, 225
Behr, John, 99, 166–67, 226
being, 27–28, 33–34, 38–39, 56,
    69–70, 77, 81–82, 103, 165–
    66, 169, 196–97, 199, 207–8,
    215–19, 222
beliefs, 65–66, 70, 78, 85, 92, 97,
    128–29, 142, 146–47, 155,
    161
Benedict XVI, Pope, 100–101
Bhaskar, Roy, 68–69, 173–74, 226
biological evolution, 60, 85–86, 96,
    102, 104, 189
body, 40–41, 63, 133–35, 142, 144,
    157, 170–72, 175, 197–98,
    213, 216, 219, 227–28
body-self dualism, 186–88
Boltzmann's constant, 180
Bouteneff, Peter, 90, 99, 226
brain, 36, 39–41, 43–44, 63, 128–29,
    138, 140, 142–44, 148, 151–
    52, 176, 179, 181, 186, 228
brain chemistry, 4, 179–80, 214
brain Imaging, 2, 228
brain plasticity, 232
brain states, 4–5, 143, 146, 148
breath of life, 214

C
Calvin, John, 94
capacities, 4, 10, 75–76, 127, 144–
    45, 147–48, 152–53, 181,
    183–84, 186–87, 196, 202,
    219, 221–22, 228–29
    emergent, 168
causal closure, 136, 138–39, 157,
    182
causality, 4–5, 11, 19, 94, 159, 161,
    169–71, 183, 188, 229, 237

causal powers, 4, 174, 176, 182–83,
    235
causation, 10, 94, 120, 136–37, 145,
    158–59, 162, 170, 172, 174
cause, 1, 11, 23–24, 26, 28, 35, 94,
    128, 136–37, 141, 170–73
Chalcedonian Definition, 166–68
choices, 12, 42, 47, 68, 133, 152,
    164–65, 171, 187
Christ, 4–5, 17–18, 71, 78–79, 86–
    87, 98–99, 166 69, 194–95,
    197–98, 200–201, 214, 218–
    20, 222–23, 226, 228
Christology, 4, 79, 81, 165–67, 195,
    222
church, 4, 19, 21, 55–56, 71–72,
    75–78, 97, 194, 197–98, 207,
    226
Churchland, Patricia, 176–81, 226
Cicero, 13–14, 19, 226
city, 7, 10, 14, 122–23, 206, 212–13
Clark, Stephen R.L., 147, 149, 166,
    226, 228–29, 232–33
Coakley, Sarah, 77, 79–81, 95, 227
Cobb, John, 61, 63, 227
cognition, 1, 69, 120, 145, 235
command, 16, 29, 32, 34–35, 125,
    169, 195, 203–4, 216–17
commandments, 15, 32–33, 35, 215
conceptual thought, 186–87
continental philosophy, 98, 227
contingency, 23, 33, 189, 199
Coyne, George V., 74–75, 234
creation, 15–17, 23–25, 37–38,
    53–56, 58–59, 79, 81–82,
    86–87, 89–90, 94–96, 102–3,
    120, 160–61, 165, 169, 181,
    190–91, 195–96, 199–201,
    218–19, 222–23
creationism, young-earth, 59, 64, 87,
    90, 96–97
creationists, young-earth, 58–59, 64,
    97, 214
Creation Museum, 59, 97, 227
creatures, 2, 5, 7, 24, 27, 29–30,
    33–34, 115, 117, 122, 124,
    196, 199, 201, 221

critical realism, 67, 69, 73, 78, 84,
    87, 90–91, 173, 192, 226, 229
critical realists, 67–68, 71, 73, 79, 90,
    92, 191
cultural explosion, 7, 117–19, 122,
    125, 214, 221
Cultural Revolution, 149
culture, 15–16, 68–69, 79, 83, 126,
    128–29, 151, 194, 200, 234
Cunningham, Conor, 55–56, 59–60,
    82–83, 85–87, 99–100, 102,
    147, 212, 227

D
Dembski, William J., 59–60, 227
Dennett, Daniel, 66, 88, 154–55, 227
Derrida, Jacques, 206–10, 227
Descartes, Renee, 84, 133–34, 153
design, 59–60, 66, 73, 94, 147, 151,
    161, 188
determinism, 23, 140–41, 171, 190
divine action, 66, 80–81, 93–94,
    160–64, 172, 233, 235
divine commands, 34–35, 104, 169,
    183, 203, 219, 222
divine freedom, 6, 32–33, 37
doctrine, 53, 56, 71, 73, 76–77, 81,
    92, 94, 99–100, 214, 222
Dore, Isaak, 10, 12, 14–15, 46,
    48–49, 227
dualism, 87, 133, 135, 154, 173

E
Eagleman, David, 41–45, 47, 140,
    148–51, 228
earth, 5, 14, 16, 21, 55–56, 58–60,
    66, 69, 122, 124, 189
economics, 3, 6, 45, 47, 49–51, 83,
    95, 230, 237
    behavioral, 50–51
eliminativists, 132–34, 138–39
Elshtain, Jean Behkte, 38–39, 228
emergence, 39, 89, 138, 157–60, 172,
    176, 182–83, 214, 227, 233,
    235–36
emergentism, 133, 138, 157–58
emergentists, 138–39, 165

emergent properties, 88, 157, 182–
    83, 199, 219
Enlightenment, 9, 26, 28, 161
environment, 43, 63, 99, 118, 147,
    149, 157, 189, 217
epiphenomenal, 130, 132
epiphenomena, 6, 97, 104, 189, 221
epistemology, 54, 64, 82, 94, 97,
    133, 214
Epperly, Bruce, 61–63, 89, 228
essence, 21, 23–24, 27, 33, 167, 172,
    184, 208, 218, 222
ethics, 38, 52, 148, 152, 176, 181,
    183, 188, 190–91, 195–96,
    228, 232, 235
Euthyphro Dilemma, 195
evidence, 2, 36, 41, 61, 66, 107, 115–
    17, 120, 122, 140, 144
evolution, human, 7, 53, 57, 100–
    101, 106–7, 120, 214, 217,
    223, 230, 236
evolutionary biology, 41, 45, 60, 64,
    86, 98, 124, 150, 188, 190,
    228
evolutionary history, 41, 63, 130,
    154, 156, 189, 222
evolutionary psychology and
    sociobiology, 7
existence, 23, 25, 27, 79–80, 91,
    103–4, 163, 167, 180, 190,
    192, 196–98, 203
experience, 24, 61, 63, 67, 71, 81, 91,
    98, 170, 178, 210

F
faith, 53, 55–58, 61, 64–65, 75–76,
    81, 91–95, 98, 101–2, 125–
    26, 190, 234, 236
faith and science, 66, 73, 85, 96, 98,
    163
Fall, 86, 99, 101, 158–60, 225–26,
    231, 233, 235
Feyerabend, Paul, 70, 84, 96, 228
Finnis, John, 48–49, 185–86, 228
fitness landscapes, 95, 149–51
force, 12–13, 30, 58, 124, 153, 203,
    206–7, 209, 217, 227
formal cause, 11–12, 172

foundationalism, 90, 190
freedom, 2, 4, 23, 29–30, 41, 43,
    88–89, 94, 103, 169, 171,
    196, 198–201, 219, 234–35
    human, 22, 142, 165, 196,
    200–201
free will, 35, 41–42, 129

G
Galileo, 21, 55–56, 160, 233
Garden of Eden, 24, 86, 103, 107,
    203, 214–19
Genesis, 54, 56, 58–59, 64, 99, 101,
    125, 169–70, 214, 221,
    236–37
George, Robert, 185–88, 228,
    230–32
Gifford Lectures, 38, 77, 79, 81, 227
God, 5–6, 13–21, 23–35, 37–39,
    48–49, 52–54, 61–66,
    71–72, 75–77, 79–82, 88–97,
    99–100, 102–4, 161–69, 181,
    190–91, 193–204, 214–19,
    221–23, 227–29
God of the gaps, 153–54
goodness, 16, 23–24, 29, 33, 36, 76,
    85, 98, 126–27, 147, 156
goods, 14, 20, 154, 165, 180, 185,
    202
governments, 10, 13, 44, 148
Graziano, Brian, 128, 228
Greco, John, 229, 235
Greene, Joel, 163–64, 228
Gregory of Nazianzus, 23, 27, 54, 89,
    102, 228
Grisez, Germain, 185–86, 228
Groff, Ruth, 173–75, 228–29, 235,
    237
Grotius, Hugo, 6, 19, 35, 37–38, 233

H
Habermas Jürgen, 152
Hamm, Ken, 97
Harrison, Peter, 20–21, 54, 217, 229
Hart, David Bentley, 48, 54, 82, 99,
    165–66, 229
Hartwig, Melvyn, 173, 229

Hauerwas, Stanley, 77–79, 184, 193–
    95, 200–201, 219, 229
Haught, John, 73–74, 229
Hedley, John, 226
Heisenberg Uncertainty Principle,
    188
history, 5–6, 10–11, 14, 18, 20,
    23, 47–48, 69–70, 101–2,
    122–23, 209, 211, 218, 220,
    230–31
Hittinger, Russell, 185–86, 190–91,
    229
Hobbes, Thomas, 6, 35–39, 229
Holmes, Oliver Wendell, 46–47, 230
Holy Spirit, 64–65, 93, 98, 167
homo habilis, 112
Homo heidelbergensis, 118
Homo rudolfensis, 111
Homo sapiens, 117–19, 171
homo sapiens sapiens, 107, 115, 129,
    168, 214
Horst, Stephen, 132–33, 135, 139–
    40, 147, 153–54, 230
human existence, 121, 147, 155,
    196–97, 203
human life, 16, 43, 133, 157, 191,
    228
human nature, 4, 6, 8, 19, 43, 45,
    52–53, 166, 168, 192–93,
    198, 200, 229–30, 236–37
human relationships, 32, 101, 202
humans, 5, 13, 24–26, 104, 106–7,
    112–13, 124–26, 132–33,
    177, 179, 187, 201–2, 214–
    16, 218–19, 221
human society, 9, 14, 18, 63, 83–84
human understanding, 61, 170, 230
Hume, David, 161, 170, 174–75,
    177, 230
Hunter, James Davidson, 20, 26,
    154, 176, 181, 230

I
idealism, 21–22, 202
ideas, 6, 10–11, 14, 32, 35, 39, 41,
    82, 128, 147–48, 150, 154,
    170
imagination, 24–25, 150, 170, 232

incarnation, 71, 86, 94, 166, 214–19, 222, 225
inerrancy, 57, 64, 227, 235
intelligent design (ID), 59, 66, 85, 148, 153, 188, 202, 227, 233
intentionality, 6, 40, 42–43, 122, 128, 131, 142, 155, 157
is/ought fallacy, 176

J
Jesus, 17, 38, 77, 102–3, 195
John Paul II, Pope, 74–76, 87, 91, 234
judges, 47, 180, 210
judgment, 15–16, 46, 197, 203, 205, 211
Justinian, Emperor, 13, 237

K
Kenny, Anthony, 230–32, 237
kind, 7, 27–28, 53, 90–91, 94–95, 122–23, 125–26, 132–33, 138, 145, 154–55, 179–81, 192, 196–97, 201–2, 221–23
knowledge, 23–24, 26–27, 47, 65, 68–69, 75, 79, 104, 125, 140, 142, 198, 201–2
    natural, 24, 92
    scientific, 36, 70, 162

L
Lactantius, Caecilius Firmianus, 17, 19
Lagash, 123
language, 24, 33, 58, 67–69, 117–19, 121–22, 124, 128, 194–95, 206–7, 214
law of love, 5, 8, 102, 104, 184, 214, 216, 219, 221–23
law of nature, 32–33, 35, 37
Lee, Patrick, 13, 186–88, 231, 235, 237
legal positivism, 36, 38, 45–46, 48–49, 130, 222
Letwin, Shirley Robin, 10–11, 231
Lewis, C.S., 154, 231
libertarian, 42, 171, 219

liberty, 34, 36, 38, 50, 237
life, 8, 11, 16, 28, 89, 189, 195, 197–201, 212, 214–19, 222, 226, 229
logical positivism, 69, 130–31
love, 5, 7–8, 18, 32, 34, 101–2, 104, 193–94, 196–97, 201, 203–4, 213–16, 219, 221–23
Lowe, E.J., 133–38, 146–47, 231

M
MacIntyre, Alasdair, 76, 78, 191, 195
material, 11, 22, 25, 68, 81, 124, 129, 154, 172, 182
matter, 5, 11, 97–98, 100, 141–42, 147, 153, 160, 162–63, 170, 177, 182–83, 186
McGrath, Alister, 54, 57, 60–61, 67–68, 71–73, 84, 87, 90–92, 96, 128, 151
medieval philosophy, 227, 230–32, 237
medieval synthesis, 21–22, 56
memology, 128–29
mental states, 132, 136–38, 141–42, 146–47
Milbank, John, 39, 77, 81–85, 96, 103, 206, 232–34
mind, human, 3, 27, 69, 103, 119–20, 130
mind/body problem, 159–60, 236
Mithen, Stephen, 117, 119–20, 122, 125, 128, 233
morality, 3, 10, 14, 33–34, 47–48, 176, 194, 196–98, 225–26, 230, 235, 237
moral principles, 183, 185, 189, 232
Morse, Stephen, 140–42
multiverses, 164–65, 189–90
Murphy, Nancey, 40, 122, 133, 157–60, 162–65, 167–68, 172, 227, 233, 235–36
mysterians, 132, 138

N
Nagel, Thomas, 88–89, 138, 142, 145–46, 148, 233
natural, 51, 83, 194, 229, 232

Naturalism, 21, 68–69, 85, 97, 177,
    226, 234
  absolute, 127
  biological, 173
  legal, 10
  metaphysical, 20–21
  reductive, 102
naturalism and human progress, 21
naturalistic fallacy, 175–77, 180–81,
    183–85
natural law, 3, 5–6, 12, 18–20, 29,
    31–35, 37, 95, 106–7, 171,
    183–85, 191–94, 200–204,
    208–9, 233–34
natural law theory, 10, 13, 16, 46,
    48–49, 185, 191, 193, 200
natural lawyers, new, 188–91
natural sciences, 20–21, 28, 52–53,
    58, 61, 71–74, 82–85, 88,
    90–92, 96, 131, 202
natural selection, 149, 152–53, 188
natural theology, 57, 72, 77–79,
    90–92, 161, 188, 229, 232
natura pura, 87, 91
nature, 2–5, 14, 28, 32–35, 37, 60–
    61, 75–76, 90–91, 154–55,
    161–62, 166–67, 169–70,
    173–76, 183–84, 186–88,
    190–95, 197, 213–15, 225–
    26, 233–34
  animal, 103
  book of, 57
  dual, 166
  dynamic, 61
  essential, 174
  fragmented, 197
  laws of, 4, 21, 29, 103, 133, 162,
    175, 202
  prerational, 193
  proper, 8
  rational, 215
  stochastic, 89
  ultimate, 147
  uncreated, 27
Nazianzus, Gregory of, 23, 228
Nedelisky, Jennifer, 20, 26, 176
neurochemistry, 51, 176, 178
neuroethics, 41

neurolaw, 2–3, 6–8, 41, 44, 51–52,
    106–7, 130, 139–42, 145,
    152, 154
neurolaw scholars, 2, 41, 104, 140,
    204, 221
neuroscience, 2, 40–42, 44–45, 53,
    97–98, 140–44, 149, 152,
    204, 221, 226
new Aristotelianism, 4–5, 7, 169,
    175, 181, 183–84, 202, 204,
    226, 228–29, 235
new natural law theory, 185–86,
    190–91, 228–29
Newtonianism, 56
Nicene Creed, 167
NOMA, 60, 87, 90
nominalism, 6, 22, 38, 85, 96
nominalist, 39, 87, 96
normal distribution, 120–22, 129,
    150, 180
Nyssa, Gregory of, 23, 27, 89, 102

O
Oakley, Francis, 34–35, 233
Ockham, William of, 6, 22, 28, 33–
    35, 37, 225, 231, 233, 235
Ockham's Razor, 3, 152–53
O'Donovan, Oliver, 19, 37–38, 233,
    235
omega point, 89
ontotheology, 81, 93–94, 235, 237
order, 12, 16, 30–31, 38, 45, 53, 75,
    91, 162, 189, 222
  cosmic, 14, 134
  social, 45, 124
original sin, 8, 63, 86, 96, 99–102,
    203–19, 221, 231
Orr, James, 58
orthodoxy, 82, 99, 103, 217

P
participation, 17, 25, 28, 76, 81, 87,
    102, 191, 198, 215, 217–19
Pascal, Blaise, 207–10, 234
Paul of Tarsus, 99, 198, 219, 227–28,
    234, 236
Pemberton, John, 174, 226

Pemberton, Nancy, 174–75
perfections, 14, 23, 62, 87, 89, 94, 117
persons, 3, 36–37, 43, 82–83, 103, 106, 133, 140–41, 143–44, 166–69, 175, 182, 185–87, 192–93, 196–99, 201, 203, 212–17, 222–23, 235–36
phenomena, 1, 8, 79–80, 82, 104, 106, 119, 128, 131–32, 145, 148
philosophy of mind, 7, 131–39, 146–47, 157, 231
philosophy of nature, 186, 190
philosophy of science, 4, 7, 22, 68, 79, 130, 139–40, 168, 170, 175, 183
physicalism, 134–35, 168
physicalists, nonreductive, 135, 146, 168
physical states, 132, 135–38, 146
Plantinga, Alvin, 64–67, 93–94, 227, 234, 236
Plato, 5, 10–11, 13–14, 21, 25–26, 81, 181, 200
Polanyi, Michael, 68–70, 79, 84, 234
politics, 12, 18–19, 26, 39, 77, 82, 209, 212, 228–29, 231–32, 236–37
Pontifical Academy of Sciences, 76, 234
Porter, Jean, 184, 191–93, 195, 200–201, 219, 234
postliberal theology, 76, 81, 98, 232
potentiality, 172, 175, 211–12, 223
powers, 5, 30–31, 33–34, 36–39, 46, 155, 169–70, 172–76, 181–84, 204–5, 208, 213, 215–16, 218–19, 228–29, 235–36
    absolute, 30–31, 34
    basic, 202
    constituted, 211–12
    constitutive, 211
    dominant, 70
    emergent, 174–75
    essential, 175
    legislative, 207
    mental, 144

natural, 175, 181, 219
persuasive, 70
police, 206
political, 204
potential, 171
rational, 144
spiritual, 207
powers of entities, 184
practical reason, 11, 31, 47, 185–86
process theology, 61–64, 81, 87–90, 133, 138, 158, 161, 227–28
properties, 14, 123, 166, 168, 170, 173, 177–78, 180–81, 187, 196, 199
    dispositional, 175
    emergent non-reducible, 173
    intrinsic, 34
    mental, 138
    necessary, 189
    powerful, 175
    transcendental, 168
providence, 56, 66, 88–89, 93–94, 96, 165, 218
purposes, 2, 4, 9–12, 19, 78–79, 81–82, 88–89, 93, 121–22, 147, 173, 177, 195–96

Q
quantum indeterminacy, 138
quantum mechanics, 66, 134, 163–64
quantum thermodynamics, 179

R
Radical Orthodoxy, 7, 81–83, 85, 96, 232–33, 236
Ramm, Bernard, 58–59
rationality, 53, 71, 134, 141–42, 155, 187–89, 231
    minimal, 141
    scientific, 155
Rawls, John, 49–50, 113, 152, 235
realism
    epistemic, 145
    ethical, 95
    legal, 3, 50
    medieval, 38

metaphysical, 3, 129
naïve, 192
representative, 173
speculative, 192
realist, 90–91, 146, 154, 174, 202
realist account of mental states, 147
realist personalism, 84
reality, 18, 21, 25, 61–62, 67–69, 71,
    83–84, 90, 93, 96, 98–100,
    132–34, 199
reason, 3–4, 10–14, 18–19, 33–34,
    37–39, 49–51, 53–54, 79–80,
    91, 94–95, 98, 134–35,
    144–45, 189–93, 195, 200,
    205, 208–9, 219
    conceptual, 142
    historical, 128
    human, 3–4, 38, 73, 190
    natural, 29, 53, 75–77, 98
    pure, 90, 191
redemption, 79, 102, 194–95, 204
reductionism, 7, 22, 130, 139–40,
    142, 145, 147, 153–54, 158–
    60, 172–73, 178
regularities, 65, 92, 120
religion, 19–20, 22, 41, 54–55, 57,
    60–61, 66–67, 72–74, 123,
    125–26, 128–29, 132, 226–
    27, 229, 231–34
Renaissance, 6, 21–22
resurrection, 37–38, 71, 81, 94, 187,
    200, 214, 223, 233
rights, 4, 19, 31, 37, 50, 194, 237
Rorty, Richard, 152
rule of law, 7, 13, 38, 121, 123–24,
    203, 205, 207, 236
rules, 9, 11, 15, 32, 40–41, 123–24,
    131, 136, 138, 205, 210
Russell, Robert John, 160–62, 165,
    229–30, 235

S
Sahelanthropus tchadensis, 107–8,
    115, 125
salvation, 3, 75, 86–87
science, 2–7, 20–22, 42–43, 45,
    51–106, 128, 130–32, 135,
    139–40, 145–47, 151,

156–57, 163–64, 170, 173–
    76, 191–92, 202, 226–27,
    229–35
science and religion, 54–55, 59–61,
    66–67, 73, 226–27, 229,
    231–33
scientific community, 70–71
scientific creationism, 53, 59, 85,
    233
scientific method, 56, 59, 73, 132,
    188
scientific revolution, 21, 57, 229
scientism, 64, 181
Scotus, John Duns, 6, 22, 26–34, 37,
    231, 235
scripture, 23, 26, 35, 57–58, 62, 64,
    76, 96, 100, 206, 237
self-knowledge, 198–99, 201
self-reflection, 187, 200
self-transcendence, 200–201
sin, 18, 24, 86–87, 93, 99, 101, 104,
    201, 204, 209, 218–19
Sloan Wilson, David, 60, 125–27
social contract, 37–38, 43, 205–6
social evolution, 179–80
social ordering, 20, 124
social sciences, 50, 83, 173, 229, 237
society, 16, 18, 21–22, 41, 43, 48, 50,
    68–70, 125–26, 141–42, 152,
    155, 158
Socrates, 10
soul, 10, 40, 63, 88, 90, 127–28,
    133–34, 157–58, 166–67,
    171–72, 183–201, 214, 216,
    218, 227–28
    animal, 166
    human, 63, 157, 166–67, 214
    rational, 40
    reasonable, 166
    sensitive, 40
sovereign, 31, 208, 211
sovereign power, 212, 225
sovereignty, 38–39, 211, 228
    earthly, 39
    political, 38
Spaemann, Robert, 184, 198–201,
    219, 235

species, 21, 27, 103, 107, 109, 112,
        115, 117, 121–22, 125–26,
        129
state, natural, 215, 217
Stout, Jeffrey, 52, 235
string theory, 164–65, 235
Stump, Eleanore, 182–83, 235
subjects, 30, 33–34, 78–79, 82, 108,
        138, 144, 161, 165, 170, 173
supernatural, 21, 87
systems
    based prediction/prevention,
        140
    complex biological, 59
    criminal justice, 150
    deterministic, 41, 163
    forward-looking, 43
    intellectual, 78
    irreducibly complex
        biomechanical, 188
    legal, 2, 41, 43–44, 154, 190
    organized, 182
    physical, 148, 157
    prison, 206
    whole-part, 162

T
Tamanaha, Brian, 45–46, 50, 236
Tattersall, Ian, 107, 117–23, 125,
        128, 236
Taylor, Charles, 35–36, 54, 56, 134,
        147, 236
technology, 43, 115–17, 125, 151
Tertullian, Quintus Septimius
        Florens, 17–18
theism, 66, 77, 80–82, 98
theology and science, 3, 6, 52–106,
        130, 140, 157, 189, 191, 222
theory, 39, 41, 43, 48, 84–85, 118,
        164, 169, 181, 183, 188–89
thought, 21, 25, 28, 39, 43, 63, 67,
        97–98, 131, 134, 144, 147,
        227–28
time, 38–39, 45, 47, 56, 58–60, 63,
        78–81, 101–2, 113, 115, 117,
        122, 148–49, 207–8, 213–15
tools, 1, 46, 67–68, 115–16, 171–72
Torah, 15–17, 103, 169, 197, 216

Torrance, Ian, 71–72, 91, 236
transcendence, 6, 20, 26, 51–52, 76,
        78, 82, 87, 120–21, 198–99,
        221–22
transcendent, 29, 81, 94–95, 125,
        127, 173, 190
    beauty, 120
    creator, 54, 222
    divine source, 106
    ethics, 3
    goodness, 33
    norms, 5
    purposes, 3
    source, 6, 33, 45–46, 51–52, 61,
        104, 184, 203, 208
    virtues, 127
transcendentals, 28, 127, 152, 166,
        168–69, 173, 237
transmission of beliefs, 70
Trinity, 8, 39, 81, 94, 103, 167, 196,
        198, 222
truth, 2–3, 8, 67, 75, 78, 80, 85–86,
        88, 141, 146–47, 152–54,
        209, 213
    basic, 92
    complementary, 57
    discrete, 84
    empirical, 96
    metaphysical, 53
    necessary, 146
    objective, 104, 145
    propositional, 64
    transcendent, 4, 11, 14
    universal, 83

U
United States, 49, 150
universals, 21–22, 25, 36, 52, 96,
        120–22, 128–29, 180
univocal, 25, 27–28, 33, 190
univocity, 28, 33–34
univocity of being, 22, 28, 33, 96
upper paleolithic revolution, 117,
        225
Ur-Nammu, 122–23

Urukagina, 123

V
value, 6, 74, 115, 145–46, 152, 180,
    205
Van Gulick, Robert, 159–60, 162,
    236
violence, 7–8, 15, 84, 88, 106, 155,
    194, 203–19
virtue ethics, 177
virtues, 10, 12, 14, 19, 25, 27, 36–37,
    115, 190–93, 198, 200
voluntarism, 6, 22, 32–33, 38, 96,
    195

W
Ward, Keith, 38, 142, 147, 213,
    236–37

Warfield, B.B., 56–57, 237
warrant, 65, 94, 234
Whitcomb, John, 59
Whitehead, Alfred North, 63, 227
Wilberforce, William, 56-57, 231
wisdom, 15–16, 18, 24, 28, 169, 192,
    216
Witt, Charlotte, 176, 237
Witte, John, 19, 237
word, 13, 15, 17, 23–25, 30, 33, 36–
    37, 47, 71–72, 78, 165–66,
    168–70, 214–19
Word of God, 71

Y
Yannaras, Christos, 196–201, 219,
    237

Lightning Source UK Ltd.
Milton Keynes UK
UKHW012025021121
393276UK00001B/46

9 781498 223898